Contentious Liberties

RACE IN THE ATLANTIC WORLD, 1700–1900

SERIES EDITORS
Richard S. Newman, *Rochester Institute of Technology*
Patrick Rael, *Bowdoin College*
Manisha Sinha, *University of Massachusetts, Amherst*

ADVISORY BOARD
Edward Baptist, *Cornell University*
Christopher Brown, *Columbia University*
Vincent Carretta, *University of Maryland*
Laurent Dubois, *Duke University*
Douglas Egerton, *LeMoyne College*
Leslie Harris, *Emory University*
Joanne Pope Melish, *University of Kentucky*
Sue Peabody, *Washington State University, Vancouver*
Erik Seeman, *State University of New York, Buffalo*
John Stauffer, *Harvard University*

Contentious Liberties

American Abolitionists in Post-emancipation Jamaica, 1834–1866

Gale L. Kenny

The University of Georgia Press   *Athens and London*

Paperback edition, 2011
© 2010 by the University of Georgia Press
Athens, Georgia 30602
www.ugapress.org
All rights reserved
Set in 11/14 Adobe Garamond Pro by BookComp, Inc.

Printed digitally in the United States of America

The Library of Congress has cataloged the hardcover
edition of this book as follows:
Kenny, Gale L., 1979–
Contentious liberties : American abolitionists in post-emancipation
Jamaica, 1834–1866 / Gale L. Kenny.
xi, 257 p. ; 24 cm. — (Race in the Atlantic world, 1700–1900)
Includes bibliographical references and index.
ISBN-13: 978-0-8203-3399-1 (hardcover : alk. paper)
ISBN-10: 0-8203-3399-9 (hardcover : alk. paper)
1. Antislavery movements—Jamaica—History—19th century.
2. Antislavery movements—United States—History—19th century.
3. Abolitionists—United States—History—19th century.
4. Liberty—History—19th century.
5. Jamaica—Social conditions. I. Title.
E449.K374 2010
972.92'04—dc22   2009039133

Paperback ISBN-13: 978-0-8203-4045-6
          ISBN-10: 0-8203-4045-6

British Library Cataloging-in-Publication Data available

For my family

CONTENTS

Acknowledgments ix

Introduction 1

Part One. 15

1. Revivals, Antislavery, and Christian Liberty 21
2. Slavery and Freedom in Jamaica 46

Part Two. 69

3. Religion and the Civilizing Mission 75
4. From Spiritual Liberty to Sexual License 100
5. Cultivating Land, Cultivating Families 129

Part Three. 149

6. Civilizing Domesticity 156
7. Revival, Rebellions, and Colonial Subordination 181

Epilogue 206

Notes 211

Bibliography 231

Index 247

ACKNOWLEDGMENTS

I am most grateful for the encouragement, criticism, and ongoing support of John Boles, Allison Sneider, Ussama Makdisi, and Caroline Levander. Their very different perspectives enriched and guided this project from its inception. I would also like to thank the various groups who provided me with funding to conduct my research and to write, including the Rice History Department, the Andrew Mellon Foundation, the Rice Humanities Center, a Serafim Graduate Stipend, and the Currie Fund for Research in Southern History, and especially the generosity of Gary Wihl, Martin Wiener, and Carl Caldwell. Paula Platt and Rachel Zepeda made sure that all of this ran smoothly, and I owe them a great deal of thanks. Edward Cox and Shani Roper helped me to coordinate my research trip to Jamaica. This book's research benefited enormously from the assistance of Ken Grossi and Roland Baumann, both from the Oberlin College Archives; Lee Hampton and Brenda Square at the Amistad Research Center at Tulane University in New Orleans; John Aarons and the staff of the Jamaica Archives in Spanish Town; and Nicole Bryant at the National Library of Jamaica. Materials from the Jamaica Archives appear courtesy of the Jamaica Archives and Records Department, and those from the National Library appear courtesy of the National Library of Jamaica. The quotations from the papers of Amos Phelps are courtesy of the trustees of the Boston Public Library, and I thank Susan Glover, Sean Casey, and Kimberly Reynolds for their research assistance in Boston. Charles Gosselink generously shared his knowledge and his research into the history of the Penfield family, and his transcriptions of their letters were invaluable to this project. Thanks also go to Carolyn Barrett, who drove me through the Jamaican mountains to see what still exists of the Jamaica Mission today. Her knowledge of Jamaican culture enriched my understanding of the people and places I had come to know in the archives.

This project has taken some of its shape from the suggestions and thoughts of many different readers. The Mellon-funded research seminar "Toward a Hemispheric Americas" inspired me to glance at the Jamaica Mission in the first place. Caroline Levander, the seminar's leader, and its participants, Molly Robey, Benjamin Wise, Cory LeDoux, David Messmer, and Elizabeth Fenton, provided an intellectual climate that nurtured my seedling idea to put AMA missionaries in relation to the bigger foreign mission movement. The Mellon Seminar's guests, especially Matthew Guterl and Timothy Marr, also offered recommendations and thought-provoking questions. Toward the end of the writing process, another of Rice's Mellon Seminars also read and critiqued the manuscript, and I thank Ussama Makdisi and his students for their insights. Editors Derek Krissoff and John Joerschke guided the manuscript through the publishing process, and it has been a pleasure working with both of them. I am grateful to copy editor Bob Land for his time and his close attention to detail, and to Julianne Means for compiling the index. I would like to thank the anonymous readers at *Slavery and Abolition* for their critiques of an article about the Jamaica Mission, and the readers for the University of Georgia Press for their recommendations.

Along the way, many people have raised questions, offered guidance, and pointed me in the right direction. Amy Murrell Taylor, Cynthia Kennedy, Derek Chang, Nancy Hardesty, and Emily Clark commented on various iterations of the project during conferences. My teachers and colleagues also deserve recognition, and I am grateful to Alex Byrd, Ira Gruber, Randal Hall, Alex Lichtenstein, Paula Sanders, Kerry Ward, Lora Wildenthal, Joseph Abel, Jessica Cannon, Laura Renée Chandler, Anne Chao, David L. Davis, David Getman, Luke Harlow, Rusty Hawkins, Meg Nunnelly Olsen, Wesley Phelps, David Sehat, Catherine Fitzgerald Wyatt, and Nancy Zey, as well as the members of the Houston Area Southern Historians. I want to thank Caleb McDaniel for helping me put my work in perspective, and our conversations enriched my understanding of abolitionists and transnational history. I also owe an enormous debt to Ann Ziker, Ben Wise, and Molly Robey for being wonderful colleagues, willing readers, and dear friends.

Finally, I owe much to those who have helped in other ways: Jackie Schmitt and Tim Hall and their accommodating children for hosting me during research trips to Boston. Sidney Touchstone kindly offered housing and company in New Orleans. Erin Williams, Jeremy Cleveland, Laura Trice, Amy Gentry, Inés Guariguata, Shirin Baskey, and Joyce Cheng have always been patient sounding boards and the best of friends. My sister, Lizzy, and my parents, Mike and Barbara Kenny, offered support in innumerable ways, and it is to them that I dedicate this book.

Introduction

On August 1, 1838, Americans looked south to the West Indies with great anticipation as they waited to see how Britain's great experiment of emancipation would proceed. Five years before, Britain had passed the Abolition Act, and the first stages of the gradual abolition of colonial slavery took effect in August 1834. While Antigua proceeded to emancipate all slaves, Jamaica and Barbados reclassified most enslaved people as apprentices. American and British abolitionists alike had condemned the apprenticeship system as a useless half-measure, and Parliament eventually agreed, bringing apprenticeship to an early end in 1838. For many observers, full emancipation began a test of free-labor ideology and the efficacy of the civilizing mission: would ex-slaves work for wages? Would black people adopt "civilized"—that is, English—Christianity? Over the ensuing years, scholars, politicians, philanthropists, and journalists presented their views on the subject. With its declining sugar exports, increasing indebtedness,

{1}

and its white and black inhabitants' notorious licentiousness, Jamaica became the example of emancipation gone wrong. While abolitionists attributed Jamaica's problems to the obstinate and greedy proprietors of sugar estates who had a stranglehold on the colonial government, proslavery writers blamed lazy and ungovernable blacks.[1] By the late 1840s, the latter perspective had triumphed in Thomas Carlyle's caustic article, "Occasional Discourses on the Negro Question." His depiction of indolent blacks eating pumpkins while refusing to work more than a few hours a week represented the attitudes of many whites in Britain and the United States who believed that the experiment of emancipation had proved that blacks were inferior to whites. A similar shift in public opinion would happen in the United States in the 1880s. After emancipation in 1863 and the Union's defeat of the South in 1865, radical abolitionists in Congress passed a number of remarkable legislative acts and constitutional amendments that instituted an interracial democracy for the first time in American history. By the 1890s, however, the resurgence of the Ku Klux Klan, black codes passed in state legislatures, and the cultural climate promoting reconciliation between white northerners and southerners had rolled back Reconstruction, and black Americans became second-class citizens.[2]

This book approaches this familiar motif in both American and British imperial history from a different perspective: an American abolitionist mission to freed people in post-emancipation Jamaica. Beginning in 1837, the American missionaries to Jamaica came from Oberlin College in northern Ohio, a hotbed of radicalism. At Oberlin, the future missionaries learned Christian perfectionism and worked to do away with all sinfulness, including the evils of slavery and racial prejudice. Oberlin also aimed to educate self-sufficient and independent men along with pious and morally righteous women. As radical abolitionists, the white missionaries had African American classmates, co-religionists, and organizational allies, and once in Jamaica, the missionaries expected black Jamaicans to fill a similar role in the mission's churches and schools. In 1847, the Jamaica Mission became a part of the American Missionary Association (AMA) an abolitionist society based in New York City. The missionaries promoted "Christian liberty," to balance freedom and manly independence with strict adherence to evangelical Christian morality. They did so in the hopes that they could save souls and improve Jamaican society while providing to the abolitionist press in the United States a useful test case for emancipation.

For their part, black Jamaicans saw the American missionaries as frustrating allies. Just as the missionaries' articulation of freedom grew out of their experiences as evangelicals and abolitionists in the antebellum North, the meaning of freedom to enslaved Jamaicans derived from a very different set of social and cultural conditions. Many black Jamaican Christians practiced a creole religion inflected with African, European, and African American beliefs and practices and shaped by the experience of Jamaican slave culture. Freed people also had their own ideas about what constituted freedom when it came to landownership and family practices. The freedom for mothers and fathers, rather than former masters, to control the division of labor in their families ranked first in importance. The American missionaries, on the other hand, looked for signs of "pure" Christianity, the middle-class family, and the gender ideology of domesticity as indicators that black people understood the proper use of freedom. Although the American missionaries provided resources and political advocacy for education and land rights, they only rarely allowed black Jamaicans to be equal partners in the mission's churches, schools, and households. Believing black Jamaicans to be in need of fatherly guidance and a moral education, the mission's white men enforced strict church discipline in the mission churches and governed their homes with patriarchal authority. The same religious principles that made these men and women support black freedom also made them imperious defenders of the hierarchies of the civilizing mission.

The mission served as a site for encounters, and out of these arose unsettling disruptions to the mission's hierarchies of white/black, civilized/barbaric, and Christian/heathen. Not only were there cross-cultural encounters between Jamaicans and Americans, but the work of the mission also generated friction among the missionaries and among black Jamaicans. Issues like women's rights, religious authority, and interracial cooperation preoccupied American abolitionists in the United States, and they often took surprising turns in Jamaica. In the context of a civilizing mission and up against the backdrop of a licentious society, evangelical abolitionists handled themselves differently. For black Jamaicans, the mission could be a place for social advancement, but, for example, when black parents sent their children to live with a missionary couple, their children confronted a sense of alienation, belonging fully to neither world. In *Contentious Liberties*, I seek to move beyond the question of whether white abolitionists and missionaries were good or bad, racist or egalitarian, and instead, to consider the predictable and unpredictable consequences that arose when they attempted to put their ideology into action. The Jamaica Mission allows us to look underneath the great experiment of emancipation to see how white and black individuals engaged with one another on a daily basis within households, churches, and schools.

Contentious Liberties grows out of the vibrant scholarship that has made it necessary to understand the antislavery movement as a transnational phenomenon. From the time the first slave ships departed West Africa with human cargo bound for the New World, Africans resisted their enslavement. In the eighteenth century, enslaved blacks in Great Britain and in France gained their freedom, and they wrote and lectured about their experiences in order to recruit sympathetic whites to take an interest in ending the slave trade and slavery. White Quakers in the American colonies and in Britain turned against the trade and the institution in the mid-1700s, and some evangelical Anglicans and Protestant Christians followed their lead. The British movement to end the slave trade gained momentum in the last two decades of the eighteenth century, and these British abolitionists attracted the attention of like-minded Americans. Meanwhile, the debate over slavery took a dramatic turn in the 1790s as the first sustained and successful slave rebellion took place in the French West Indian colony of Saint-Domingue. Enslaved blacks and *gens-de-couleur* claimed the rights articulated in the French Revolution for themselves and violently overthrew the island's white rulers. In the Atlantic world, news, letters, and tactics circulated from one country to another and throughout imperial channels.[3]

After the American Revolution, most northern states passed laws mandating immediate or gradual emancipation. In the British West Indies, evangelical missionaries began an intensive effort to Christianize slaves, against the wishes of many planters. The missionaries found that many black West Indians, particularly in Jamaica, had already become Christians, many having been converted by African American Loyalists, Baptist refugees who fled the United States at the end of the Revolutionary War. The white missionaries also built churches and facilitated networks of black religious leaders, and they unwittingly contributed to a more coordinated antislavery movement in Jamaica. As news about growing antislavery in

England and parliamentary debates about the institution filtered into Jamaica, enslaved Jamaicans believed that they had been freed, but that the island's colonial assembly had refused to obey the wishes of the Queen. After the Baptist War in Jamaica, a slave uprising during Christmas 1831, the colonial assembly blamed the British missionaries for fomenting rebellion, and the assembly exiled the missionaries from Jamaica. Events like the Jamaican Baptist War and British antislavery petitions became international news stories, and they had an effect on the debate over slavery already under way in the United States. While the British abolition of slavery in 1833 encouraged northern abolitionists, the lessons from the Baptist War concerning the danger of antislavery missionaries worried white southerners. They grew intensely suspicious of any abolitionist propaganda, believing that the Baptist War proved that "contented" slaves would only rebel after abolitionist interference.[4]

While missionaries in Jamaica were linked to slave rebellions, antislavery, and emancipation, the relationship between missionaries and slaves in the United States had a different history before 1830. The violence of the Haitian revolution made some white Americans feel that slavery must be eradicated in order to protect whites from black vengeance. One plan appealed to white northerners as well as to some white southern slaveholders: the strategy to deport freed slaves to Liberia, far away from their former masters. Established in 1816, the American Colonization Society (ACS) copied a British plan to relocate former slaves to Sierra Leone, raising money and trying to recruit free blacks to move to Liberia. The ACS was the most popular antislavery option in the early national period, and it attracted northern and southern white supporters who wanted to see a gradual end to slavery in the United States. Significantly, the ACS came into existence only a few years after American evangelicals had launched the interdenominational American Board of Commissioners for Foreign Missions in 1810. Many supporters of colonization invoked missionary language, describing slavery as a "civilizing mission" to African heathen, and now that slavery had run its course, it was time for African American Christians to bring the light of Christianity to darkest Africa. Colonizationist theory held that only by leaving the United States could blacks prove themselves as worthy exemplars of Christianity and civilization.[5]

For many reasons, the early 1830s brought about a radical challenge to gradualist antislavery in the United States. As in Great Britain in the 1700s, evangelical revivalism in New England and in New York during the 1820s stirred many new converts to humanitarianism and moral reform. In the wake of this Second Great Awakening, white northerners were primed to take on the sinful corruption of slavery, and many religiously awakened reformers saw slavery as a great evil that besmirched the Christian soul of the United States.[6] After all, white abolitionists fiercely guarded their own liberty as much as they sought an end to slavery, and it seemed the South gained more national political clout every year. These new radical white abolitionists also learned from listening to African Americans—freed slaves, fugitives, and free blacks. Another major factor contributing to the coalescing abolitionist movement in the United States was the 1833 passage of the Emancipation Act in Great Britain. The law mandated an end to slavery in all British colonies beginning on August 1, 1834, and it charted a timeline for the complete end to all indentured servitude. Months after the Emancipation Act passed, white and black Americans who had belonged to a variety of local abolitionist organizations across the U.S. North joined together to form the American Anti-Slavery Society in Philadelphia.

Abolitionists associated with the society traveled widely to organize local abolitionist organizations and to organize petitions against the peculiar institution. Abolitionist tracts, newspapers, and pamphlets poured out of printing presses in Boston and New York, quickly spreading the abolitionist message and stirring up a great deal of antiabolitionist sentiment along the way. In response, Congress put a gag order on the slavery question, quashing the flood of abolitionist petitions calling on the legislative branch to end slavery in Washington, D.C. Mobs attacked and burned abolitionists' homes and meetings throughout the 1830s, even killing an abolitionist editor in Illinois. The movement's fervor took a turn in the early 1840s as schisms over women's rights, religious institutions, and the need for an abolitionist political party divided the American Anti-Slavery Society, and evangelical abolitionists, guided by New Yorker Lewis Tappan, broke with William Lloyd Garrison and his Boston-based movement. During the 1840s and 1850s, the antislavery movement in the North expanded to include a spectrum of supporters, from the radicals calling for immediate emancipation and myriad other reforms to racially conservative whites who supported abolitionism as a means to remove all blacks from the nation.[7]

While thinking about antislavery as an Atlantic world phenomenon has long been a part of scholarship on colonial America and the early republic, the history of American abolitionism after 1833 has been surprisingly isolationist, focusing on the national story of sectionalism and the march toward the Civil War. There are exceptions, to be sure. For example, the British abolitionists' refusal to seat the female American delegates at the 1840 World's Anti-Slavery Convention in London has served as a critical turning point for American women's historians because Elizabeth Cady Stanton traced her interest in the "woman question" to this event.[8] More recently, historians have begun to provide the same level of analysis of the mid-nineteenth century as others had done for earlier periods. Essay collections juxtaposing, if not fully integrating, the process of emancipation in the Atlantic world have pointed toward the importance of seeing antislavery and emancipation as well as slavery in a transnational context.[9] This work is not necessarily comparative, but instead provides a more interwoven history that represents more accurately the world of nineteenth-century people. Black and white abolitionists could and did read newspapers and books published in London, Boston, and Kingston. They traveled widely and corresponded with like-minded reformers throughout the world. As Richard Blackett and Edward Rugemer's books show, a richer understanding of abolitionists and their ideas comes from seeing them in the world they lived in—a world that encompassed more than the United States. The Jamaica Mission was yet another tether between the United States and the Caribbean in the nineteenth century, showing how even white northern abolitionists made up what Matthew Guterl has called the American Mediterranean.[10]

American abolitionists did not just look to the British West Indies for a model of emancipation; some moved there to enact the world they could not yet have in their own nation. The records the missionaries left behind reveal the underlying assumptions of American evangelical abolitionism, ideas made manifest in their mission to post-emancipation Jamaica. In the United States, evangelical abolitionists believed that churches should discipline sinful slaveholders, and the abolitionist "come outers" left churches and religious bodies that refused to exclude slaveholders from their ranks.[11] Religious ties had also brought white abolitionists together with some black activists because they shared a similar commitment to morality and respectability, even if, as James Brewer Stewart has argued, they supported racial uplift programs for quite different reasons.[12] In the Jamaica Mission, the same rigorous pursuit of moral perfection drove American ministers to invoke church discipline against black Jamaicans who had unorthodox beliefs or who led lives that the ministers considered to be sufficiently immoral. The Christian perfectionism born out of the Second Great Awakening had influenced many whites to become supporters of immediate emancipation, and the same rigid moralizing would be put to use in a racialized way in the Jamaica Mission. Some of the ministers resisted this position of authority as contrary to abolitionist principles, but most of the Americans embraced their role as fatherly guides for blacks who frequently strayed from the righteous path.

The confluence of abolitionism and the missionary movement also reconfigures how we understand the relationship between the two. Abolitionists focused on race at home also became interested in race abroad, and they had much to say on the subject of foreign missions. With the exception of the impressive scholarship on the American Board of Commissioners for Foreign Missions and the Cherokee, few historians of missionaries contend with slavery in the United States, and few historians of abolitionism have looked at the overlap between abolitionists and missionaries.[13] The American Missionary Association was formed in 1846 as an explicit rejection of the American Board because this much larger organization refused to condemn slavery. Further, the slavery question at home was never far from the minds of the missionaries and black Jamaicans involved in the Jamaica Mission, and the Oberlin ministers led their congregations in prayer for an end to barbarous slavery in the supposedly civilized United States. In tracing the connections between evangelical abolitionism and racial ideology in the antebellum North with both British and American missionary work in Jamaica, the Jamaica Mission calls for a more integrated history of race abroad and race at home. In this light, the work of the AMA in the South after the Civil War can be seen as a continuation of decades of missionary work, and as an extension of the missionary movement as well as abolitionism.[14] In analyzing the logic of those southern slaveholders who claimed that the institution of slavery was itself a part of a larger "civilizing mission," historians of religion have unwittingly cast proslavery Christianity as the missionary religion in the nineteenth-century United

States. The Jamaica Mission proves otherwise, showing how white abolitionists also could discuss converting and "civilizing" racial others even as they opposed the institution of slavery.

The other component of evangelical abolitionism that took unexpected turns in the Jamaica Mission was the ideology of domesticity. Although coeducational and interracial Oberlin is known for its radicalism, the college's administration tried to contain the school's political commitments by imposing policies and rules to guard against any "licentiousness" or overly free behavior, whether sexual or otherwise. Particularly during Oberlin's early years, its governors believed that if the male and female students could be contained within their proper spheres, Christian liberty would prevail in spite of the school's support for abolitionism and spiritual freedom. This stance also served as a measure to protect the school from antiabolitionist mobs and critics. Responding to accusations linking emancipation to interracial sex and to moral degeneracy, Oberlin advocated male self-control and female respectability in order to stave off such accusations, even if this gender ideology conflicted with abolitionism's message of personal freedom.[15] This conservative interpretation of domesticity in which parents and husbands always trumped children and wives defined the mission family in Jamaica.

The patriarchal mission family in the Jamaica Mission became increasingly out of sync with white abolitionist families and the evolving ideology of domesticity in the U.S. North. At Oberlin, the culture of radicalism led some female students to women's rights, and even those women who did not become suffragists took on more public roles through their moral reform and abolitionist activism.[16] *Contentious Liberties* examines how the changing currents of domesticity in the United States were brought to the mission by single women missionaries and ministers' wives, and how these women had limited success in gaining any authority within the mission family. As Catherine Hall has described for British Baptist missionaries in Jamaica, the American missionaries drew on the language of family both to signify "religious kinship" and to institute hierarchies.[17] Consequently, white women in the mission had few opportunities to expand domesticity to work as a justification for female moral authority in Jamaica, as did their peers in the United States. This characteristic of the Jamaica Mission shows domesticity to be an ideology contingent on context. In the interracial mission households—a setting comparable to colonial settlements and even, in some ways, to southern plantations—white men were suspicious of white women's attempts to increase their authority because they believed that any disruptions to the Christian family would disrupt the mission's racial order.[18]

Gender also served an important role in the mission as a marker of "civilization." Historians Diana Paton and Pamela Scully contend that the movement toward slave emancipation "meshed with efforts of missionaries and reformers to 'civilize' native peoples in many societies in the Atlantic world." Abolitionists, like other "proponents of liberalism attacked 'old fashioned' forms of patriarchy such as the slaveholding household, the aristocratic patriarchy of the European and Latin American great landed estates," among other traditional social customs.[19] Changing the gendered behavior of black Jamaicans formed a central component of the mission, and attacks on the unmanly and unchaste behaviors of black men and women were missionary shorthand for illustrating the distance that black Jamaicans had to go before they could be considered civilized Christians.

The ideology of domesticity was much more than a measure of civilization, however, and it was also a set of practices that the missionaries used as "civilizing" tools. Along with the practices of church discipline and education, the missionaries believed that their domestic habits acted as civilizing influences for the black children who lived with them in the mission's stations. Building on the work of Amy Kaplan, Ann Laura Stoler, and others who have uncovered the nationalist and racial assumptions embedded in the ideology of domesticity, *Contentious Liberties* shows how this unfolded in the Jamaica Mission. While female missionaries in Jamaica felt stymied by the patriarchal mission family, they acquired a sense of authority as white women civilizers. Further, as the ideology of domesticity evolved in the United States, the changing views of household management would, like the nascent women's rights movement, influence the households of the Jamaica Mission.[20]

Unlike the history of American emancipation, the history of Jamaican emancipation cannot be told without Protestant missionaries, their supporters and opponents, and the impact they had on slavery and emancipation. Beginning with the small Moravian mission to enslaved Jamaicans in 1754, the history of Jamaican religion is composed of waves of missionaries ranging from black Baptist loyalists from the U.S. South to dissenting

English ministers who saw the British Empire as a pathway to spread their faith and to convert the world.[21] The American missionaries, however, are almost entirely absent from accounts of post-emancipation Jamaica.[22] *Contentious Liberties* argues that the American missionaries differed from their British counterparts, both because of the makeup of their home audience and their apprehensiveness toward imperialism.

Writing about the British Baptist missionary William Knibb's "missionary dream" for Jamaica, Catherine Hall noted that his "love for Jamaica was based on a conception of black people which both gave and denied equality in the present, while promising it for the future."[23] Like the English Baptist missionaries, the American Congregationalists in Jamaica met with a similar predicament, but the Americans reported their results to an audience still debating the slavery question. Thus, first, their letters and reports to the American Missionary Association carried a responsibility toward politics at home, and the missionaries often protested the demands for good news when they had little to report. As a consequence, the ministers and schoolteachers mastered the technique of simultaneously praising emancipation while also railing against "corrupted" Christianity and black licentiousness in Jamaica. Second, the fact that a national abolitionist movement continued to grow and change during the Jamaica Mission's history also meant that new missionaries brought evolving ideas of racial ideology, religion, and gender to the mission, and the new arrivals did not always meet the approval of the older ministers—both because they differed from the abolitionists of the 1830s and because the older ministers had changed during their time on the island. For the American missionaries in Jamaica, exactly what the missionary dream entailed remained a moving target in the 1840s through the 1870s.

The Jamaica Mission also contributes to a better understanding of how black Jamaicans engaged with white mission churches after emancipation. Historian Thomas Holt observed that freed people "valued most the very things persistently denied them as slaves—a home and control over their family's labor."[24] This was repeatedly made clear in the American missionaries' letters, and the ministers' ultimate failure to create "pure" churches also shows how important religious autonomy was to freed people. But rather than seeing the post-emancipation missionary landscape as a binary pitting white missionaries against black Jamaicans, the Jamaica Mission also shows the ways that black Jamaicans and white missionaries together created a world that was both American and Jamaican. American ministers sometimes chose to look the other way when their church members showed that they had not abandoned all of their old ways, and the evidence indicates that many Jamaicans did join the mission churches. Their reasons for doing so are harder to find, which is one question that I cannot answer in any certain terms. Knowing that freed people were not a homogenous community, it seems likely that some participated in the mission's churches and schools because they liked the American ministers, while others may have joined as a way to obtain an affordable education for their children and the chance of social advancement. Church members also fought among themselves about whether to keep an American minister. In one case, a congregation almost split over the question of alcohol, as some members supported the requirement that they sign a temperance pledge, while rum merchants in the church proposed that they seek out an Anglican minister who would not enforce rules that would hinder the merchants' business.[25] The missionaries' letters provide a portrait of a complex creole society. By the mission's end in the early 1870s, the churches and schools bearing the names of the famed English missionaries in colonial America—Eliot and Brainerd—as well as the missionaries' alma mater, Oberlin, had become entirely Jamaican institutions that had an American past.

The book is divided into three parts. Part 1 focuses on the American origins of the missionaries and the Jamaican context for the mission. As the opening story about the founding of Oberlin illustrates, evangelical abolitionists saw orthodox Christianity as a way to separate good from evil and to build protective walls around a good society. In Jamaica, in contrast, slaves combined dissenting Christianity from English and African American missionaries and African religious practices to forge a creole community out of people who spoke different languages and came from different places. The religious differences also led the abolitionist Americans and Jamaican freed people to have conflicting ideas about the meaning of freedom. Part 2 turns to the mission's first decade. It focuses on the American attempts to impose a Christian culture based on church discipline and specific gender roles and family practices, and the challenges Americans faced from black Jamaicans who opposed the missionaries' claim to religious authority, and also from some of their fellow American missionaries. Chapters 3, 4, and 5 demonstrate the fragility of the civilizing mission, and they also chart a broader evolution of the mission as the abolitionist ministers became more interested in social control. Part 3 takes a closer look at the inner workings of the civilizing mission, particularly the schools and the mission households, as a younger generation of missionaries joined the Jamaica Mission. Part 3 also examines how the mission adapted to changes taking place in the United States and in Jamaica, and the different ways that the missionaries responded to shifting ideas of domesticity, the emancipation of slaves in the United States, and the Morant Bay Rebellion in Jamaica.

Part One

After the Revolutionary War, New Englanders moved west to the Ohio River Valley, spreading across the lands ceded by Iroquois tribes in western New York as well as the Western Reserve, what would become Ohio in 1803. For many migrants, this settlement was seen as the latest stage in the fulfillment of a national destiny, and the settlement in Ohio drew comparisons to the Puritan settlement of New England. One account even told of a group of settlers floating along the Ohio River on a boat named the *Mayflower*, and after landing in Marietta, Ohio, they "reenacted the arrival of the Pilgrim Fathers at Plymouth." The Protestant clergy, particularly those located in Connecticut, followed this settlement of the Western Reserve closely, watching speculators and land companies map out the land into frontier towns for adventurous Yankee settlers. In the 1810s, members of the Connecticut Missionary Society saw the Western Reserve as more than an opportunity for material riches, and they believed that this "New Connecticut" offered a chance for moral regeneration for the descendants of English Puritans. In speaking and writing about the Western Reserve, they condensed history, recalling images of the New World in the 1600s as well as locales recently selected for Protestant foreign missions. The West was at once a "howling wilderness" and a "garden paradise," awaiting the attention of godly men and women who would prepare a fruitful harvest.[1]

While some in the East believed that the frontier would reanimate the Puritan spirit of two centuries earlier, anxiety also existed that the white settlers leaving the "civilized" settlements of New England might degenerate into savages. Consequently, after a brief failed attempt to convert the Indians of the Western Reserve to Christianity, the missionaries sent out by the Connecticut Missionary Society shifted their attention to the souls of white settlers. Harrowing accounts of white frontier families relied on descriptors more commonly applied to Natives than to white Americans. As an example, New Englander Zerah Hawley's dismal travel narrative written in the early 1820s observed that the residents of Ohio were "literally barefoot" and their houses contained little furniture.[2] Indicating the amount of regression among the westerners, Hawley commented that the women's clothing "is very ancient, similar to the fashion of our grandmothers," and older women wore their hair in braids, "much in the manner of Chinese gentlemen."[3] Far more disturbing to Hawley, families and unrelated guests slept together "*promiscuously* in one room . . . without anything to screen them from view of each other." While dress and living conditions may be explained and forgiven, Hawley could not tolerate this breach of the gender order, and to him it indicated that these white settlers had taken a "great step toward a state of barbarism."[4] Hawley's commentary also reflected his fluency with the emerging Protestant missionary movement in the United States, and its underlying theory that all the world's peoples existed on different rungs of the ladder toward Christian civilization. Indeed, he perhaps had the recently launched American mission to the Sandwich Islands in mind when he wrote, "Missionaries are, as appears to me, almost as much needed here as in the Islands of the Seas; and as these people are our own brethren according to the flesh, there appears to be a duty incumbent on those who possess the means" to save these frontier families who "are groping in Heathenish darkness."[5] For Hawley and many other easterners traveling to the Western Reserve, the signs that their fellow white Protestants were backsliding into savagery were deeply disturbing.

Almost a decade later, Oberlin's founder, John Jay Shipherd, shared Hawley's view of the creeping barbarism of the frontier, and the need for religious and moral institutions to protect white settlers from backsliding. Shipherd, his wife, and their two young sons moved from upstate New York to Elyria, Ohio, a six-year-old town southwest of Cleveland. Shipherd found the discomforts of frontier life physically and spiritually taxing. One night on the way home at twilight, he wrote his mother, "I lost my way, as I could not see the marked trees or tracks which were covered with leaves—and to comfort me while searching for the road a gang of wolves set up a howling which make the woods ring." But, he reassured his mother, the wolves had yet to kill anyone in his neighborhood, and that "wolfish men are much more to be dreaded."[6] For Shipherd, the truly fearsome part of the frontier was not the forests, wild animals, or even Indians, but rather the antagonistic white men and women who refused to accept the light of Christ. Dejected with the difficulties of missionary work, Shipherd left Elyria for a nearby settlement where he established a town of his own: Oberlin. He believed that this colony would serve as a beacon of morality in the Western Reserve, or the "Valley of Moral Death" as he and his colleagues had taken to calling it.[7]

Shipherd intended Oberlin to be a covenant town: all the residents would live morally upright lives and pledge their faith in God, and students from the Oberlin Institute would spread the gospel throughout the West. Oberlin indeed became influential, although perhaps not for the precise reasons Shipherd envisioned in 1832. Within its first five years, the school not only accepted female students, as had been part of Shipherd's plan, but after an influx of radical abolitionists moved to Oberlin and made it their home, the school opened its doors to African Americans as well, making it the first interracial and coeducational college in the United States. Writing an appeal for donations from British philanthropists, abolitionist Theodore Dwight Weld and his wife, Angelina Grimké Weld, laid out Oberlin's destiny: "We believe it to be accomplishing more for freedom of thought, speech, and conscience, more for the great cause of human liberty and equal rights, the annihilating of prejudice and caste in every form, more to honor God, exalt his truth, and purify a corrupted Church and Ministry, than any other Institution in the United States."[8]

While the frontier may or may not have been as dreary as it appeared in the accounts of Zerah Hawley and John Jay Shipherd, it is telling that both men compared their fellow white Americans to heathen savages. At the same time that the Connecticut Missionary Society and other New Englanders sent ministers to the West, the American Board of Commissioners for Foreign Missions had been established in 1810. Soon after, it sent out its first missionary couples to Burma, the Holy Land, and the Sandwich Islands.[9] Missionary letters describing the conditions of "heathens" around the world combined with the existing literature on Native Americans gave Hawley and Shipherd a framework for understanding race, religion, gender, and civilization. At this particular moment, white easterners feared that white westerners were falling backward, losing the clothing habits, gender roles, and religious beliefs that were the outward markers of civilization. Less than a decade later, however, Oberlin's first graduates, young men and women who were products of the frontier, would be setting up a civilizing mission of their own in Jamaica in which their race and their nationality marked them clearly as civilized Christians. Further, the mission offered them a way to live out their political and religious abolitionist beliefs as they performed the good works required for salvation. These farmers-turned-missionaries from Oberlin mirrored British missionaries, many of whom were working-class members of dissenting churches in England, hailing from provincial English towns rather than London, the metropole's center.[10] While their status at home may have been questionable, once abroad, these men and women easily secured their position as civilized white Christians living among the benighted heathen.

For the American missionaries in Jamaica, the move to the West Indies could be jarring, a sudden break with the climate and culture to which they were accustomed, and they quickly found that black Jamaicans were quite different from their black classmates at Oberlin and the African Americans they had met as volunteer teachers and preachers in the black communities of Cincinnati and Cleveland.[11] In contrast, for Jamaicans—black, colored or brown, and white—the American mission was nothing special or even particularly new, only the latest wave of proselytizers. Although Jamaica had been a British colony since the late 1600s, the Anglican Church and missionaries from the Society for the Propagation of the Gospel made few inroads among Jamaican slaves in the seventeenth and eighteenth centuries. More successful were the Moravians, who came to Jamaica in 1754 and taught slaves to submit to their masters, even as all Christians were equal in the eyes of God. In the 1790s, African Americans who had been loyal to Britain during the American Revolution sought sanctuary in Jamaica, and these free blacks imported their southern Baptist faith, an evangelical Protestantism that had grown out of the Great Awakening in the United States. By the early 1800s, nonconformist Methodists, and later, Baptists and Congregationalists from England sent out missionaries to the West Indies with the intention of converting slaves and slaveholders. Even evangelical Anglicans from the Church Missionary Society grew interested in reaching out to the West Indies in the early 1800s.[12]

In addition to European and African American missionaries, the last decades of the 1700s brought Jamaica hurricanes, earthquakes, drought, and epidemic diseases, all of which acutely worsened the misery of enslavement. Although the end of the slave trade in 1807 was meant to improve the condition of slaves, evidence shows that planters demanded more labor from a shrinking population of workers. Nonetheless, black Jamaicans created communities, kinship networks, and culture, an Afro-creole culture that incorporated elements of European Christianity as well as qualities born from the experiences of the Caribbean. Just as evangelical religion sparked a missionary movement in England and in the United States, black leaders in Jamaica drew on religious iconography and the religious community to mobilize and demand their freedom. In the so-called Baptist War of 1831–32, a black Baptist deacon led an uprising that set into motion a series of events ending with the passage of the Emancipation Act in 1833, declaring an end to slavery on August 1, 1834. Religion and its relationship to political and spiritual liberation developed differently in the United States and Jamaica. American evangelicals like Shipherd believed Christianity to be the necessary restraint on what would otherwise be unfettered freedom, whether to "uncivilized" whites in the West or to foreign heathen who had not yet encountered the gospel. Black Jamaicans, in contrast, took the antiauthoritarian message of evangelical Christianity to justify slave revolts, and later, after emancipation, to protest the hypocrisy of white missionaries.[13]

The meaning of freedom and its relationship to religion, gender, and race in the United States and in Jamaica is the central concern of the first two chapters. The first chapter shows the context of the American missionaries in the revivals of the Second Great Awakening and in the early stages of radical abolitionism in the antebellum North. It also shows how manual labor education, the gender ideology of domesticity, and the religious doctrine of Christian perfectionism influenced Oberlin College and became the grounding ideology for the civilization that was at the heart of the Jamaica Mission. The second chapter turns to Jamaica, and to a related but very different history of the relationship between black abolitionists, white missionaries, and religion. While few Jamaican freed people wrote detailed letters and articles about what freedom meant to them, as did the American abolitionists, the Jamaicans' actions—reported by missionaries, overseers, and colonial officials—revealed how they acted on freedom in terms of their labor, families, and churches.

I Revivals, Antislavery, and Christian Liberty

In 1825 two events occurred that would change the physical and spiritual landscape of New York state: the completion of the Erie Canal and the evangelical revivals of the Second Great Awakening. The Erie Canal created an efficient means of transportation for farm produce, manufactured goods, and people. Small settlements became towns and cities, and commercial centers like Utica and Rochester attracted young men and women from the hinterlands. Wage-labor jobs in factories and domestic work for the rising middle class provided an escape route for young people who wanted to leave behind the old order of the family farm. The growth of the market economy served as the backdrop for the Second Great Awakening as rootless individuals in canal towns constituted new communities of the converted. The message of evangelists like Charles Grandison Finney proved attractive to the social mobility of the day, and upstart preachers questioned the relevance of older clergymen and their orthodox beliefs.

{ 21 }

Finney called for a new moral order. God called on his children to repent and be reborn, and once they had been transformed by God's spirit, they were to perfect the world around them through the eradication of all sin. The converted were to establish a new social order, one no longer complacent with society's sinfulness, and anyone who opposed the young zealots was to be overthrown.[1]

In the 1820s and 1830s, Finney's evangelicalism inspired men and women to seek ways to live out their faith through good works. For evangelical women, moral reform societies became a means to act without compromising the ideology of true womanhood. Evangelical women could remain pious, pure, and even submissive while also mobilizing to raise money for charities and missionary work.[2] Christian duty justified the creation of a social space between the private and the public spheres. Evangelical men also committed themselves to moral reform, and because they had greater freedom and mobility than evangelical women, they followed a different path. Many of Finney's male converts left home to attend manual-labor schools as a means of obtaining both an intellectual and a spiritual education. Most prominently, a number of Finney's Holy Band attended the Oneida Institute near Utica, New York, where they performed manual labor, attended classes, and adhered to the school's strict disciplinary policies.

At manual-labor schools, young evangelical men faced an ongoing struggle to reconcile their fierce defense of self-reliance, individual liberty, and free speech with their equally vigorous support for an evangelical moral order. Attempts to wed individualism with communal order were not uncommon in the early republic, as John Andrew's biography of missionary organizer Jeremiah Evarts makes clear: "Evarts believed that self-discipline, individual virtue, and Christian principles were essential to harness the centrifugal tendencies evident in American life." Indeed, rather than seeing individualism as antagonistic toward republicanism and community morals, Evarts "refused to uncouple individual freedom of the marketplace from moral self-restraint, seeking instead a fusion of republicanism, capitalism, and revivalism."[3] As many supporters of manual-labor education embraced abolitionism in the early 1830s, they grew even more outspoken against anything that limited their independence or forced them to compromise their religious beliefs. They also quickly learned the difficulty of finding a balance between supporting individual rights and cultivating community norms.

In 1834, a group of theology students led by Theodore Weld left Lane Seminary in Cincinnati when the administration prohibited them from agitating for immediate emancipation. These same students who protested restraints on their freedom of speech soon found themselves having to create their own rules at their new home, Oberlin College. Like Jeremiah Evarts before them, Oberlin's leaders tried to cultivate an ideology of Christian liberty that combined their support for individual liberty and free speech with rules intended to preserve the school's moral foundations. Oberlin, after all, was different from other manual-labor schools like the Oneida Institute or Lane Seminary because it educated female students alongside male students, and, critically, it enrolled a small number of African Americans as well. The mobs who attacked abolitionist meetings and activists' homes would hardly allow such a school to stand. In response to their own religious convictions as well as antiabolitionist threats, the men and women in charge of Oberlin elevated the bonds of the Christian family to new heights. By strictly enforcing certain rules governing Oberlin's students, the school's leaders believed that they had created an adequate order to guard against licentiousness and the possibility of extramarital sex without diminishing their commitment to individual liberty.[4] This chapter unravels the strains of religious doctrine, gender ideology, and racial thinking that led to the school's policies and to the foundational beliefs of the missionaries in Jamaica.

In the 1820s, the orthodox Calvinist clergy in New England saw the raucous western revivals as a dangerous trend that would, like the rational Unitarians in Boston, peel away more people from their churches. Earlier in the century, the Presbyterians and Congregationalists had joined to form a united front of orthodox Calvinism as their church members migrated out of New England and into New York state. The Plan of Union in 1801 provided a way to maximize "Presbygationalist" assets and clergy as they planted new churches across the New York frontier, but it seemed that traveling evangelists, northerners like Charles Finney as well as itinerant Methodists and Baptists from the South, had more success. The revivalists held mass meetings outdoors or in municipal buildings.[5] With meetings continuing for several days, men and women who came to witness the spectacle were pulled into the frenzy of public confessions drawn from repenting sinners and of sermons exhorting listeners to let Christ into their hearts. To the established clergy nervously observing these revivals, it appeared that the preachers believed people had a role to play in their own salvation and that they advocated the heretical position that it was not God alone who predestined those who would go to heaven or hell.

While based in Calvinism, Finney's religious inclinations responded to the needs of the people as much as to traditional understandings of God. Converted at the age of twenty-nine while living in Adams, New York, Finney drew his beliefs more from "common sense and democratic values" than from the theological formulations of Yale professors. Although Finney's theology of Christian perfectionism would become more complex in later decades, he initially held only a few simple tenets of faith. Christ's crucifixion offered salvation to all people, but in order to be saved, people must be brought to their knees with "self-abasement" before the redeeming goodness of the Holy Spirit could enter their soul. For Finney, the stance of orthodox Christianity placing all powers of salvation in God's hands and holding that only an elect would be saved hindered evangelism, and orthodox Calvinist clergy actually worked *against* God.[6] Finney lambasted "cold," and usually older, clergy, many of whom thought him to be an unorthodox upstart. At one revival meeting, for example, Finney prayed, "Lord wake up these stupid sleeping ministers; [else] . . . they wake in hell."[7] Finney's converts agreed with their preacher, and one young man registered his discontent by shouting down his own minister, reportedly yelling, "You old grey headed sinner, you deserved to be in hell long ago."[8] Controversially, Finney also encouraged women to speak out in revival meetings; as one of Finney's band, Theodore Weld, later recounted, "It made a great deal of talk and discussion, and the subject of female praying and speaking in public was discussed throughout western New York."[9] In the opinions of many, Finney's disregard for the church's traditional stances was fast leading to the disintegration of civilization. Although time and institutionalization reined in Finney's radicalism, the antiauthoritarianism and self-righteousness that animated it in the 1820s would occasionally resurface, even among the order-seeking missionaries in Jamaica.

Aside from the theological differences, orthodox Calvinists also feared the more general social disorder that accompanied religious enthusiasm—the new measures Finney and others had instituted to elicit conversions. Lyman Beecher, a popular Connecticut minister, gained both fame and notoriety when he adopted some of the revivalists' techniques in his sermons, yet he remained a firm critic of what he viewed as the chaos of Charles Finney's revivals. Lyman Beecher described Charles Finney as a man who stormed through a town and left the ground ripe for lawlessness and licentiousness. In the minds of the Finneyites, Beecher argued, "Truth" was more "frequently admitted than the importance of order."[10] The order in question was the patriarchal family in which younger people obeyed their fathers, wives submitted to their husbands, and younger clergy heeded the advice of older and wiser ministers. One minister warned that the tactics used in their revivals threatened "a civil war in Zion—a domestic broil in the household of faith."[11] For Beecher and other established clergy, religious belief should reinforce the social order, not attack it, yet as Finney's converts questioned the ministerial authority of the establishment and often the legitimacy of earthly sources of authority as well, they brought an anarchic spirit to the burned-over communities of New York and Ohio.

The orthodox ministers viewed Finney's revivals in a broader context of radical sects, utopian experiments, and fierce anti-Catholicism. Like Finney, these groups fostered social disorder and alternative family structures in addition to suspect theological stances. Joseph Smith's Latter-Day Saints emerged in western New York in the 1820s, and while this was before Smith's formal declaration in favor of "celestial marriage," rumors of the community's alternative sexual practices already abounded.[12] Another sect, the Shakers, believed Christ had returned in the form of their leader, Ann Lee. The Shakers and the Quakers permitted women ministers, a serious affront to the leading orthodox ministers.[13] Even more loathsome to the New England clergy were the ideas of freethinkers like Frances Wright. Because both Lee and Wright opposed marriage (Lee and the Shakers were celibate; Wright opposed marriage and the laws punishing illegitimate children), orthodox clergy easily connected such dissenting sects with disorderly gender systems that truncated male power and promoted "abnormal" sexuality.[14] For the Protestant establishment, these movements provided living proof that, when taken too far, liberty would lead to licentiousness and particularly sexual misconduct. On the other end of the spectrum but with the same ultimate consequences, despotic Roman Catholic priests and nuns, beholden to the undemocratic pope, also came under attack in the 1820s. Lurid tales of abuse and sexual exploitation in nunneries contributed to the fear of spreading Catholicism in the frontier states, spurring Lyman Beecher to author *A Plea for the West*.[15]

While evangelical revivals brought momentary disorder in some cases, the men and women converts rarely turned out to be sex radicals and free lovers. Instead evangelicalism helped to shape new forms of manhood and womanhood that would become part and parcel of the ideology of domesticity in antebellum America. Evangelicalism found an eager audience among young white men who were trying to find a way of expressing their independence and manliness in the new market economy. A wage worker who could not afford his own land or who had little hope of reigning as a patriarch over a large farming family could, through his religious faith, assert his independence from his father's generation and from his employer. One did not have to be a Finney convert to find a new purpose in religious conversion, as more and more orthodox Calvinists became open to the possibility that missionary work and good works could be combined with the doctrine of predestination. Indeed, the young men who established and who served as missionaries for the American Board of Commissioners for Foreign Missionaries, for example, rejected the comforts of a bourgeois home and instead embraced the self-sufficiency and self-sacrifice required to labor in a foreign mission field. For Finney's converts in western New York and, later, at Oberlin College, this same ideology was put into practice in the form of manual-labor schools—where young men were taught individual self-reliance and were required to obey strict rules governing their diets and work habits, while fostering a Christian community.[16]

In contrast to their male counterparts, white female converts to evangelicalism during the Second Great Awakening acted on their faith in a very different way. Rather than seeking personal independence from old hierarchies and newfound ways of exercising self-reliance, evangelical women embraced the qualities of true womanhood. True women demonstrated selfless attention toward others, religious piety, sexual purity, and submission. Through self-abnegation, evangelical women gained moral strength precisely because they rejected self-interest, and in the name of service, they organized moral reform societies. More confrontational than the benevolence organizations that had existed since the American Revolution, moral-reform women wanted to do more than merely aid the victims of vice; they wanted to stamp it out entirely. In New York City, for example, women organized against prostitution, and New York City Female Moral Reform Society members held public prayer vigils in front of Manhattan's brothels. The moral-reform women went so far as to publish the names of men who frequented prostitutes, showing that while evangelical women may have drawn on a language of submission, their actions demonstrated that they sometimes put their moral obligations first.[17]

More often, however, evangelical women chose less controversial modes of moral influence.[18] When evangelical men experienced their conversion experience as a call to stand up for their religious beliefs, women's historians have shown that evangelical women viewed their conversion experience as a submission to God, a step typically made during adolescence and a precursor to their submission to their husband during marriage. Significantly, Christian women were to serve as a complement to their independent husbands, and they were not supposed to manifest the same independence of spirit. In the female seminaries that proliferated in the 1820s as a means for educating women to become mothers, teachers, and missionary wives, the lessons focused on self-denial instead of self-reliance and autonomy, as predominated in all-male manual-labor schools. While female organizing on behalf of moral reform and abolitionism directed some women to form the woman's rights movement, the vast majority of evangelical women did not go down this path to become suffragists. Instead, evangelical women sought to influence their husbands and children, gradually extending their sphere of influence to include certain moral issues in the public sphere. For example, when some evangelical women became abolitionists, they viewed slavery as a moral wrong that corrupted white and black families in the South, and therefore deserved northern women's attention.[19]

Evangelical men, however, had the largest role in shaping Oberlin and the Jamaica Mission. The well-documented life of Theodore Dwight Weld provides a way to trace how revivalists moved to construct a new moral order and value system in the manual-labor schools that dotted the frontier, and why they became committed to immediate emancipation in the early 1830s. In addition to being a well-known abolitionist orator, Weld was a friend, classmate, and colleague of the first missionaries to Jamaica. Before his marriage to women's rights activist Angelina Grimké, Weld focused little on ideas related to women (he even swore off marrying until emancipation occurred), and his writing and speeches instead seemed more intent on developing an ideology of evangelical manhood. Weld and his white evangelical abolitionist colleagues developed a gender ideology of evangelical manhood based in strict morality, manual labor and self-sufficiency, and economic and intellectual independence—an ideology they shared with many northern black allies. This stance would become the core of the "civilization" that the Oberlin missionaries to Jamaica wanted to impart to freed people in Jamaica.[20]

The son of an orthodox Congregationalist minister, Weld resisted conversion until his twenties, at which time an aunt insisted that he attend one of Finney's revival meetings. After some resistance, he was converted, and Weld followed his evangelical work with a stint at the Oneida Institute, a manual-labor school in Whitestown, New York.[21] Although manual labor or industrial education brings to mind Booker T. Washington and black education in the post–Civil War South, the origins of many of those abolitionist-founded southern schools rested in the industrializing antebellum North. In his perceptive analysis of why manual labor appealed to those who would become radical abolitionists, historian Paul Goodman noted that "manual labor, abolitionism, and racial integration" all acted as "expressions of a communitarian, egalitarian ethos at odds with the dominant strain of competitive individualism, an effort to balance moral values against market values."[22] Manual-labor education offered a middle path: a new social order compatible with the democratic impulses of evangelicalism that still provided a moral rigor found lacking in the anything-goes capitalism of the market towns. Schools like the Oneida Institute encouraged self-sufficiency, and they built character and fostered manly independence. Students learned to think, but they also learned to support themselves: to hew wood, to build houses, to fix machines, and to grow crops. In writing about the benefits of manual labor, Weld noted that "modern education has indeed achieved wonders," but it had not paid adequate attention to the formation of the body in which the mind was housed. Physical activity kept licentiousness at bay without too much supervision from overbearing authorities. Activity served as a self-regulator. Anticipating its later role in foreign and domestic missions, Weld maintained manual-labor education's importance as a civilizing force: "it would preserve the equilibrium of the system, moderate the inordinate demands of animal excitability, and quell the insurrection of appetite."[23]

The wealthy philanthropist Lewis Tappan could not agree more, and he sent two of his sons to be educated at Oneida. When Tappan met Theodore Weld at the school in 1831, he hired Weld to go on a lecture tour as an agent for the Society for the Promotion of Manual Labor, one of the

Tappan brothers' many reform organizations.²⁴ As Finney converts, Lewis and Arthur Tappan had been funding moral-reform causes in New York City for several years when they became interested in manual labor. Lewis believed that "physical and intellectual education" should "be considered inseparable." Lewis Tappan's support for manual labor would be a constant all of his life, from 1831 when he told his brother, Benjamin, that "it has been the disgrace of this country that education has made most men ashamed of manual labor," to his work in the 1860s to establish manual-labor schools for free blacks in the South. Already known for his speaking abilities, the talented and charismatic Weld seemed an obvious choice for spreading the word about manual labor around the country.²⁵

The Oneida Institute served as a model in Weld's speeches about manual labor. The strict moral code of the Oneida Institute required its students to abstain from alcohol, of course, but also coffee, tea, and other stimulants, and many of the students were practicing vegetarians, some adhering to the Graham diet that prescribed simple meals of mostly raw fruits and vegetables. There was also a work requirement for all enrolled students; by this mandate, some poor students funded their education, and wealthier students, like Lewis Tappan's two sons who attended Oneida, learned to value work. The Oneida students prided themselves on crafting an "amalgam of primitive-Christian and common-man" in their dress, labor habits, and meals.²⁶ Unsurprisingly, many students had an interest in missionary work, and they praised the practical component of the school's curriculum. One Oneida student and a future missionary to Jamaica, Charles Stewart Renshaw, rejected any kind of scholarship to help him afford his education, and instead praised Oneida's system that required him to work, to become "more of a self-made man." Renshaw had, according to Theodore Weld, served for seven years in the navy before attending Oneida, and was "a man of rare mind and heart, uncommon power as a speaker and writer, great common sense, tact, perseverance, energy, unswerving principle, benevolence, conscientiousness, self-denial."²⁷ Like Weld, Stewart Renshaw also praised manual labor as an ideal education for a future missionary. He found little use in studying Latin and Greek, for "it would not aid me in telling a heathen sinner the way to go to the saviour's feet." Missionary work excited him, though, as he felt "it is mocking the woes of Hell to sit here calmly studying, when we ought to be in the field, persuading and beseeching men to flee from the wrath to come."²⁸ The labor-intensive and practical education provided at Oneida was meant to develop skills that missionaries could use, whether they were stationed abroad or in the western United States.

As Weld traveled the country on behalf of manual labor in 1832, Arthur Tappan worked to convince Lyman Beecher, the renowned preacher, to become a part of the effort to train young ministers for the West. While the men had not always seen eye to eye on the subject of Charles Finney and revivalism, they both could agree on the need to train Protestant ministers for the new settlements in the western territories. Tappan asked Beecher to leave his Connecticut church and to serve as the president of Lane Seminary in Cincinnati; at around the same time, Theodore Weld and Lewis Tappan agreed that Lane would be an ideal location to establish a model manual-labor program. Weld enrolled at Lane Seminary in order to help develop the manual-labor curriculum, and he went forward with the plan that he and his fellow seminarians would be trained in practical skills that they could then take with them when they moved out to plant churches in rural outposts.

The shared commitment to evangelism, however, could not maintain the Beecher-Tappan alliance. In 1832, as Lyman Beecher and his daughter Catharine moved to Lane Seminary, Theodore Weld and the Tappan brothers encountered and embraced the early stirrings of the radical abolitionist movement. During his speaking tour on behalf of manual-labor education, Weld had met several early supporters of William Lloyd Garrison, the abolitionist editor of a new Boston newspaper, the *Liberator*. Defending the rights of enslaved men and women struck a chord with Weld, who already had a deep interest in the cause of manly independence. At almost the same time, in New York City, Garrison's newspaper had drawn the attention of the Tappan brothers. Meanwhile in Cincinnati, Lyman Beecher showed no interest in shifting his support away from the long-standing gradualist American Colonization Society. Like many northern and even southern evangelicals, Beecher recognized the moral dilemma that slavery presented, but he felt that a gradual end to the institution, accompanied by the removal of black Americans from the United States, offered a better and less divisive solution than immediate emancipation.[29]

In one sense, the evangelical reformers' sudden devotion to immediate abolitionism can be interpreted as the natural progression of a commitment to self-sufficiency and independence turning into an even broader critique of the institution of slavery, a system that denied independence and liberty for millions of people. For Weld, liberty was a Christian imperative, not something that could be granted or withheld by a human government. Like the Jamaica missionaries, he was, in effect, converted to abolition, and just as assuredly as he knew God, he now knew that slaves had to be freed. Yet after adopting abolitionism as his new cause, the struggle that became most important involved his own freedom to express abolitionist ideas and to act on his beliefs. At Lane Seminary, Weld led a rebellion against those who wanted to put limits on his own liberty. The battle between the students and trustees of Lane Seminary that took place in 1833 and 1834 reinforced the importance of independence in the minds of the young evangelical abolitionists standing up to the older establishment.

Even before immediate emancipation became their rallying cry, the Oneida students who had followed Theodore Weld to Lane Seminary proved difficult to control. They continued to follow the lifestyle that had reigned at Oneida, where they had risen at four in the morning and regulated their diets by avoiding meat or any stimulants. At Lane, the Oneida students would boycott lectures of faculty members they disliked, and they protested the hiring of any man who might "lay abed late of mornings" or who "profaned his body with tea and coffee."[30] One of Lyman Beecher's sons commented that the group was "uncommonly strong, a little uncivilized, entirely radical, and terribly in earnest . . . a kind of *imperium in imperio*."[31] Beecher himself complained about the Oneida students: they "are the offspring of the Oneida denunciatory revivals, and are made up of vinegar, aqua fortis, and oil of vitriol, with brimstone, saltpeter, and charcoal, to explode and scatter corrosive matter."[32] Unsurprisingly, Weld had little success in converting Beecher to the abolitionist cause, and Weld decided to take a bold step on behalf of his new reform agenda.[33]

Freshly apprised of the first meeting of the American Anti-Slavery Society in Philadelphia, Weld organized a series of debates at the seminary between supporters of colonization and immediate abolitionism. Scheduled for February 1834, the meetings incorporated seventeen speakers who had experiences with slavery in the South, including James Thome, the son of a Kentucky slaveholder, and a former slave who was the only black student at Lane, James Bradley. Most of the faculty and students attended the meetings spread over nine evenings, and they listened to speakers discuss documents from the American Colonization Society as well as the newly founded American Anti-Slavery Society. Lyman Beecher even sat in on some of the meetings, and had a student read out an essay of his gradualist views that his daughter, Catharine, had drafted (but did not read publicly) for him.[34]

The passionate speeches and dramatic narratives of slavery worked like an evangelical revival in persuading most of the student attendees to convert to immediate abolitionism, and almost all of the students concluded the debates by voting against colonization.[35] They agreed that slavery was a sin, and those Christians who continued to countenance slavery were sinners. In addition to condemning slaveholders, the radical abolitionists also faulted northern colonizationists and gradualists for compromising with sinners, which surely went against God. One former advocate of colonization learned the error of his ways after hearing from free blacks in Cincinnati of "their preference to remain in their native land, rather than to emigrate 'home' to a foreign shore."[36] The students at Lane planned to employ the power of moral suasion to convince their co-religionists of their mistaken commitment to gradualism, and they would also turn their attention to slaveholders in the South, opening "the minds of slave holders [with] the truth, in the spirit of the Gospel."[37] In the wake of the meetings, an abolitionist student group formed, and the participants intended to act on their ideals and to reach out to the black community in Cincinnati. Critically, the seminarians' sense of freedom and manly independence was tied up in their advocacy for immediate emancipation. When the Lane Anti-Slavery Society declared that a black man was "a moral agent, a keeper of his own happiness, the executive of his own powers, the accountable arbiter of his own choice," they were also talking about themselves.[38]

In addition to organizing their abolitionist society, the Lane students took their activism into Cincinnati's black community as volunteer teachers. The young men discovered many African Americans to be far more interested in the teachers' philanthropy than working-class whites. Augustus Wattles, a theology student at Lane who became the superintendent for colored schools in the city, reported to the Ohio Anti-Slavery Convention in 1835 that black people demonstrated "a docility and readiness to be benefited which invites effort in their behalf." As James Brewer Stewart has argued, white abolitionists and northern blacks found common ground in the language of respectability and the task of education, even if they came to this common ground for quite different reasons. In Cincinnati, the white evangelicals found people whom they could defend and improve, and they worked out a mode of activism that they hoped would redeem white America and themselves. Black people, many of whom had been born into slavery, gained white allies who could offer the resources otherwise denied them under Cincinnati's draconian race laws. Although Ohio laws forbade slavery, Cincinnati's location as a trading hub on the Ohio River, just across from slaveholding Kentucky, made it a destination for fugitive slaves, and the city government responded with restrictive black codes. In 1829, a few years before the Lane students initiated their abolitionist society and activism, a white mob had conducted a reign of terror in the city for three days, and over one thousand blacks left Cincinnati for Canada. In this climate, the efforts of the students from Lane Seminary must have seemed a welcome and surprising turn of events.[39]

The visibility of the student activists in the black community and their use of the school's facilities as a base for their operations antagonized Lane's trustees, four of whom served on the American Colonization Society's board. The trustees also sought to protect Lane Seminary's reputation from the gathering storm of accusations of interracial social mixing. For northern whites, the fear of interracial sex informed most attacks on abolitionism.[40] Political cartoons parodied abolitionist women as masculine beings or as overly sexual creatures drawn to black men. These sexist and racist vilifications were more than mere words and pictures, and they antagonized white mobs who launched physical attacks against abolitionists' homes and meetings, as well as black neighborhoods, as had happened in Cincinnati in 1829. Aware that such accusations of familiarity between blacks and whites threatened the safety of his school and his students, Lyman Beecher warned Weld that he would gladly "fill your pockets with money" to open "colored schools," but "if you will visit in colored families, and walk with them in the streets, you will be overwhelmed."[41] Christian benevolence, with the implied social distance between the generous donor and thankful recipient, was acceptable; socializing between the races should be condemned. Theodore Weld and the other Lane students ignored Beecher's advice, and they declared their belief in "social intercourse according to character, irrespective of color," and made no motion to desist attending black churches or joining black families for meals, parties, and funerals.[42] Indeed, for Lane's apprehensive trustees, the most shocking stories about the Lane students involved actions like that of white seminarian Augustus Wattles, who was seen escorting a black woman, or the attempt of the students to seat a black woman next to "one of the most prominent white ladies in the city" at a church service.[43] Black and white mixing may have been allowed in the all-male confines of the Lane Seminary, but when the Lane students attempted to integrate Cincinnati and openly transgressed gender boundaries, their behavior stirred resentment and led to scenes of mob violence.

In order to attempt some kind of damage control, the trustees denounced the "exciting topics" that had become so interesting to students at Lane, and the local newspaper agreed, commenting that "there may be room enough in the wide world for abolitionism and perfectionism, and many other isms; but a school, to prepare pious youth for preaching the gospel, has not legitimate place for these."[44] In the summer of 1834, with Lyman Beecher in New York, the board passed a series of regulations that banned the school's abolitionist society and prohibited the discussion of slavery even in private conversations. The board further decided to fire the faculty member who supported the students and moved to expel the students' leaders, Theodore Weld, James Thome, and Henry B. Stanton, the future husband of woman's rights activist Elizabeth Cady Stanton.[45] Echoing his earlier criticisms of the disorderly tendencies coming out of Charles Finney's evangelical revival meetings, Lyman Beecher complained that the students' support of abolitionism represented an affront to their elders and to the God-given social hierarchy. Beecher affirmed that the school's "plan of Parental and evangelical government is right and would have carried all before it but for one headlong power mind too powerful and too unsafe to be trusted."[46] In the opinion of Beecher and the members of the seminary's board, the students' complaints that their freedom of inquiry was being circumscribed made no sense as they were not independent men but sons with a dependent place in the family hierarchy. Weld was leading them into rebellion. To the board members, the threatening mobs opposing abolitionism and the disobedient behavior of the students were both "signs of the times," revealing the "strong and growing propensity to insubordination—a disposition to set up individual notions or constructions in opposition to lawful authority," whether that order was local government or the patriarchal family.[47] Much to Weld's irritation, the *Western Monthly Magazine*, published in Cincinnati, agreed, calling the students "embryo clergymen" and "precocious undergraduates," and blaming them for disrupting public order.⁴⁸

The students were hardly shamed into submission. Instead they embraced their insubordinate status and protested the administration's attempts to control their freedom of speech. When school resumed in October 1834, seventy-five students withdrew from the seminary. Out of the larger group, the core members—about a dozen students, including Theodore Weld, the Kentuckian James Thome, and the future corresponding secretary for the American Missionary Association, George Whipple—removed to Cumminsville, Ohio. In December the Lane Rebels launched a public attack against those who had sought to quell their moral opposition to slavery, and in January 1835, they published their *Statement of the Reasons Which Induced the Students of Lane Seminary, to Dissolve Their Connection with that Institution*, signed by fifty-one students. In it, they framed their experience at Lane as one in which their speech had been suppressed, but they left the subject of their speech, abolitionism, out of their report. Perhaps they did so in order to gain broader support, as more northerners would agree with their rights to free speech and to organize than with their stance on abolitionism. Notably, the document said little about the institution of slavery or the racist attitudes of Lane's trustees, a point that Theodore Weld mentioned in a letter written in 1835. He first made the point that his opposition to racism was "expressed in our Expose of the Lane Sem." but then remembered "that a long paragraph was stricken out by a vote of the majority of the brethren which they thought was so strong *amalgamationally* that the Anti Slavery community would kick."⁴⁹ Rather than focusing on what might be a controversial issue for even abolitionists, Weld agreed to leave out the paragraph condemning racism and in favor of interracial interactions.

Instead, the Lane Rebels appealed to a broader audience of white men, and they wrote in a democratic language that defended the rebels' rights. They wrote that if schools had the power to control what students discussed, then they defeated the entire point of education. "Better, infinitely better, that the mob demolish every building . . . than that our theological seminaries should become Bastiles, our theological students, thinkers by *permission*, and the right of free discussion tamed down into a soulless thing of gracious, condescending sufferance."⁵⁰ In contrast, Beecher and the trustees of Lane reflected an older generation's belief that the school, like society at large, should reflect a family order in which younger students needed to demonstrate proper deference to their elders. The students, in contrast, exhibited aspects of Jacksonian democracy in their self-conception as the egalitarian faithful. God had entrusted them with a moral duty to act, and their right to "free discussion" was a "right conferred by God, and its proscription would be 'sacrilege.'"[51]

The Lane Rebels arranged to continue their education on terms acceptable to them at Oberlin. The Oberlin Institute, as it was then called, already had a secondary school and a college, and in December 1834 arrangements were made between John Shipherd, the Tappans, and others to create a seminary at Oberlin. While only men were to be enrolled in the seminary, the college and preparatory school had both male and female pupils. Arthur Tappan pledged twenty thousand dollars to the school, with others sympathetic to the Lane Rebels offering to pay for the salaries of eight new faculty, under two conditions: first, the revivalist Charles Finney was to be hired as a theology professor, and second, Oberlin would accept black students. After a good deal of debate and a vote on the proposal conducted by the students, the measure passed, and Oberlin welcomed the new influx of cash, faculty, and the Lane Rebels.[52]

After Shipherd agreed to accept the Lane Rebels and abolitionist funding, he found himself the recipient of a great deal of friendly and not-so-friendly advice. One man wrote Shipherd about his concern for the school's reputation: "New England will scarcely bear to have young Ladies at the same sem[inar]y [with white gentlemen]." While conceding the point that coeducational institutions would eventually have their day, he wrote that there was no possibility that interracial schools would ever gain popular acceptance. "To place black and white together on the same standing will not most certainly be endured . . . and in trying to do this you will lose the other object, nay you lose Oberlin." The writer further warned Shipherd that when black students arrived at the school, "the whites will begin to leave" and that Oberlin would become a black college. "Why not have a black Institution, 'Dyed in the wool'—and let Oberlin be?" Unless "you do not at least keep the blacks entirely separate, so as to *veto* the notion of amalgamation I am persuaded that the Colony . . . will be blown *sky high* and you will have a black establishment there thro out!"[53] While some protested the interracial aspect of Oberlin, others found fault with the coeducational component. The former Lane professor and friend of the rebels, John Morgan, maintained that he would only move to Oberlin if black students were allowed to matriculate. The question of women, however, was more problematic: "the mixing of young men and women together in the same institution strikes me as not at all judicious," Morgan confided to Theodore Weld.[54]

The perils of operating an interracial and coeducational school were amplified at Oberlin precisely because of the evangelical abolitionists' tendency to attack the existing and accepted social order. Yet very few of even the most radical abolitionists had wholeheartedly endorsed interracial marriage, with most dodging the question, suggesting that black people and white people would prefer not to marry each other, and pointing to slavery as the real cause of interracial sex. Responding to accusations that emancipation would result in "amalgamation," evangelical abolitionist Amos Phelps offered a typical rejoinder:

> [G]ive that slave girl her freedom, and instead of courting the unhallowed embrace of her master or his sons as an honor, she would have a character of her own, and would stand upon it, and reject that embrace . . . So long as the present prejudice exists there is no danger. Do you think, Mr. Objector, that with your present feeling there is any danger of your amalgamating? . . . Only keep your prejudice alive, and instill it in your children, and rely upon it, neither you nor they will ever marry a negro.[55]

A freed slave would seek a husband of her own color, and if so prejudiced, white people would not seek black spouses. If in the distant future, "this prejudice should melt away," Phelps continued, then there would be no basis for any "objection to amalgamation." Taking a moment to imagine this future, Phelps presented the commonly shared view among white and black abolitionists that with education would come respectability, and racial differences would cease to be an issue among people of the same refined morals.[56]

At Oberlin, teaching respectability meant reinforcing separate spheres for men and women, and the ideology of domesticity, for the dual purposes of forming morally upstanding young people and countering accusations that the school sponsored licentiousness. Although male and female students largely followed the same curriculum, the school's policies kept them separated and heavily supervised to guard against any romantic liaisons.

Students also had work assignments intended to teach proper gendered behavior, and as farmers, carpenters, mechanics, and printers, young men learned how to support themselves and their families, while young women trained to be housekeepers, mothers, and moral reformers. The unprecedented step of educating men alongside women, and blacks alongside whites, was answered with a rigid structure meant to preserve order and proper gender roles.[57]

Not long after the Lane Rebels moved to Oberlin, however, a small minority of radical abolitionist men and women in the North issued a challenge to these very gender roles. Women's general participation in the antislavery movement was never in question, given that most abolitionist men, whether evangelical or otherwise, felt that women, as the morally superior sex and as politically disinterested reformers, would lend credibility to their cause. Consequently, from the early 1830s, male abolitionists encouraged women to petition the federal government to end slavery in Washington, D.C.; to form female antislavery societies; and to influence their families and friends. Both men and women emphasized the point that slavery was a *moral* question, not only a *political* concern, and therefore a perfectly acceptable cause for benevolent Christian women. Yet in the late 1830s some white women steeped in the abolitionist men's language of freedom and equal rights for African Americans began to see a larger role for themselves that moved beyond this limited activism. When the southern-born Philadelphia Quakers, Angelina and Sarah Grimké, went on an abolitionist speaking tour in 1837, they upset many abolitionist men who felt that women speaking in front of "promiscuous" mixed-sex audiences ended up hurting the cause more than helping it. The Grimkés' critics saw their speaking tour as evidence that abolitionists wanted to destroy the existing social order and turn the United States over to anarchism and sexual license. As more conservative antislavery supporters as well as some abolitionists spoke out against the Grimké sisters, the two women fired back: might not women have the same rights as men to act on their faith?[58]

At the 1840 meeting of the American Anti-Slavery Society, the pro–woman's rights supporters of William Lloyd Garrison nominated a woman, Abby Kelley, to serve on one of the group's committees, much to the distress of Lewis Tappan and his evangelical allies. The Garrisonians outnumbered the Tappanites at the meeting, and Kelley was elected. For the evangelical men and women at Oberlin, and those who would form the American Missionary Association, the "woman question" distracted from the primary goal of abolitionism: the immediate abolition of slavery in the South. New conversations about the emancipation of women muddied the movement, and, importantly, compromised the ideology of domesticity that kept women morally above the fray of politics. Evangelical abolitionist men and women adhered to the ideology of domesticity; God had decreed that women and men occupy different spheres and modes of activism, and this division would be broken if women began to speak publicly before men and women and if women became full members of the same organizations as men. Michael Pierson has argued that this conservative patriarchal interpretation of domesticity could be seen in abolitionist politics as well, especially in the Liberty Party's newspapers in the 1840s.[59]

The arguments in favor of sexual equality made by abolitionist lecturers Angelina and Sarah Grimké in the late 1830s and their successors in the 1840s, including Abby Kelley, had little to do with Oberlin's coeducational policy. Shipherd had initiated the education of women at Oberlin in order to provide educated and pious women as wives for the mission-minded men he educated for the conversion of the West. Thus, the ideology of domesticity, not women's rights or female equality, prevailed at Oberlin during its first decade. In accordance with the ideology of domesticity, the administrators at Oberlin expected the school's female students to be above reproach and to exemplify submissiveness, sexual purity, and morality. Mary Welch Cowles, the head of the Female Department at Oberlin from 1835 to 1839, offered practical advice to her young ladies—"Be accurate in everything . . . be scrupulously honest in very little things . . . cultivate a cheerful countenance . . . make short calls"—and a note to the fashion-conscious: "never wear dark skirts under light skirts or dresses." She also gave talks titled "Learning" and "Marriage," and addressed the subject of being a minister's wife.[60] These were not the lessons of sexual equality. Instead, they harmonized with the position of the Lane Rebels' old nemesis, Catharine Beecher, and her growing opus on domesticity. While Oberlin's professors might have disagreed with the Beecher family's moderate antislavery and support of colonization, they fully supported the family's views about the roles of women in public life. The radicalism of Oberlin's male students and its obvious attachment to the abolitionist movement was therefore tempered by an emphasis on particular gender roles. Although the work ethic and moral zeal at Oberlin made the school's students stand apart from the predominant culture of the northern middle class, Oberlin's early faculty and students did not promote sexual equality.[61]

The work assignments handed to the school's female students provided one way of teaching domesticity. Unlike some of the utopian communities whose members experimented in new gender roles through their plans for collective living in the antebellum years, Oberlin's rules ensured that their boarding houses' dining halls modeled the dining room of a family home. Male and female students ate together in Oberlin's boarding houses' dining rooms with assigned seats for the entire year—benches for the men and proper chairs for the ladies. One student wrote, "The ladies set around among the gentlemen to wait on the table, get milk, bread, etc. when wanted."[62] In addition to serving at table, the female students prepared the food and washed the dishes after meals. Far from relying on the girls' education before coming to Oberlin on these matters, the head of the Female Department, Alice Cowles, prepared numbered instructions for each task. Cleaning silverware, for example, had eight separate steps.[63] The rules concerning preparing the food and removing it from the tables, mopping the floors, and washing clothes and linens were similarly precise, showing that perfectionism could be applied to the scientific management of the domestic sphere as well as to the moral improvement of the outside world.

As the young women at Oberlin fulfilled their manual-labor requirements in selfless domestic service, the male students learned the work associated with independence and self-sufficiency cultivated at other all-male manual-labor schools. The young men worked on the school's farm, performed mechanical repairs on equipment, and worked on the printing press, following instructions for each task just as specifically written out as were the girls' instructions for their dishwashing. While manual labor changed form over the course of the 1830s and 1840s, moving from an obligation to an elective department, it remained critical in the minds of many students and alumni who persisted in their commitment to Theodore Weld's vision for the tasks and the concept. One wrote that the "pecuniary disadvantages" of the college's farm "can never counter-balance the moral, intellectual, and physical advantages that he derives from manual labor."[64] The orderliness of their manual-labor obligations also appeared in their daily schedules, and it structured their days just as it had done at the Oneida Institute in the 1820s. Both sexes kept strict schedules: rising between four and five in the morning when the bell rang, spending a half hour in prayer, and then breakfast, work, classes, and other meals until the evening when they retired at nine-thirty.[65]

Just as men and women had interpreted their conversion experiences in gendered ways, young women at Oberlin did not see the manual-labor requirement as a means to greater autonomy and independence, as did young men. Female students praised the manual-labor system, and one, writing to the school's agent in England, explained that it was "the very thing we need. After having our minds absorbed in some abstract subject until we become weary with intense thought, we repair to some household duty and the mind and body become relaxed." As the rigors of the classroom tired the female mind, domestic work repaired it. The student continued, "While the majority of well educated ladies are ignorant of domestic affairs, here the two are blended, here domestic economy which is true should be inculcated by the mother is carried on to still greater perfection, here knowledge of domestic affairs, high intellectual culture, and even refinement of manners are considered as consistent with each other."[66] For women and for men, Oberlin paired a thoroughly eastern education with the expectation that its students be prepared to live practical lives rooted in the soil, for the men, and in the home, for the women.

In addition to providing its students with many regimented and gendered tasks, the school also had numerous rules governing any social interaction between the sexes. Marriages among the students were strictly forbidden, and the faculty expelled married students. Young women were prohibited from going on walks around town on Sundays, from walking in "the fields or woods without special permission from the Principal," and in order to leave her room, she had to obtain permission from the house mother.[67] In spite of faculty attempts to control the Oberlin students, some were asked to leave because they violated the rules and formed attachments. One young man was expelled because his "habits of associating with young ladies are not such as will sustain the character of this Institution or the honor of the Christian name." He was warned that at Oberlin in particular, "Their example and influence cannot fail to be most pernicious!"[68] The Ladies' Board, which constantly reviewed the characters of female students, and the watchful faculty kept most sexual or even flirtatious liaisons between students from occurring in the name of protecting the reputation of the school. In looking closely at the infractions handed out by the Ladies' Board, historian Carol Lasser observed that black students received a disproportionate number of disciplinary warnings. She suggests that for "black women, gendered deference implied racialized subordination," and that while the women on the Ladies' Board favored "public invisibility" as an attribute of evangelical womanhood, black women sought public involvement as a way to live out their abolitionist commitments. At Oberlin, the ties that had connected black and white abolitionists began to fray.[69]

In spite of its religious orthodoxy and conservative gender ideology, Oberlin's reputation for radicalism in the antebellum decades is not unwarranted because of its students who critiqued its harsher policies. Most famous is the story of Lucy Stone, a twenty-five-year-old supporter of William Lloyd Garrison, who matriculated in 1843. Stone came to Oberlin as a supporter of woman's rights and an opponent to institutional religion.[70] At Oberlin, however, she found that its radical reputation only extended to a degree. She wrote to her parents of her irritation with some of the school's policies: "I was never in a place where women are so rigidly taught that they must not speak in public." Stone also complained of the antagonism between the administration and the radicals who had overtaken the American Anti-Slavery Society. "They hate Garrison, and woman's rights . . . I love both, and often find myself at swords' points with them." But the history of woman's rights at Oberlin was not as clear-cut as Stone implied.[71]

Before Stone enrolled at Oberlin, some of the school's Lane Rebels supported a move to make speech and rhetoric classes coeducational, but apparently, most of the school's young ladies protested. Later, when Lucy Stone and her friend and future sister-in-law Antoinette Brown asked to debate with their male classmates in 1846, their professor, Lane Rebel James Thome, granted the request. The faculty quickly vetoed Thome's decision and prevented any repeated public speeches by women, even those requesting especially to read their commencement addresses themselves. Another incident showing the difficulties of restricting some of Oberlin's female scholars took place when Lucy Stone accepted an invitation to speak at a black school in 1846 on the anniversary of West Indian emancipation. That same year, Stone had invited the Garrisonian abolitionists Abby Kelley Foster and her husband Stephen Foster to campus to speak on abolitionism and woman's rights, and many in the Oberlin community disapproved, especially when Abby Kelley took to the stage. In spite of the ongoing resistance from Oberlin's Ladies' Board and many of the male faculty to woman's rights activism at the school, for a number of Oberlin's graduates, including Stone, Brown, Sallie Holley, and Betsey Cowles, their education had not taught them to submit to domesticity, but they had instead imbibed the abolitionist lessons about independence and applied it to themselves. The lesson of Oberlin's more radical female students shows the difficulty in limiting the radicalism of abolitionism to a select few, and the inherent problems of mixing one kind of hierarchy—domesticity—with calls for equality. It is not hard to imagine that the Jamaica Mission's combined focus on abolitionism and the structure of a hierarchical civilizing mission would spark similar protests.[72]

Unlike Stone, however, most of Oberlin's female students preferred to engage in less controversial avenues of moral reform. The ideology of domesticity underwrote the Oberlin Female Moral Reform Society, and even Lucy Stone joined this organization rooted in the ideology of domesticity and gender distinctions. This organization along with other familiar causes of female benevolence revealed the rift between the principles of the ideology of domesticity that kept white women silent and secluded in their homes and the reasoning invoked by women that their gender made them ideal commentators on social problems. Women reformers who did not support sexual equality connected the ideology of domesticity to broader issues with ease. A representative of the New York Female Moral Reform Society lectured to the Oberlin organization that immorality stemmed from a wide variety of causes that they needed to guard against, including "Impure imagination, Dress of females, Slavery, Public opinion licenses the evil, Females receiving visits of gentlemen protracted to a late hour, Low prices of labor in cities, Voluptuousness, Balls, Parties, Theaters, Novel Reading, Classics, Prints, and Books."[73] For the women at Oberlin—students and teachers alike—female education provided a rational way to teach domesticity and to instill morality; the classroom was not a place for women to become supporters of equal rights. Yet by upholding women as the defenders of morality and social order, Oberlin trained them to be outspoken about some matters. Even women who had no interest in women's rights, suffrage, or sexual equality would become thorns in the side of men who dared depart from the doctrines of Christian perfectionism.

The fiery sermons of Charles Finney sparked an initial outburst of religious radicalism that affected young men and women alike who were seeking a new way to understand themselves and their relation to God, their families, and their fellow citizens. As New Englanders migrated west, settled in booming canal towns, worked for wages, and started families, the old social order based in close-knit communities and patriarchal farming families seemed to be falling apart. Although Finney and his followers attacked religious authorities and constraining hierarchies, they did not support anarchy. They organized a new social order for themselves, and out of Finney's revivals came the manual-labor schools that taught evangelical men to value independence from their elders and to appreciate self-discipline and self-reliance. For these men, abolitionism was a claim at independence from the older and established Protestant clergy as well as from their actual fathers, and their activism against slavery allowed them to express their manly independence in such a way that did not contradict their obedience to a rigorous moral code. The freedom and liberty exalted in abolitionism also blended with their own personal desires for independence in the market society being created around them. Yet as the 1830s progressed and some Garrisonian abolitionists rejected organized religion and politics, the more moderate evangelical abolitionists at Oberlin sought to temper freedom with the bonds of family and of church discipline, relying on Christian liberty to keep the dangers of despotism and license at bay.

The abolitionist and evangelical beliefs informing the Jamaica Mission combined a fervent commitment to individual liberty with the constraints of sexual purity, womanly submission, and religious discipline. For the abolitionists at Oberlin who would become involved in the AMA, slavery's end would best be worked out in these terms. In their imagined version of an emancipated society, freed people would be instantly changed with the knowledge of their freedom. This change would come quickly, abolitionists predicted, just like how the abolitionists experienced awakenings in the evangelical revivals and abolitionist meetings. The freed people of a post-emancipation society would eagerly sign up to be educated in manual-labor schools where black men and women would learn proper gender roles and the importance of religious piety and moral behavior. They would then form families and become darker-skinned versions of their white abolitionist teachers. These expectations provided little flexibility for incorporating what black Jamaicans wanted from freedom, nor did they take into consideration the persistent racism of former slaveholders or a whole host of economic and political obstacles that accompanied emancipation. All of these unexpected hurdles would make themselves known in the British West Indies, the location where the American abolitionists had an opportunity to put their ideas into practice.

2 Slavery and Freedom in Jamaica

Although New England and Jamaica shared a common heritage as British colonies, they were separated by a social and cultural gulf as well as geographical distance. As the forefathers of the American missionaries built up their city on a hill in Massachusetts, another Puritan, Oliver Cromwell, oversaw the British Navy's capture of Jamaica from the Catholic Spanish in 1655. During its first decades as a British colony, Jamaica hardly lived up to the rigorous moral standards of the Lord Protector, and it became a notorious haven for pirates interested in acquiring gold and silver from Spanish ships departing from Mexico. By the eighteenth century, however, stealing material wealth had become secondary to the riches derived from the labor of African slaves on sugar estates. Europeans and Americans had acquired a taste for sugar, and planters who had been given land grants on the island were eager to supply the need. Like the British colonies of Virginia and Barbados, Jamaica became an important agricultural producer fitting into a transatlantic triangle connecting the mother country with her North American and Caribbean possessions.

Vast numbers of African slaves were imported to Jamaica, and for those who survived the Middle Passage, a period of seasoning occurred, in which Africans were "broken," as well as tested with new diseases and a new labor regime. Throughout the eighteenth century, newly imported captives replenished an ever-decreasing population of slaves in the West Indies. As a testament to the brutality of Jamaican slavery, although 750,000 Africans had been brought to the island, only 311,000 people were emancipated in 1834, a stark contrast to the reproducing slave population in the U.S. South that had gone from around 650,000 imported Africans to four million enslaved people on the eve of the Civil War.[1] As Alexander Byrd has described, the harsh labor conditions were only one part of what made life in Jamaica especially difficult at the end of the eighteenth century. In the 1780s and 1790s, "successive environmental tragedies and disasters," including hurricanes, droughts, earthquakes, and epidemics, merged with "the general disasters and tragedies of Jamaican servitude," and "inflected a significant portion of this generation with a fatalism that went beyond that of mere enslavement."[2]

The violence and upheaval of slavery had many consequences. Byrd and other historians of slavery have pointed out the problem of understanding a slave society as divided only along lines of planter and slave, white and black, because the slave community itself hardly represented a united front.[3] A significant number of African slaves in Jamaica had fled their captivity and had settled in the mountains, creating Maroon villages that waged a decades-long war against those who would reenslave them. The British and Maroons signed a treaty in 1739 in which the Maroons agreed to defend the island and not to harbor fugitive slaves in exchange for their freedom. Among the enslaved people, divisions between different groups of Africans, and African-born and Jamaican-born people existed, although after the end of the slave trade in 1807, the Jamaican-born creoles became a majority. The growing population of free "browns" or colored people, many of whom were the manumitted children of whites and their slave mistresses, or "housekeepers," settled in town, and often tried to separate themselves from the rural enslaved blacks, creating more fractures along class and color lines. Geography and work also separated enslaved people in Jamaica. Jamaica's terrain meant that it had more agricultural diversity than other sugar-dominated islands. Large sugar estates prevailed on the coastal plains, and the cooler temperatures in the mountainous interior of the island made the land conducive to coffee plants. Animal pens raising beasts of burden and cattle for food also marked the Jamaican landscape. Historian Barry Higman estimates that, in 1832, fewer than half of Jamaican slaves worked on sugar estates. Fourteen percent worked on coffee properties, and almost 13 percent for livestock pens. Smaller numbers of slaves lived in town or were hired out by their masters for jobs repairing roads or as seasonal labor.[4]

Amid this diversity, an Afro-creole culture developed in Jamaica. Creole religious practices and beliefs, as well as creole understandings of land, property, and gender, all informed how black Jamaicans conceptualized and actualized freedom.[5] Jamaica was very different from the American South, and black Jamaican culture shared little in common with the African American northerners who had been the allies and friends of the future American missionaries. These differences were not always clear to white abolitionists. When the American Anti-Slavery Society sent James Thome and J. Horace Kimball to investigate the state of emancipation in the West Indies, for example, their resulting book depicted black Jamaicans as blank slates, eager to adopt the culture of Christian civilization.[6] Consequently, when the American missionaries arrived in Jamaica in the late 1830s, they were surprised to find a thriving cultural landscape of African-inflected Myal religion and black-led Native Baptist churches, while the white British mission churches had begun a long decline. Disputes between freed people and landowners disrupted the wage-labor economy, and perhaps most irritating to the missionaries, few black Jamaican men and women shared the same notions of middle-class respectability as the missionaries. This chapter addresses how black Jamaicans imagined freedom before and after emancipation in 1834, and the obstacles they faced during the apprenticeship period and immediately after full emancipation in 1838.

During and after emancipation, slave drivers served as important spiritual leaders in the mission churches and in the black Baptist churches; these men attracted the attention of the first five Oberlin ministers in Jamaica. Unsurprisingly, given their background in the United States, the Americans looked for black Christian men, and not women, to be their liaisons with communities in search of a minister. Their approach did not necessarily lead to mutual respect. The *Oberlin Evangelist* reported that one Jamaican neighborhood "had chosen a minister of their own number, after having built and furnished a chapel; but he was so ignorant that they dismissed him." They hired the American Charles Stewart Renshaw as his replacement. Missionary Ralph Tyler's congregation at Devon Pen "built a chapel, furnished it with a Bible (when none could read), and then set themselves for praying for a minister," and Amos Dresser stepped into the role previously filled by "an aged man, who had been a slave" but who "kept up meetings for a long time."[7] The mission churches were not created out of nothing, but were built around and within preexisting religious communities. The choice to change out an aging black minister for a young American who promised resources, teachers, and schools shows how adaptable creole religion could be. When the American minister became a burden instead of a blessing, he could just as easily be replaced. For the American missionaries, however, these narratives of churches choosing an American over an "ignorant" black leader indicated how eager black Jamaicans were to advance toward the light of civilization.

As these accounts show, when the Americans first arrived in Jamaica, they knew little of the religious history of the people they sought to convert to their version of Christianity. Indeed, like other nineteenth-century Protestant missionaries, the Oberlin graduates dismissed creole religion as a collection of superstitions instead of seeing it as a coherent religious system. But just as industrialization, the Second Great Awakening, and western migration, among other factors, had shaped the contours of the Americans' faith, Afro-Jamaican religion took its form from the many people living on the island. The religious practices and beliefs of white and black Jamaicans drew on African belief systems, Anglican liturgics, African American Baptists, and the dissenting theology of English missionaries. As historian Vincent Brown explains, "The cultural forms that sacred authority took underwent a continual process of convergence and re-definition as they resonated with the practical demands of domination on the one side, and of survival struggles within slavery on the other."[8] White and black Jamaicans both adapted religion to serve their purposes. For the enslaved, religion provided one way for Africans and Jamaican-born slaves to assert control over their souls and to validate their humanity while they were treated as human chattel, even though planters also learned to use religious symbols as a way to put down slave resistance.

The terminology for the creole religions practiced on the island deserves some discussion. White accounts from the pre-emancipation period show that components of African religions survived in burial ceremonies, conceptions of the afterlife, and deity myths, but that these elements also took on modified forms in Jamaica. For commentators on Jamaican religion in the 1600s and 1700s, "Obeah men" (or women) were akin to witches who could work negative and positive magic on others. In historian Mary Turner's words, Obeah men were "spiritual leaders with authority as headmen and drivers" who "united the attributes of diviners and medicine men . . . conversant with good and bad magic and with herbs."[9] Historians have pointed to the importance of Obeah in slave resistance from poisonings to more coordinated events, as well as the willingness of professing Christians to seek out Obeah men for backup supernatural assistance.[10] After 1760, a more ritualized Afro-Jamaican religion, Myal, emerged. Generally, Myal has been described as a "positive" and community-affirming religion, while the term "Obeah" delineated individualist and "negative" witchcraft.[11] This perception perhaps emerged because by the late eighteenth century, Myal became mixed in with the Native Baptist churches, while Obeah, whose practitioners could be punished with death, remained underground and private. Diana Stewart has argued that the distinction between the two only came into being during the Myal Revival of the 1840s when Myalists defined themselves against Obeah. Because most of the uses of the terms "Obeah" and "Myal" derive from white observers who each came up with their own definitions, I am going to simplify matters here by referring to Afro-Jamaican creole religion as "Myal." As the American missionaries came to Jamaica after emancipation and just as the Myal Revival was taking place, they tended to use this term. Further, while the missionaries occasionally reported on "Obeah men" near their mission stations, they felt that Myal and Myal-influenced black-led churches were a larger threat to their missionary goals.[12]

Before emancipation, Myal developed as a way for Africans from different places to unite with a common creole faith and language, and to develop a way to exact justice for misdeeds within the slave community. Myal had core beliefs reflecting general attributes of western African religions: a communion of deities or spirits, ancestral veneration, possession trance, food offerings and animal sacrifice, divination and herbalism, and a belief in a strong, neutral sacred power. Myalists believed invisible and visible powers controlled the world, and that these powers needed to be kept in balance for the well-being of humankind. Black Jamaicans did not assign an inherent moral value of "good" or "evil" to people or objects in Myal rituals; rather they believed that each person had the capacity for either. Consequently, the general goal of practicing Myalists was to achieve neutrality, for the sake of the community's temporal greater good, rather than salvation. Unlike the American missionaries' singular focus on an individual's conversion, Myal emphasized the community's well-being rather than the state of an individual soul.[13]

Second, Myal differed from the American missionaries' Christian perfectionism in its pluralism. Whereas Oberlin's evangelicalism called for the purity of the church and the exclusion of those who did not obey church teachings, Myal served a more diverse society and consequently proved highly adaptable to a multitude of believers. It enabled linguistically and culturally diffuse Africans to formulate a common creole religious lexicon that existed as perhaps the sole black institution in Jamaica. Myal, as Monica Schuler points out, "was the first Jamaican religion known to have addressed itself to the affairs of the entire heterogeneous slave society rather than to the narrower concerns of separate ethnic groups."[14] Myal was born in a context where enslaved people needed to form a common religious framework in order to consolidate a community that would enable them to cultivate a sense of humanity under brutalizing circumstances. In contrast, the evangelicalism of the American missionaries to Jamaica grew out of an impulse of separatism rather than commonality. As evangelicals who opposed slavery, the future missionaries had divided themselves from orthodox churches that remained silent on the slavery question. Because of their very different settings, antislavery evangelicals belonged to a religious culture of purity and exclusiveness; creole Jamaicans formulated a relatively pluralist religious culture.

With this pluralistic quality of creole religion in mind, we can understand how easily African American Protestantism fused with Myalism in the late eighteenth century after the arrival of black American Loyalists to Jamaica. The best known of these émigrés was George Liele, who had founded one of the first African American Baptist churches near Savannah, Georgia. Liele's conversion reportedly occurred during the Great Awakening of the mid-eighteenth century, and he demonstrated the spiritual gifts of ministry and was allowed to preach on several plantations in his neighborhood. Liele's Loyalist owner, who died during the Revolutionary War, freed Liele a few years before his own death. Liele, along with his wife and children, left the new nation as an indentured servant to a British soldier headed for Jamaica. In 1784 Liele began a small church in a Kingston house along with four other black Americans. Liele described himself as a farmer, but he regularly traveled around the island baptizing black Jamaicans and the occasional white person as well.[15]

Liele structured his Baptist church around a system of deacons and elders, leaders whom the people chose and he approved. As the Baptists converted enslaved people on the plantations around the island, the church existed beyond the urban brethren who were both slave and free, black and colored. Those interested in the church were divided into classes, a system that had originated with Wesleyans but that would become widely known as a Baptist practice. Tickets were issued and sometimes sold to individuals as a way to raise money, and the ticket identified one's status, or class, in the church.[16] In spite of this, the Baptist ministers had little financial support, given that their congregations were primarily enslaved people. In the words of one of Liele's deacons, he traveled around the island to "preach, baptize, marry, attend funerals, and go through every work of the ministry without fee or reward." The deacon emphasized his poverty, comparing himself to St. Paul in that he had not received anything for his pastoral work and instead "had to labour with my hands for the things I stand in need of to support myself and my family, and to let the church of Christ be free from incumberances."[17] The free black Baptist churches and their ministers worked in addition to performing their ministerial duties, and the financial strain caused by having a church made up of enslaved people led the Jamaican Baptists to reach out for assistance to their white Baptist brethren in England.

In seeking the support of their English brethren, the black Baptists and other clergy on the island testified to the respectability of the denomination and presented their denomination in a "civilized" fashion. Black Jamaicans once "were living in slavery to sin and satan" but "the Lord hath redeemed our souls to a state of happiness to praise his glorious and blessed name." The church's leaders, most of whom were U.S.-American-born, wanted to make Jamaica into a "Christian country," and they did so by working with planters who hired them to educate the slaves in Christianity. For example, as planters had to give their slaves permission to attend Baptist services,

Liele encouraged them to peruse his covenant, a document of scriptural extracts read once a month to his largely illiterate congregations. At least in letters to their potential British patrons, the key words denoting a civilizing mission were present: Liele "was an industriousness man—decent and humble in his manners," and he encouraged education and literacy, as well as marriage instead of sexual wantonness.[18]

In spite of the black Baptist leadership's outspoken advocacy of European cultural values that lent themselves to the perpetuation of slavery, the Afro-Jamaicans who joined the churches incorporated Baptist doctrine and rituals into their lives without necessarily adopting European habits. It could be argued that the success of the Baptist Church on the island was due in part to the numerous sects that emerged with the name "Baptist," a fact that the Baptist Missionary Society probably did not fully understand until their missionaries arrived.[19] Baptism provides one example of how a religious rite could work in Myal and European Protestantism. For most non-Baptist European Christians, baptism occurred once, usually at infancy, and represented a child's initiation into the life of the church. For some evangelical Christians, and Baptist sects in particular, one received the rite of baptism a second time after having an adult conversion experience. For followers of Myal in Jamaica and for Liele's earlier black converts in the United States, this central component of Baptist doctrine resonated with their African-derived understanding of the importance of immersion. The symbolic language of baptism made sense within an Afro-Jamaican religious perspective, and as Myal, like early Christianity, had its roots as an integrated faith, it brought elements of Liele's understanding of baptism into its practices.

Growing numbers of English missionaries joined the African American proselytizers in the first decades of the nineteenth century. Increasing evangelicalism and philanthropy in England directed a number of dissenting sects to send missionaries to the West Indies. The Wesleyans opened a mission to the West Indies in the 1790s, and the first English Baptists arrived in 1814. Not to be outdone by their dissenting brethren, evangelical Anglicans also sent some missionaries out to the West Indies, and all of these men and women joined a long-standing Moravian effort in the western part of the island. The missionaries met with numerous challenges to their evangelism. First, a majority of whites on the island distrusted the missionaries, and they had to work with what little support they could gain from reform-minded planters who believed that Christian slaves would be more obedient slaves. Second, the European missionaries found many slaves already to be self-professed Christians, even if the Christianity being practiced seemed highly unorthodox to the English ministers.[20]

The missionaries from the English Baptist Missionary Society tried to remedy the religious mélange, and they drew lines distinguishing their orthodox Christianity from the "Native Baptists" or "black Baptists"—terms that could be applied to a variety of the island's black-led Christian churches. Yet in spite of their anxiety, the English missionaries "seemed blind to the possibility that their most trusted converts might make independent use of the knowledge and skills they had acquired." As an evangelization strategy, the Baptist missionaries appointed leaders to oversee church communities on different estates. The black men chosen to be deacons and church leaders, however, tended to be men with a history of religious authority in their community. As a consequence, the Baptists' black leaders were usually drivers or other prominent men, and they might have already been Native Baptist ministers or even Obeah men. The leaders effectively created a church within a church in Jamaica, working with the missionaries and also transforming the "missionaries' religious teaching for their own ends."[21]

The ticket system illustrates how missionary practices gained creole interpretations. As noted earlier, the English Baptists borrowed this missionary tactic from the Wesleyans; black Jamaican preachers and churchgoers, at Native Baptist and mission churches, gave the ticket system their own meaning.[22] Oberlin missionary Charles Stewart Renshaw remarked that this system might have been "an innocent device at first," but it gained "tremendous power in the hands of the leaders." According to Renshaw, black leaders had taught their church members that the tickets were "passports to heaven."[23] Several years later, another American missionary's comments on the ticket system described the use of the tickets in funerals: "A native preacher in this vicinity, took from a bundle of tickets, laid upon the breast of a corpse, about to be lowered into the grave—the last one recd by the deceased, and addressing him, bade him present that when he should arrive at the gate of heaven, and 'massa Jesus' would open and let him in!" Although the Oberlin minister passed on this story to the AMA "to show what superstitious, soul-destroying notions are instilled into the minds of this deluded people, by some who set themselves up as native preachers," it also illustrates the complexity of religious traditions facing the American ministers.[24] The AMA missionaries were late to discover what the English Baptist missionaries had already learned in the early 1830s: the symbols and lessons of Christianity, particularly dissenting Protestantism, were impossible to contain within the mission churches.

The tenuous relationship between the Myal-inflected Native Baptists and the English missionaries burst onto center stage during the Baptist War, a slave rebellion that occurred during the Christmas holidays of 1831.[25] The revolt happened in part because white Jamaican planters overreacted to the news of the ameliorative acts being pushed by the antislavery movement in England, and after the Jamaican colonial assembly had been forced to grant equal rights to the free colored population in 1830. Planters feared the imminent end of slavery, and at the time of the Baptist War, it was common for planters to give "inflammatory speeches" that were "duly published in the newspapers." Many whites supported "armed revolt" against Britain.[26] For black slaves, however, the whites' anger seemed to prove that Britain had in fact issued an order for emancipation, and that the white colonial officials in Jamaica resisted enacting it.

In the social networks created by English Baptist mission churches and operated by black church leaders, news of the possible emancipation order circulated; Sam Sharpe, a black Baptist and member of an English missionary church, began to plan. According to Sharpe's narrative of the rebellion, it was initially designed to be a labor strike that would force the white colonial government to implement the supposed emancipation laws passed by the English. The enslaved people would refuse to process the cane crop until they were paid wages. But soon after the strike began, it escalated into armed conflict. On the days before and after Christmas, traditionally a holiday for the slaves, labor strikes erupted on plantations around the island, and workers burned the cane harvest, the sugar works, and the estate houses of their masters, destroying over one million pounds of property by the rebellion's end.

Once they had quelled the uprising, the Jamaican militia promptly arrested and "tried" 621 slaves. The colonial government quickly executed the plot's leaders and over three hundred of the Baptist War's alleged participants. Believing the Baptist missionaries to be the source of the agitation, angry white mobs responded by setting fire to chapels and other mission buildings, and the government officially banned missionaries from operating on the island, a statute that lasted until emancipation in 1834. For their part, the English Baptists denied any involvement in rebellion, claiming instead that they had tried to suppress it. The long-term effects of the Baptist War on the Baptist Missionary Society, however, led them to end their official line of neutrality on the slavery question and to take on a fully articulated antislavery position. Following the Baptist War, expelled white Baptist and Wesleyan missionaries became the best propagandists in England's antislavery movement until the first stage of emancipation began in 1834.[27]

The understanding of Christianity and freedom that black leaders developed before and after the Baptist War provides quite a different conception of liberty than that which took shape within evangelical abolitionism in the northern United States at this time. The divergence between these two concepts of Christianity and black freedom, on the one hand, and spiritual liberty, on the other, points to problems that would develop between the perfectionist Christian missionaries and the recently freed people in Jamaica. In the 1830s, those who would become American missionaries to Jamaica framed Christian liberty in terms of sexual morality and evangelism, and they opposed sinful "bondage" ranging from "unmanly" dependence on alcohol or prostitution to the more obvious captivity created by slavery. Afro-Jamaicans, in contrast, drew on an interpretation of Christianity based on adaptability rather than exclusion, and significantly, they drew on the dissenting theology of English missionaries to resist slavery and white power. Jamaican slaves lived in a society replete with rigid hierarchies and physical and social bondage, and freedom meant an end to this tyrannical system of control.

The actions of slaves during the Baptist War raised questions about slavery in England, and the uprising fueled a concentrated antislavery effort by the expelled missionaries, ultimately pushing Parliament to pass the first Act of Emancipation in 1833. The act decreed that on August 1, 1834, all slaves under the age of six would be freed. All other slaves would become apprentices—until 1838 for nonpraedial, or domestic, slaves, and until 1840 for praedials, or those who worked in the fields. Dissatisfaction with apprenticeship from antislavery politicians and from the imperial officials monitoring the process of emancipation led to a revised timeline, and the Emancipation Act of 1838 fully freed all slaves on August 1, 1838. During apprenticeship and after 1838, observers speculated on whether former slaves would work for wages on the West Indian sugar estates. Framed as a "great experiment," Seymour Drescher writes, Jamaica and the other British colonies "had become the world's operating theater for the anatomy of emancipation."[28] Problematically, American and British observers paid little attention to what made economic and social sense to black Jamaicans, and what former slaves expected their lives to be like in a postslavery world.[29]

During the apprenticeship period, British and American abolitionists wrote favorably of Antiguan immediate emancipation as compared to the unsatisfactory neoslavery of the apprenticeship in Jamaica and Barbados.[30] The American Anti-Slavery Society (AASS) in the United States added its voice to this debate in 1836. The newly founded organization arranged for James A. Thome, one of the Lane Rebels, and J. Horace Kimball, a New England newspaper editor, to visit the West Indian islands of Antigua, Barbados, and Jamaica to investigate the process of emancipation. Kimball's death soon after the men returned to the United States left the bulk of the writing to Thome and his editor and friend, Theodore Weld. The resulting volume, *Emancipation in the West Indies*, centered on the differences between Antigua, a colony that had granted full freedom in 1834, and the apprenticeship laws put into place in Jamaica and Barbados. Thome and Kimball commented that Jamaica's "apprentices are improving, not, however, in consequence of the apprenticeship, but in spite of it, and in consequence of the great act of abolition!"[31] This interpretive perspective corroborated the American abolitionist contention that Antigua's immediate emancipation worked better than any kind of gradualism, as seen in the other two islands.[32] Thome and Kimball, and their British counterparts, Thomas Harvey and Joseph Sturge, condemned the apprenticeship system as an utter failure. It had been designed to ease slaves into freedom and to teach them to work for wages instead of by force, but in practice, planters took advantage of the system and, alarmingly, continued to physically abuse women. Writing for a British audience, Harvey and Sturge begged for black Jamaicans to be given the "protection of the law as British subjects."[33] Thome and Kimball had a similar demand, although their message to Americans was that the United States should not follow along the mistaken path of gradualism that the British government had taken.

As Americans and Britons engaged in their own debates about free-labor ideology, black Jamaicans saw the apprenticeship period—and, later, emancipation—as a chance to fulfill their own desires for the future, which centered on access to and control of family lands. Even before emancipation, enslaved Jamaicans had a sense of what it meant to own land. Unlike the slave societies in the American South, it was customary in Jamaica for planters to apportion unused land on their property to slaves as provision grounds. Slaves grew and marketed their produce and passed down this land along hereditary lines.[34] Historians of slavery have described slaves' land rights as a type of slave resistance because although property themselves, enslaved people developed a strong notion of property rights on the land apportioned to them, what Jean Besson has called a "tremendous paradox within the slavery system."[35]

During the apprenticeship period and after emancipation, estate managers feared that ex-slaves would quit estate work and live off their provision grounds, a move that would effectively drive sugar estates out of business. In 1833, the well-connected Colonial Office clerk Henry Taylor filed a memo with this exact scenario: freed people could survive and make a living working on their grounds alone, and unless the population were "condensed" and guided by white missionaries to develop civilization, emancipated men and women would live as "squatters and idlers . . . beasts in the woods."[36] To combat this threat, as early as the apprenticeship period, property managers kept a watchful eye on their laborers. In St. Mary Parish, near where the American missionaries would build their mission churches, an English Wesleyan minister, Peter Samuel, discussed the emerging conflicts between laborers and estate owners. Simon Taylor had once owned Montrose and Flint River pens and the Llanrumney sugar estate, and after his death in 1813, they had fallen into the hands of a series of attorneys. The pens had more slaves than needed, and the crop accounts show that much of Montrose and Flint River's income came from leasing out gang labor to neighboring estates, including Esher, White Hall, Charlottenburgh, and Richmond.[37] This situation would have given the apprentices a fair amount of geographical knowledge about the neighborhood and available land, as well as contacts on other plantations.

The first time Peter Samuel visited Montrose Pen, a property neighboring Charlottenburgh Estate—where the Americans' Eliot Station would be formed—he noted its isolation from missionary influence. Montrose was ten miles from his station at Grateful Hill, and the roads were "impassable in bad weather." Samuel also commented on the necessity of reaching out to the apprentices, noting that if "proper attention be paid to the inhabitants of that neighborhood, many might be brought to forsake sin and flee from the wrath to come." The overseer of Lewisburgh Estate, William Lindop, invited Samuel to preach to his apprentices, and complained that "some of the people [were] behaving very ill and the work of the estate [was] being very much neglected."[38] Like others in the Wesleyan mission, Samuel embraced a conciliatory role in the process of emancipation.[39] Drawing on a biblical lesson calling on all men to repent their sins, Samuel concluded his sermon by telling the apprentices, "Should I hear that they neglected the estate work or otherwise conducted themselves badly, I would never again visit them so that they might choose what was best for themselves."[40] Samuel allied himself with the white overseer rather than the apprentices in the evolving circumstances concerning labor after slavery. Like many whites in Jamaica, Samuel and Lindop feared that emancipated blacks would retreat from estate labor and tend only their provision grounds. For apprentices at Lewisburgh, the white missionaries appeared to be in league with the overseers, and as the origin stories of the American mission churches show, black-led congregations existed, even if unsanctioned by the visiting white English clergymen.

Lindop and Samuel invoked religion as a way to encourage apprentices to work on the estate land, but other whites had a different idea in mind. In writing up reports on the estates owned by the heirs of Simon Taylor, John Cooper recommended that English peasant stock be imported to run the land more efficiently. Regarding Montrose Pen, Cooper remarked that male apprentices were typically leased out to nearby sugar estates in order to dig cane holes, and that forty-five men could dig one acre per day. He suggested instead that "a Suffolk Ploughman with good Horses could do just as much in the same time." Cooper was not alone in his proposal to import European laborers and technology to Jamaica, and while a few attempts to do this were made, none succeeded. Nonetheless it demonstrates the widespread belief in the 1830s that new labor solutions were needed in the post-emancipation era. Cooper's letters unintentionally revealed the tasks that black Jamaicans pursued instead of the estate labor. Writing about another of Taylor's pens, Cooper commented that the second and third gang of laborers were either "cleaning pastures or idling their time away at home. As there is no white person to look after them it cannot be supposed they will be industrious by themselves." What Cooper saw as idling at home was likely apprentices taking time on their provision grounds, time that he felt was wasted because his priority was cultivating sugar for export. Like other skeptical white observers, Cooper also expressed the common belief that apprenticeship was showing that blacks would not work—in the cane fields, at least—without being coerced.[41]

Even in unflattering reports of black workers, evidence of the importance of family lands—the provision grounds and yards claimed by freed people as their own—appeared. In one account, an overseer destroyed fences around apprentices' provision grounds and the livestock trampled their crops. When he later tried to hire the apprentices out to work on a different estate, they refused and "went to the woods." On this estate, the apprentices resisted being hired out because "it often takes them miles from their homes, and they are still required to supply themselves with food from their own provision grounds."[42] The abolitionist writers sided with the workers and explained the reasons for their protest. A less sympathetic account of family lands came from John Cooper, the agent inspecting Simon Taylor's heirs' estates. He noticed a field of Guinea grass that had no animals grazing on it, and when he asked about it, he "was told that it was formerly in Negro Provisions and that one man still cultivated ½ an acre in the middle, and consequently stock could not be turned in to molest his garden." Cooper took no time in attributing this practice to what he viewed as the backward culture that slavery had produced: "I need not mention this is not *law* but custom."[43] In spite of his disparaging intent, Cooper offered insights into the way black Jamaicans used and thought about land. For freed people, land was more than an economic investment. It represented ownership for people who were themselves property, and it opened up a physical space for autonomy within the confines of a slave society.

In the years immediately following emancipation in 1838, freed people demonstrated a diversity of opinions about what would be best for them and for their families when it came to waged work and landownership. These choices largely depended on the particulars of their situation. On some estates freed people voiced their willingness to remain as workers, as long as they could keep their provision grounds and homes, and earn an adequate living. Smaller numbers of ex-slaves left their estates in 1838 to live in free villages that sprouted up across the island. The English Baptist missionaries played a part in organizing some free villages, especially in the western parishes where the denomination had the largest presence. Notably, the white missionaries expected to have complete control over the free villages they helped to build. When they purchased and organized free villages, they laid out plans for houses, streets, and churches so that the villages resembled a preindustrial English town, and they paid little attention to the historical patterns of provision grounds and black landownership on the island.[44]

Frustrated with ex-slaves, Jamaican planters appealed to the British public for aid, and in 1839, they presented numerous testimonies about the unwillingness of black Jamaicans to work for wages. On the other side of the Atlantic, Britons could not have failed to notice that the cost of sugar had increased almost 60 percent.[45] One colonial official complained that "the want of continuous labor is still very much felt on many estates, as the Labourers generally work *very irregularly*, without any regard to the wants or wishes of their employers."[46] In response, planters thought of ways to force freed people to work a certain number of hours per day, and planters also began to require labor in exchange for rent on houses, yards, and provision grounds.[47] The planters focused their attention on the fact that many women with children and married women had withdrawn from field labor; thus, their rental policies demanded that each member of a household pay rent or its equivalent in labor, or face eviction. Black families resisted this reexertion of control over domestic arrangements, and by the early 1840s, those freed people who could not blend wage labor with their desired level of control over their family life left their homes and family land to find arrangements elsewhere, a phenomenon that historians call the "flight from the estates." Some moved to the island's interior as squatters or small freeholders, while others looked for better wages on other estates.[48]

When freed people moved away from low wages and limited autonomy on sugar estates and instead sought their own freeholds, some of the observers who had been waiting to see the results of this experiment turned to racial explanations for the "failure." In 1849, Thomas Carlyle published his sarcastic essay mocking abolitionists and freed people, "Occasional Discourse on the Negro (Nigger) Question." In it he made the case that blacks were lazy, and they preferred to work one day a week and live in a state of savagery instead of working for six days a week and earning money for the comforts of civilization; consequently, he argued, black labor required coercion.[49] Not all Europeans and Americans shared the perspective that wage-earning blacks would be the marker of emancipation's success, and Baptist missionaries defended the rights of black men to own land rather than work as dependents on sugar estates.[50] The Americans James Thome and J. Horace Kimball also supported black landownership from the time of their visit to Jamaica in 1836. Landownership, they argued, "would relieve [them] from some of that dependence which they must feel so long as they live on the estate and in the houses of the planters."[51] For black Jamaicans, the cultural meanings invested in landownership were rooted in the history of slavery, in the importance of place for a rootless people, and in the connections between parents and children. For the future American missionaries, who in the early 1830s were leaving their families' farms to be educated at manual-labor schools, land was a sign of independence, not a reminder of one's connection to a long-existing community. The township of Oberlin, only a few years old when the Lane Rebels moved there in 1835, was a new Zion for the evangelical abolitionists to remake themselves. In Jamaica, freed people hoped to remain on their old land, and they only left their provision grounds when it became economically impossible to survive.

As the previous section showed, contests over gender ideology and family arrangements were embedded in post-emancipation labor disputes. Unlike the stirrings of woman's rights in the North in the 1830s that caused consternation among the orthodox evangelicals at Oberlin, the woman question in Jamaica concerned whether freed women would continue to work in the fields. Would freed men, freed women, or planters have control over black family arrangements? When James Thome and Horace Kimball visited Jamaica in 1836, they, like many abolitionists, found much fault with the ongoing practice of having black women work in the fields during the apprenticeship period. Like other abolitionists in the United States and in Britain, the American travelers were used to condemning slavery for disrupting what they considered to be a Christian and civilized gender order, and Jamaican slavery was no different from its cousin in the American South. The men asked their readers,

> What could more effectually force woman from her sphere, than slavery has done by dragging her to the field, subjecting her to the obscene

remarks, and to the vile abominations of licentious drivers and overseers; by compelling her to wield the heavy hoe, until advancing pregnancy rendered her useless, than at the earliest possible period driving her back to the field with her infant swung at her back, or torn from her and committed to a stranger.[52]

Thome and Kimball illustrated the cruelty of slavery—and now apprenticeship—through the way it punished women, and especially mothers. They spent several pages detailing the horrors of the treadmill as a punishment for women who had stopped work to care for young children.[53] Thome and Kimball placed their hope in full emancipation, and they seconded the wishes of one white Antiguan official that "the day would come when the principal part of the agriculture of the island would be performed by males, and that the women would be occupied in keeping their cottages in order and in increasing their domestic comforts."[54]

When examining the predicament of female field laborers, Thome and Kimball predicted a new era of domesticity in Jamaica, and they pointed to green shoots where they thought they glimpsed examples of the ideology of separate spheres. When writing about provision grounds Thome and Kimball glossed over the fact that the produce of these plots fueled the island's internal market economy. Instead they described "men, women, and children laboring industriously in their little gardens," just as a family at Oberlin might do.[55] In another anecdote, they recounted their visit with a "brown young woman" on her way home after a day at the Kingston market. She had bought and sold goods for her husband's shop, and when the Americans asked if she wanted to keep the money she made for herself, she replied, "What for him for me."[56] The American writers substituted their ideas of marital unity for a long-standing custom that had granted black women economic independence. More common in *Emancipation in the West Indies*, however, was the change that emancipation had wrought on extramarital sex. Emancipation had provided "the death blow to open vice" that had once proliferated during slavery. In the newly free society, "the proper restraints upon vice" were restored, and the conditions of free labor "supplied the incentives to virtue."[57]

For many reasons, Jamaican gender ideology after emancipation did not reflect the triumph of separate-spheres gender ideology and the ensuing public morality that Thome and Kimball predicted. After emancipation, many black women, and especially mothers, withdrew from field labor, much to the distress of planters.[58] Indeed, the magistrates monitoring the process of emancipation reported that, on one estate in Trelawney, freed women had been told that they needed to return to work in order to keep their houses. The women "had devoted their attention to their husbands and families who are working on the same estate," and the planter wanted them "to relinquish their attention to their domestic duties, and apply themselves unremittingly to the labours of the field."[59] Freed men also defended their rights to control their families' labor. In July 1839, black men stockpiled weapons to protect themselves against rumors that "the white and brown people were going to surround the chapel on the 1st August, and kill the black men, and make the women slaves again."[60] This plot did not come to fruition, but it shows the contested nature of women's labor in the post-emancipation period.

While these pieces of evidence suggest black women moved to the private sphere, Bridget Brereton argues that in withdrawing from field labor, black women furthered their family's chance to become independent cultivators. It was not, then, a decision meant to produce domesticated housewives, but familial independence.[61] After emancipation, few freed people fully accepted all European or American gender norms, but instead they crafted their own conceptions of respectability. When it came to land and labor, the predominant family strategy after emancipation was for black men to work for wages on the estates, while freed women cared for their children and worked the provision grounds, the family land. Women then contributed to the family income by selling the produce at the weekly market. Also, the family Brereton describes was not always the nuclear family—a husband, wife, and children. The sexual division of labor in Jamaica, and family structures that did not always resemble the middle-class ideal, would prove frustrating to the American missionaries who came to Jamaica with very different expectations.[62]

The gendered customs associated with family lands created a connection between marriage and property that baffled the Americans, accustomed to legal concepts of marital unity and coverture. Derived from English common law, the doctrine of coverture meant that a married woman was legally "covered" by her husband; her property went to him as well. Marital unity meant that the wife and husband functioned as a single legal subject. As

Jean Besson observes in her field research of one of the Baptist free villages, Martha Brae, land in Jamaica was passed down to male and female children, who were expected to hold the land in common ownership. It was not to be divided among individuals, and daughters, once married, did not give over their portion to their husbands.[63] As a result, a married couple might work on land that was their personal hereditary right rather than on land that the spouses owned together. A married woman could have rights to land that was not her husband's, and a wife had no obligation to turn over her property to her husband upon marriage. American missionary Stewart Renshaw thought that these practices indicated surviving relics of barbaric African culture. He observed how "husbands and wives frequently rent and cultivate different 'grounds,' keep separate purses, and defend their rights against each other as rigidly as against strangers." While decrying the lack of affection in Jamaican marriages, he added, "It must not be inferred that the people live together unhappily; not at all."[64]

While some black Jamaicans and many more colored Jamaicans (who numbered few in the mountainous area of the American missions) adopted the middle-class gender ideology of Anglo-American missionaries, most rural freed people had a different view of what the family should look like. As can be seen in Renshaw's observation, marriage was not the most important social bond for freed people, and the nuclear family was not the only or even the most obvious way to organize men and women. Diana Paton writes, "There was no expectation that women would marry before bearing children. Nor did bearing children necessarily imply that a woman would live with the father of her child. She could expect support from other family members, especially her mother and the other older female relatives, but bore primary responsibility for the economic support, as well as physical and emotional care, of her children."[65] Generations of scholars have described the Jamaican family as matriarchal or matrifocal, with various judgments being made about whether or not this is inherently good or bad, while other scholars countered with the argument that black Jamaicans desired a male head of household, but economic circumstances made this difficult.[66] The array of evidence suggests that freed people formed different kinds of families, which would explain why the American missions had hundreds of church members who lived in monogamous nuclear families, while the ministers could still complain about the lack of public morality and widespread sexual license. Freed slaves did not always agree about ideal gender roles and family life.

The American missionaries' frustration with Jamaican gender roles had as much to do with the society's tolerance as the actual numbers of unwed mothers or adulterous affairs. But, as historians have argued, Jamaican freed people were not without a moral order; it just was a different system than that of Anglo-American missionaries. Jamaican female respectability was not tied to the economic dependence of wives and the seclusion of women within the private sphere, as respectability was defined for women in the northern United States. Instead, black women lived by a different ideology of domesticity, one that valued a woman's right to be a mother and to have the privileges of motherhood.[67] A pregnant freed woman might refuse marriage because the potential husband lacked sufficient resources, and she lost no social standing from having a child out of wedlock. In terms of slave resistance and also women's labor and political activism after emancipation, motherhood offered black women a way to justify their activism in a way that both resonated with white notions of femininity and drew on black Jamaican customs.[68] If motherhood, rather than marriage, centered black womanhood, making choices for the benefit of children mattered more than marriage. Since slavery, strong networks between older women and young women often replaced the traditional male-headed family, or meant that a young woman might live in a household where the male head was an uncle rather than a father.[69]

In the black family after slavery, women were in charge of child rearing, working on the provision grounds, and marketing a family's produce. Many families expected men to work for wages on the sugar estates, but this was not exactly the breadwinner model of the family that contemporary observers may have perceived. Diana Paton proposes that this work—wage work—was actually "a source of marginality more than power." She further notes that most of the domestic disputes after emancipation involved sexual infidelity, one partner's loyalty to their natal household, and "women's refusal of men's demands for domestic services such as cooking."[70] The nature of these conflicts points to the transitional nature of this period in Jamaican gender roles. Clearly, some men sought to claim their rights as freedmen through marriage and controlling their family, while in other cases, the customs that had developed during slavery clashed with the expectations of Victorian marriage. Freedom initiated a reevaluation of the gender roles that had existed during slavery, but this did not always result in the rise of the "Christian civilization" for which many white abolitionists hoped.

Religion, landownership and labor, and family life had a distinct context in Jamaica, as they had in the United States, and the Americans' ideas of Christian liberty hardly matched black Jamaicans' ideas of freedom. The first American missionary, David Ingraham, like those Oberlin graduates who would join him on the island, had been educated about the British West Indies through a series of propaganda pieces that told more about what Americans and British abolitionists hoped would happen than what actual Jamaican life was like. Consequently, the American missionaries were startled to find that few ex-slaves living around the mission stations lived up to their expectations. The gap between what the missionaries imagined and what they found on the island required the white abolitionists to rethink and reformulate many of the tenets that they had developed at Oberlin and in the antislavery movement of the 1830s.

Myal and Native Baptist churches had grown in the years following emancipation as black Jamaicans left white missionary churches for their own institutions. These pluralistic religious communities would prove constant irritants to the American missionaries who structured their churches around rigorously enforced rules and church discipline. Even more detrimental to the Americans, however, was the brewing distrust of white ministers on the part of many black Jamaicans who found that all of the talk of Christian brotherhood and equality rarely trickled down into actual practice. As black Jamaicans began to lose patience with missionary allies, they also had to deal with planters who wanted to ensure ongoing cheap field labor. The American missionaries discovered that the much-discussed smooth transition from slavery to wage labor would be impossible when low wages and high rents were being used to coerce black Jamaicans into the fields. How were converts to the American churches to become truly free if they remained dependent on the fluctuating wages that resentful and economically strapped planters paid? Finally, the family strategies that Jamaican freed people employed hardly matched the American ideology of domesticity. Black families depended on black women's labor—if not for wages, then certainly on provision grounds—and the wide acceptance of premarital cohabitation shocked the missionaries. For the missionaries from Oberlin who had learned that marriage and the Christian family prevented Christian liberty from devolving into licentiousness, this seemingly unrestrained sexuality was the biggest threat to the mission's religious and political goals.

Part Two

The first Oberlin missionary to Jamaica came to the island in 1837, at the end of the apprenticeship period. After finishing seminary at Oberlin, the one-time Lane Rebel, David S. Ingraham, arrived in Jamaica with the intention of ministering to the island's apprentices. Over the next several years, Ingraham moved back and forth between Jamaica and the United States, trying to establish a mission church on the island while also raising funds and awareness, and recruiting new missionaries in the United States. During this time, he married a fellow Oberlin graduate, Elizabeth Hartson, and the couple had a daughter, Sarah, born in Jamaica in 1839. Writing a few days after the first anniversary of emancipation in 1839, Ingraham drew a direct connection between his Jamaican congregation and the slaves in the United States. On Emancipation Day, his "chapel was well filled, and as one after another prayer for the poor slaves and for the cruel masters of America, I almost felt *sure* that God would hear and that while we were yet speaking the . . . chains of some at least of our brethren in bondage would *fall*."[1]

During their trips to the United States, Ingraham spoke before antislavery meetings in Boston and New York, and made the rounds to visit nodes in the abolitionist network like Gerrit Smith and the Weld family.[2] Ingraham recruited five of his fellow Oberlin graduates, several of whom had been working as traveling agents for the American Anti-Slavery Society, to join him in Jamaica. Spread out in villages in the mountains between Kingston and Annotto Bay, the Oberlin ministers and their wives established a tentative American presence in Jamaica. What little we can glean of these early years of the Jamaica Mission comes from the missionaries' letters to their hometown *Oberlin Evangelist* newspaper and from the *Evangelist*'s frequent updates about their work. From the scant evidence available, one thing is clear: Jamaica proved a more complex and frustrating emancipated society than the Americans anticipated, or than Ingraham had told them in his letters and speeches. American missionary Henry Evarts summed up the state of affairs in 1847: "It is hard for the human mind to give up high hopes and fond anticipations, and take hold cheerfully of labors in which much more is to be endured, and less brilliant hopes can be indulged."[3]

Initially, primed with abolitionist propaganda about the happy results of West Indian emancipation, and their own experiences working with black northerners, the missionaries had little reason to doubt that black Jamaicans would quickly seek out their churches. Moreover, they had no reason to doubt that they would find eager collaborators in the black churches proliferating on the island. Indeed, having read *Emancipation in the West Indies* and other pamphlets and books on emancipation, the Oberlin ministers imagined that ex-slaves wanted to throw out all of the culture of slavery, including ignorant superstition and its constant companion, sexual licentiousness. Yet in the 1840s, a Myal revival and black-led Native Baptist churches grew out of the growing frustration that black Jamaicans had with white English missionaries. When the Americans figured out that many Jamaicans adamantly preferred "ignorant" black-led Native Baptist churches to their "orthodox" American congregations, the missionaries were crestfallen. That the black ministers working in their neighborhood did not enforce church discipline, and even welcomed disgraced ex-members of the mission churches into their fold, perplexed the American missionaries. As during Shipherd's days in the Valley of Moral Death, it was very difficult to evangelize a population to whom excommunication meant little.

Almost as disheartening to the missionaries was that black Jamaican men and women had not adopted the gender ideology of domesticity. Sexually active teenagers, unwed mothers, womanizing and abusive husbands, and other forms of sexual licentiousness filled the pages of missionary letters as proof that the purported Jamaican Christianity was nothing but a collection of spurious superstitions. Unlike most varieties of licentious Americans—the members of the Oneida Commune, for example, or even sinful slaveholders—morally suspect black Jamaicans actively sought membership in the mission churches. Patrolling church membership and punishing sinful church members who had somehow slipped into their congregations became as important a part of the Jamaica Mission as trying to recruit new converts away from the Native Baptists and other competing churches.

In addition to finding out that building an interracial and orthodox Christian community in Jamaica would not be easy, the Americans realized that their plan to cultivate black landownership and independent yeoman farmers would be difficult in the climate of economic turmoil that existed in the 1840s. Soon after emancipation, disputes broke out between freed people and planters over the terms of free labor. Many ex-slaves had been satisfied to remain as wage laborers on the estates, as long as they were allowed to retain their cottages, yards, and provision grounds and have control over which family members worked for wages. A vigorous marketing culture had developed in Jamaica during slavery, and many families preferred that women would work on the family land to raise produce to sell at local markets, while men and young adults would work for wages to supplement the household's income. Planters, however, feared that freed slaves would not work on sugar estates and coffee properties, or at least would not work the same amount of time that they had as slaves; indeed, the withdrawal of black women from gang labor after emancipation seemed to confirm their suspicions.[4] As early as 1839, abolitionist Charles Stuart commented on the conditions that would lead to the "flight from the estates," writing to Theodore Weld about the insurmountable problems that renters and wage laborers faced in Jamaica:

> The frequent and arbitrary changes of overseers, etc., and the sudden and arbitrary changes of plans consequent upon those changes; each new overseer, recklessly, if he pleases, overturning the plans and engagements of his predecessor and substituting his own. The uncertain tenure of houses and grounds, disheartening and provoking the labourers, and the uncertainty of labour (all labour in general being daily or weekly) discouraging the masters from permanent pursuits: this, it should be observed, is almost altogether the fault of the masters; and the fact that they are suffering deeply from it no more disproves the fact, that the destructive retributions which sinners bring upon themselves disprove their transgressions.[5]

Like his fellow evangelical abolitionists fixated on slavery's sinfulness, Stuart was convinced that the master class's unrepentant nature had led to the widespread battles over land rights, wages, and rent—a moral failing that harmed the planters, he thought, as much as the freed people.

In order to keep black laborers as wage workers, landowners began to charge rent for property that the freed people considered their own, often deducting rent directly from the workers' wages. The ongoing battle over the terms of labor hurt the sugar estates, as did a series of free trade acts passed in Britain in the mid-1840s. British politicians responded to the high price of sugar, and ended the tariffs that had protected West Indian sugar from competition from Cuba and Brazil, a policy that furthered the decline in sugar production in Jamaica. Many estates went bankrupt or were abandoned, while some planters tried to recover their losses in charging even higher rents without increasing their workers' wages. Many freed people refused to tolerate these policies any longer, and they left the land they claimed as their own and moved elsewhere, often buying or squatting on abandoned land in the island's largely rural and very mountainous interior.[6] On the whole, the American ministers in Jamaica focused less on the systemic economic problems in Jamaica, and instead paid more attention to the ways that economic turmoil impacted the mission's churches and schools. Low wages meant few black Jamaicans had much money to donate to the mission's coffers, and the transitory nature of wage workers and renters inhibited the mission church's growth and stability. As a consequence, the American ministers focused a great deal of their attention on black landownership as a means to improve the material conditions of the mission as well as a way to "domesticate" black men and women.

British supporters of Jamaican emancipation found themselves similarly disillusioned during the 1840s. As Thomas Holt has argued, the debate surrounding the question of how an emancipated Jamaica was to be governed revealed as early as the late 1830s the limits of abolitionist commitments to black equality. Dominated by planters angry over the early end to apprenticeship in 1838, the Jamaica Assembly thwarted the attempts to inch toward a more equitable society as made by the Colonial Office and Sir Lionel Smith, the island's pro-emancipation governor. The Americans would have been acutely aware of the obstacles that black Jamaicans faced in this political climate, and Charles Stuart made the point plainly: "A faction in Jamaica, probably not numbering more than 2000, worshipping still their great idols, sugar and rum, and insanely dreaming that fraud and force are better ways of getting sugar and rum than equity and kindness, is triumphing in the suicidal success of its machinations."[7] In England, few British abolitionists supported black political rights and a more representative assembly as a means to handle the island's political crisis. Instead they suggested that the self-governed colony be turned into a Crown colony, without an elected assembly and under the direct control of British officials who would be more equitable than white planters. The crisis eventually resolved, and the Assembly was reinstated after a temporary suspension.

The decision to support a benevolent white government in 1839 over an interracial representative democracy demonstrated the limits of black freedom for white British abolitionists. The pervading narrative, as Thomas Holt writes, was that "'the natives' had no inner controls and thus required external controllers."[8] On a similar note, historian Catherine Hall found that the abolitionist men and women who supported Baptist missionaries in Jamaica came to a similar conclusion in the 1840s. Although the Baptists supported black landownership and spoke about the need for greater black independence, they proved unwilling to relinquish their control over free villages and in the mission churches. The Baptist free villages, Hall argues, depended "on the refusal to recognize an existing black culture," so when the so-called culture of slavery persisted in spite of the efforts of white missionaries and colonial officials to erase it, the period of white tutelage was extended indefinitely.[9]

The American missionaries in Jamaica were distinct from the British missions that had been in operation for several decades. First, the timing of the American mission, begun just after emancipation, meant that the American ministers established their churches and schools amid this changing religious and economic landscape. Second, coming from the United States, the Oberlin missionaries and their supporters were quite skeptical of British imperialism and what British emancipation had accomplished in Jamaica. For the former Oberlin students, dedicated supporters of manual labor, "aristocracy" was "one of the giant evils of the civilized world," and the "bane and the curse of Old England."[10] The American mission planned to treat black Jamaicans "as men, and not as serviles," and their mission's goal would be "to make them a New England farming population, not an English peasantry." Later, the missionaries complained about the waning interest of the British in Jamaica, with one Oberlin minister writing, "I think British Christians ought to take care of Jamaica, but whether they will or not is a matter to be considered," and a former missionary had become convinced "that the regenerating power . . . for the Island in every respect, must come from the United States."[11]

Finally, the missionaries' experiences as evangelical abolitionists in the United States and the continued ways that American evangelical abolitionist ideas trickled into the Jamaica Mission shaped the way the missionaries thought about freedom and the way they viewed black Jamaicans. At the Oneida Institute, Lane Seminary, and Oberlin, the white missionaries had experience working with northern blacks, and they expected that black church leaders and ministers in Jamaica would be similarly interested in respectability and racial uplift.[12] The comments of one missionary speak to how the missionaries confronted their own ideas of racial and cultural difference: "Here we are now surrounded by almost another race of beings. And yet not another for like ourselves, they have human passions and human sympathies and like ourselves are immortal beings."[13]

3 Religion and the Civilizing Mission

A decade after the Oberlin ministers began their missionary work, the missionaries went to great pains to explain that while Jamaica had many mission churches, it had few authentic Christians. One missionary acknowledged that after emancipation in 1838 many freed people had been moved by the Holy Spirit to join churches, but after ten years it had become clear that "comparatively few conversions proved to be real and genuine." Skeptical of the authenticity of conversions, the American ministers also blamed lax church discipline, and they regretted "that greater care and strictness were not exercised in the admission of members to the church." According to one article, "The novelty of freedom and the peculiar sensations to which it gave birth gradually wore off," and black Jamaicans had become less interested in supporting mission churches over time. Whether black Jamaicans had once been legitimate Christians who had backslid, or whether the missionaries had only recognized too late that

{ 75 }

"the Christianity so largely professed was . . . a false and spurious thing" all along, it had become clear that the American missionaries and Jamaican freed people had distinctly different notions of what it meant to be free and what it meant to be a Christian.[1]

This uneasy assessment of the state of religion in post-emancipation Jamaica conveyed to the home audience why the American mission on the island was proving to be more complicated than initially anticipated. After all, if accounts like that of James Thome and Horace Kimball were to be believed, emancipation, religious conversion, and racial uplift were all part of the same process. Why had black Jamaicans not become the "civilized" people whom American abolitionists had imagined? Why had the transformative power of emancipation failed? These questions stemmed in large part from the disparities between American and Jamaican notions of freedom. From their experiences as abolitionists in the United States, the Oberlin missionaries had undergone evangelical conversion, and in their antislavery education, they had interpreted the legal emancipation of slaves to be intertwined with a more spiritual and cultural conversion. Freedmen would emerge from slavery as exemplars of independent manhood, eager to labor for their own support on their freeholds and quick to establish domestic tranquility in their free homes. Few enslaved Jamaicans had shared in this American view of emancipation, and the much-discussed backsliding in the decade after 1838 that dominated American and British reports illustrated the growing anxiety of the white missionaries.

The first Oberlin graduates to go to Jamaica in the late 1830s and early 1840s left the United States as fervent abolitionists, and they assumed that black Jamaicans awaited their arrival. Former slaves needed schools, to be sure, and this would be hard work for the missionaries, but evangelism and conversions to Christian perfectionism would come easily. After all, why would freed people shun white Americans who cared so deeply about their condition? Only when the missionary encounter began did the Americans begin to revise their abolitionist assumptions, and in this mission, it appears that the Americans were changed far more than the people whom they attempted to civilize and convert. Regardless of the amount of theoretical and theological missionary planning that occurred in the United States, Jamaicans and the religious culture of the island had a hand in shaping the Jamaica Mission. Facing black Jamaicans who claimed to be Christians but who practiced adult baptism, drank rum, and sometimes engaged in extramarital sex put the American ministers on edge, and they questioned whether they could tell a true convert from someone just trying to get into the church. The Americans were certainly not unfamiliar with religious unorthodoxy. Charles Finney's Christian perfectionism had been the target of attacks in the United States, for example, and one evangelical visitor to Jamaica remarked that the island's "superstition" was mild compared "to the extravagancies of Mormonism; or to the horrible doctrines of the Universalists."[2] The Oberlin ministers quickly racialized the threat from Jamaican Christianity. As Catherine Hall writes in regard to British Baptist missionaries' similar dilemma, "White Baptists could never be mistaken for Black or Native Baptists, but Baptists who were black were always susceptible to that possibility."[3]

Church discipline became the most important part of the missionaries' religious work in Jamaica. While church discipline was used in the United States to exclude sinful slaveholders from abolitionist churches, a factor that led to the formation of the AMA in 1846, church discipline had a different use in Jamaica. Rigorous screening processes for potential converts and frequent excommunications were the tools that American ministers used to try to exert control over what was to them a licentious society. In exercising church discipline, the ministers talked about themselves as fatherly authorities to whom God had given a duty to take care of children who would easily be led astray. As a result, the goal to support black men's independence in Jamaica faltered when it came to converts and church membership, and a different gendered language of the patriarchal mission family prevailed instead. Yet in spite of all these measures instituted to keep Jamaicans' "corrupt" Christianity from infiltrating the Americans' church community, evidence from the ministers suggests that they sometimes compromised. Whether to preserve comity within a mission chapel or because missionaries recognized something of value in the "superstition" they so often condemned, one can find small chinks in the armor of church discipline.

When David Ingraham and his colleagues—Amos Dresser, Julius Beardslee, Stewart Renshaw, Ralph Tyler, and George Hovey—settled in Jamaica in the late 1830s and early 1840s, they planned to form self-supporting churches. This decision reflected the profound importance they placed in self-reliance and their belief that any form of dependency hindered their manly independence, as well as the type of missionary ethos prevalent at Oberlin.[4] They had no desire to be in a dependent relationship with a parent society in the United States, and they thought that dependency would compromise their ability to serve as examples of independent manhood to freedmen. Further, the missionaries had read the many reports of ex-slaves eagerly adopting European Christianity, prospering as wage laborers and seeking to purchase their own land, and, of course, living out "proper" gender roles and family practices. The *Oberlin Evangelist* published a letter from a Jamaican planter that proclaimed, "All churches and Chapels of every denomination were *crowded to overflowing*" and "the orderly and correct behavior of the people was equal to what their best friends could expect of them."[5] In this scenario, it would not take long before black Jamaicans would contribute enough money to support a minister and his family, as well as a teacher, with funds enough left to build a chapel and school.

This vision hardly matched what the missionaries found. Instead, they encountered a society rife with tensions between white missionaries and black church leaders. The economic problems plaguing freed people whose rent on their property and houses increased while their wages stagnated further complicated the dream of self-supporting churches. Emancipation, the ministers were disappointed to realize, had not immediately made Jamaica into a prosperous society comprising yeoman farmers and their families. The missionaries' letters in these early years illustrated the dilemma that American ministers faced as they realized much of what they thought they had known was wrong. Between 1839 and the formation of the AMA in 1846, the missionaries failed to find a balance between the popular missionary ideology of self-sufficient missions and the monetary needs of running schools and churches for a community struck with one economic setback after another.

A mission theory in favor of self-supporting churches was very popular at Oberlin College for the Jamaica Mission as well as for other foreign missions. Those who regularly read the *Oberlin Evangelist* would have come across letters and articles from a number of different missionary efforts, all commenting on the need for "native converts" to take responsibility for mission churches rather than relying on continual American aid. For example, in 1845, a letter from a missionary in Hawaii declared that he was tired of "making apologies" for the poverty of his converts. "The people will always remain poor if the churches carry them in their arms, so to speak. I hope to show that they not only can do much toward the support of their own religious institutions, but that in doing it, they will be great gainers in every way."⁶ A similar principle applied in Jamaica; in the same issue of the *Evangelist*, a short notice on the Jamaica Mission noted that although impoverished, black Jamaicans "are learning to labor not for themselves only, but for their pastor, for their own education, and for the comforts as well as the necessaries of life."⁷ As the writer of this brief notice probably knew, describing the self-supporting nature of the Jamaica Mission resonated with Americans beyond missionary circles. A successful and self-supporting mission in Jamaica proved that black Jamaicans were willing to work for wages and displayed a very "civilized" generosity. The reality on the ground, however, proved considerably different from this assessment. Freed people made do with low wages and had to pay increasingly high rents, and few could afford to donate enough money to support a minister, his family, and a church building fund.

From the earliest days of the Jamaica Mission, the ministers were keenly aware of Americans' interest in whether former slaves would work for wages, and the ministers realized that the troubles they were having in building mission churches might reflect poorly on black Jamaicans. The refusal of ex-slaves to work was not creating the problems in Jamaica, the Oberlin ministers pointed out, but the failure of landowners and employers to pay fair wages to laborers. Like some British missionaries, the Americans in Jamaica had a strong aversion to the post-emancipation tactics that landowners used to control their workers. In one letter republished in the *Oberlin Evangelist*, David Ingraham dismissed the "doleful stories about the 'lazy niggers'" circulating in the United States in the wake of West Indian emancipation. He attested to the fact that freed people all wanted to work, but they were offered only eighteen cents for a day's labor. "The people feel, as well as they may, that they have worked for nothing, long enough," Ingraham wrote, and consequently, some were refusing to work until their wages were raised to twenty-five cents. He even included testimony from one freedman that would have certainly appealed to his Oberlin readers: "Massa mus giv twenty-five cents a day, or do he own work."⁸ Ingraham put wage disputes in Jamaica in terms that *Evangelist* subscribers would understand. Black Jamaicans who refused work did not do so out of laziness but to protest unfair wages paid by incompetent and lazy bosses.

Ingraham's testimony about the wage-rent system that left Jamaican laborers cashless and indebted to the sugar estates made his supporters at home aware of the prime difficulties preventing the formation of entirely self-supporting mission churches. In his overall analysis, however, Ingraham presented a very positive account of his work in Jamaica, one that fit quite well alongside abolitionist propaganda. During a return to the United States in the summer of 1840, Ingraham traveled and spoke about his missionary labors. He told his audiences that he had seventy-three church members, and that *"Every individual who had learned to read the Bible was hopefully converted."*[9] He had also started a Temperance Society and "a total abstinence society," and conducted 118 weddings. A moral sea change had taken place in his congregation, Ingraham testified, demonstrating the usefulness of missionaries to black Jamaicans. While only "two or three had escaped pollution" before emancipation, "now they were free and had the gospel" and "they began to be virtuous, and to practice chastity."[10] Ingraham argued that morality and marriage, Christianity and education prevailed in Jamaica, in spite of the troubles in securing fair wages. His private letters spoke of other matters, and in one letter to Amos Phelps, Ingraham confided that, as missionaries, "We are looked upon by all the whites with a jealous eye."[11]

Ingraham's bright picture of the mission's future was not the only version of events in the Jamaica Mission, and by the early 1840s, private letters from Ingraham's colleagues alerted their friends to the unexpected difficulties they had found in Jamaica. When he was planning to leave for Jamaica in 1839, Stewart Renshaw asked abolitionist Gerrit Smith for financial support, noting that "by and by the freedmen may be able to help us to some of the current necessaries of life, but for the present a school house and preaching shanty will fill, if not overburden, their hands."[12] Missionary Ralph Tyler pointed out the hardships for the Americans, and complained that David Ingraham had not suffered for money because he had been "too free in admitting to the church." Tyler refused to do this after seeing how Ingraham's "church society and school" was "almost gone to ruin."[13] In phrasing his complaint in these terms, Tyler referenced the words often used to describe sugar estates that had ceased operations and had been taken over by freeholders: estates were "thrown up" or "gone to ruin." Likewise, after Ingraham's departure from the mission, freed people had claimed his church, and this rapid creolization of the missionaries' evangelicalism served as a poignant lesson for what might happen if church discipline was not strictly enforced.

Ralph Tyler's letter suggested the growing disillusionment of the American ministers in Jamaica as they learned more about other missionary churches on the island. The Americans complained about how British missionaries had compromised true religion for merely getting along. For example, Nancy Prince, an African American New Englander whom Ingraham had recruited to join the Oberlin mission, worked briefly as a teacher for an English Baptist church in St. Ann's Bay. Like many mission churches on the island, this church divided its members into classes, and the minister, Thomas Abbott, assigned Prince to a class led by a black woman whom Prince found sorely lacking in church discipline. According to Prince, "I attended her class a few times, and when I learned the method, I stopped. She then commenced her authority and gave me to understand if I did not comply, I should not have any pay from the society." In Prince's opinion, the class leader too easily welcomed new members into the church. Prince tried to explain to her "the necessity of being born of the spirit of God before we become members of the church of Christ," but to no avail. After the class leader complained to Abbott about Prince's behavior, he fired Prince from her teaching job. When Prince tried to appeal to Abbott on theological grounds, he informed her that she was only to talk over such concerns with him. He further attested that "[the new members] have the gospel," so he "let them into the church." He also chastised Prince for intervening, perhaps alluding to the American women's request to be seated at the World's Antislavery Convention in London in 1840: "I do not approve of women societies; they destroy the world's convention; the American women have too many of them."[14] Prince left St. Ann's to teach at the American mission's schools.

Prince's experiences also offer a glimpse at how black Jamaicans viewed white missionaries. As a black woman, Prince was quite aware of the patronizing way in which missionaries treated black and brown church leaders who served as their allies. After attending a Baptist meeting in Kingston where one black man stood alongside the white missionaries, Prince observed that "it is generally the policy of these missionaries to have the sanction of colored ministers, to all their assessments and taxes" as this encouraged more donations. Prince noted, "The missionaries understand [this] very well, and know how to take advantage of it." On another occasion, Prince reported on her conversation with a man whom she met while traveling to Kingston. The man agreed with Prince that Jamaicans needed education, and when she asked him why black men could not pay to support their own teachers he replied, "Our money is taken from us so fast we cannot. Sometimes they [the missionary teachers] say we must all bring 1*l*.; to raise this, we have to sell at a loss or to borrow, so that we have nothing left for ourselves." Jamaicans referred to missionaries as "Macroon hunters," Prince noted, explaining that a "macroon" was a coin of small value.[15]

Prince's account of the mission churches also revealed the degree of creolization that went on under the British missionaries' noses. She observed that the Baptist churches had many members, but that the ministers made little effort to supervise the black class leaders who had command over the baptized. She wrote that "most of the communicants are so ignorant of the ordinance that they join the church merely to have a decent burial; for if they are not members, none will follow them to the grave, no prayers will be said over them . . . not so if they are church members." After a church member's funeral, the survivors held a wake because "they believe the spirit of the deceased is present with them for nine days, and they leave a place for them at the table and pay them all the attention they give to the visible guests." For Prince, as an American Protestant versed in the language of female moral reform, the American mission churches were a welcome change with their strict church discipline. She placed much of the blame for the state of Jamaica with British missionaries who charged too much for admission to their schools and who required people to pay for their Bibles. In her estimation, black Jamaicans were "enterprising and quick in their perceptions, determined to possess themselves, and to possess property besides, and quite able to take care of themselves."[16]

Prince's observations about the tenuous relationship between white missionaries and black and colored Jamaicans had already become a problem for the British missionary societies. In the late 1830s, a Wesleyan minister, Thomas Pennock, resigned his post when the Methodist mission refused to appoint colored men to serve as ministers and had not promoted two white ministers who had married colored women. Incidentally, the American mission employed a British schoolteacher, Charles Venning, who had married a colored woman. The mission ordained Venning in the late 1850s, and his wife was the last remaining person on the AMA payroll in the early

1880s.[17] In the mid-1840s, an even bigger controversy about the role of black church leaders developed in the Spanish Town church of Baptist missionary James Phillippo. When a majority of his congregation voted to support a different white minister, Thomas Dowson, the Baptists in Jamaica split over whether they should support Phillippo because of his seniority or Dowson because this was the wish of the congregation. In the wake of emancipation, British missionaries had to adjust to freedom. Some, like Thomas Abbott and Thomas Pennock, ceded authority to black Jamaicans, while others, like James Phillippo, insisted on the continued need for white control over the churches and over black Jamaicans. All of this occurred against the backdrop of a revival of Myalism and the arrival of a new governor in Jamaica who set his sights on prosecuting Myal practitioners. Lord Elgin called Myal "pseudo-Christianity," and noted that the use of Christian words did not "mitigate the barbarism of their rites."[18]

The American missionaries came to the island with little knowledge about the stakes of missionary work in post-emancipation Jamaica. They were therefore unprepared to respond to black Jamaicans who challenged their authority, and the missionaries were not expecting there to be an abundance of black-led churches, many established by church leaders who had left British mission stations for greater autonomy. The fracturing British mission churches indicated the limits of the universal Christian family. Catherine Hall has argued that English Baptist free villages were less a place for black people to realize freedom on their own terms and were instead "a site for acting out white visions of how black people should live."[19] Alternatively, some white ministers, like Thomas Abbot, had apparently conceded some authority to black church leaders, and in so doing, his church served as an example to the Americans of the lax church discipline that pervaded Jamaica's religious institutions.

By 1843, the members of the Jamaica Mission had realized that their self-supporting missions would not work. The ministers united to form the Jamaica Congregational Association on the island, and in the United States, their ally Amos A. Phelps formed the West India Mission Committee. The committee tried to raise funds for the Oberlin ministers, but Phelps was also aware that any whiff of "dependency" might actually hurt the mission. The importance of manly independence and self-sufficiency taught at the Oneida Institute and Oberlin stuck with the mission's men, even as they and their families suffered for lack of money. The appeals for donations that the West India Mission Committee made therefore balanced between the mission's needs and what the audience back home wanted to hear. One article noted that all of the ministers had raised money for their travel expenses, and in Jamaica, "They have depended chiefly for support upon their own manual labor, and the scanty, precarious aid afforded them by the very poor and destitute people, just emerged from slavery, among whom and for whom they labor."[20] Another appeal printed a missionary letter that interpreted hunger and hardship as God's benevolence. Awaiting a shipment of goods from the United States, the missionary and his colleagues faced hard times as the provisions failed to arrive. "No flour, and scarce any thing else for my family, or my teachers to eat, and means to get scarcely any thing." Unable to provide for his dependents and feeling forgotten by his friends in the United States, the missionary withheld his problems from his black congregation because he did not have the "heart to talk much to them of our wants."[21] The abolitionists who had fashioned themselves as rugged individualists, ready to sacrifice worldly comforts for the sake of spreading the gospel, found themselves and their abolitionist ideology tested in Jamaica. Consequently, when evangelical abolitionists established the American Missionary Association in 1846, the Jamaica Mission's ministers were offered a choice, and they decided that strict church discipline and the accompanying moral order, even if it came at the cost of the self-supporting mission, was more important than relaxing their rules and admitting more tithing church members.

The origins of the American Missionary Association highlight the way that church discipline fit into evangelical abolitionism in the United States. In the late 1830s, the men behind Oberlin College grew increasingly irritated with their fellow evangelicals' failure to condemn slavery as a sin. Invoking Charles Finney's theological position of Christian perfectionism, evangelical abolitionists chastised their fellow churchgoers for letting sinful slaveholders remain a part of their churches. Within evangelical circles, Lewis Tappan and other abolitionists began to challenge church leaders for their hesitancy to take a stand against slavery. Not only did accepting money from slaveholders corrupt religious societies, abolitionists argued, it turned foreign missionaries into hypocrites. The Salem Female Anti-Slavery Society agreed; in its 1842 annual report, the society echoed a common request for missionary organizations to condemn slavery because it was "antichristian" for Americans to try "to Christianize far distant heathen, at the expense of the heathen at home."²² Much abolitionist ire was directed toward the most prominent missionary organization, the American Board of Commissioners for Foreign Missions. The American Board's leader, Rufus Anderson, had called for missionaries to focus more on spiritual matters than social transformation, a position that Christian perfectionists and abolitionists found intolerable. For white abolitionists, like for missionary women working for the American Board, the work of evangelizing and uplift was one and the same.²³ The *Oberlin Evangelist* incredulously summarized that Anderson's policy held "that the gospel must be planted as quietly as possible, and with the least possible disturbance of organized focus on sin, and then left to work out itself, the social and moral regeneration of society."²⁴ Of particular contention was the issue of the Cherokee. The American Board had defended the Cherokee against the Indian Removal Act in the 1830s, but they had done nothing to encourage Cherokee slaveholders to manumit their African American slaves. For the AMA's founders, when the American Board permitted slaveholding Cherokee into mission churches, they were condoning sin for the sake of increased conversions, which represented a moral compromise.

After years of agitation from evangelical abolitionists, the American Board finally consented to hold a debate on slavery at its annual meeting in Brooklyn in 1845. The meeting came in the wake of a number of denominational schisms as southern and northern missionary organizations split on the question of slavery. The American Board wanted to avoid a split, even as some members, including Arthur Tappan, had already begun to withdraw support from the society for its tacit acceptance of slavery and public support of the American Colonization Society.²⁵ The ghosts of the 1834 Lane Rebellion could be found just beneath the surface in the Brooklyn church. The representatives of the American Board, Edward Beecher (Lyman's son) and Calvin Stowe (husband of Harriet Beecher), successfully defended their continued silence on the issue of slavery by classifying it as a new category of sin: an "organic sin" or "organic social wrong," which they defined as a sin that was ingrained in a people's culture and society and therefore not a transgression that an individual could be condemned for practicing. One slaveholding minister who had been born in the North but who worked in South Carolina testified that the American Board ought not to concern itself with slavery as it would only lose supporters, foment revolution (presumably slave rebellions), and make itself "as a Pope dictating to local churches."[26] Aligning the abolitionist movement with Catholic despotism was a persuasive point to the virulently anti-Catholic evangelical community. Edward Beecher agreed with his southern colleague even though he opposed slavery himself. Slavery, Beecher argued, was a "sin of the body politic," and God dealt with these sins differently than he did with individual sins.[27] Amos Phelps, the head of the West India Mission Committee, spoke on behalf of abolitionist evangelicals. He refused to go along with the notion of "organic sin," asking, "Why call the act a sin and say that he who commits it may be a Christian . . . We do not thus in the case of drunkenness, or polygamy, or any other sin—why this sin?"[28] As the meeting concluded, the American Board voted 75–0 in favor of the initial report that took no formal action against slavery other than generally wishing for its end.

Just as they had separated from the Garrisonian abolitionists in 1840, evangelical abolitionists began to plan a new missionary organization that would put them apart from the American Board. Only months after the American Board meeting in the summer of 1845, Amos Phelps addressed a crowd of twelve hundred antislavery partisans in Boston and asked, "Shall friends of the slave, who are also the friends of mission, sit down quietly, and give their silent assent to the position now taken?" He told the audience of the emerging two-pronged plan to form a new abolitionist missionary society "to reach the perishing at home and abroad, free from all contact and fellowship with slavery," all while giving "the Board no rest till its steps are retraced, and slavery has no home in its churches."[29] This statement would become the rallying cry of AMA supporters: how could Americans presume to spread "civilization" when millions of "heathen" on their own shores were left trapped in the state of slavery? Indeed, Phelps was not wrong in seeing the moderation of Stowe and Beecher as problematic, for proslavery southern clergy drew on this argument that a slaveholder could be a morally upstanding Christian as a way to defend slavery and attack abolitionism.[30]

Guided by American disputes about whether or not slavery was a sin, evangelical abolitionists in the United States gave little thought to how their doctrine of church discipline would transform once put into place in the mission field. In September 1846, Lewis Tappan, Amos Phelps, and a number of other evangelical abolitionists gathered together in Albany and made plans to unite three small missionary organizations, including the West India Mission Committee headed by Phelps, into one larger society. The other two organizations—the Oberlin-based Western Evangelical Mission Society and the Union Missionary Society that had been founded by African American clergy—had been similarly small enterprises. Combined, the fledgling AMA had three primary fields of mission labor: Jamaica; the Ojibwe Indians in the Northwest, the mission to whom had been run by the Western Evangelical Mission Society, and the African mission in Sierra Leone that had been founded there in part by the Amistad Africans, whom Tappan had financially supported during their Supreme Court case. As two of the three mission fields directly engaged with the question of slavery, the AMA made a clear statement of its intentions. Tappan wrote that the society was to spread "a pure and free Christianity" that

> wages an uncompromising warfare against all forms of sin, public as well as private: social, political, and organic, as well as individual; sins sustained, authorized, enacted, and even required and enjoined by civil rulers, as well as sins forbidden and punished by them; and ministers of the gospel, Christians, and Christian churches, should themselves abstain from, and reprove others, the one class of these sins as fully as the other; making no distinction between them in their teachings, their examples, their terms of church membership, or their administration of church discipline.[31]

In contrast to the American Board's compromised clergy, the AMA's Christian missionaries were to wage war on sin and maintain strict discipline to exclude the sinful from joining in with the body of the saved. Tappan and his allies had no toleration for those who failed to live up to their idea of Christianity.

While in the United States, church discipline had developed as a way to keep slaveholders out of churches, in the Jamaica Mission it became a tool for turning away or excommunicating black Jamaicans. The AMA persistently opposed the American Board's willingness to convert first and change the social conditions of a culture later, a mission theory developed by the American Board's Rufus Anderson.[32] It made no sense for missionaries to look the other way if converts were slaveholders or polygamists, and all potential church members should be held to a high standard. It is therefore unsurprising that the American Missionary Association endorsed the disciplinary measures of the English Wesleyan Missionary Society and republished them in the *American Missionary*. The instructions told missionaries to expel a church member who "became a Polygamist or an adulterer—who shall be idle, disorderly, or disobedient to lawful authority—who shall steal, or be in any other way immoral or irreligious." Such problems would be avoided if the church "first placed on trial" any potential church member to make sure that he "has wholly renounced all those vices to which he may have been before addicted."[33] Church discipline entailed keeping a close watch on the congregation and monitoring the behavior and any potential converts.

As a first duty, a missionary was a gatekeeper, paying close attention to the beliefs and practices of potential converts. The ministers struggled over whether they made the right decision when admitting new members in their churches. When the minister at Eliot Station, Loren Thompson, detailed the events of a revival sweeping his congregation, he also wrote about his concerns that the new spirit of religion was false. After all, the revival came in the wake of a deadly outbreak of cholera in 1850, and he acknowledged that it was possible that "some no doubt are only excited by fear . . . It is so in all revivals of religion." Indeed, he had almost been fooled in the past. He learned from men and women he had once refused to receive into the church that his instinct had been correct. They later told him that "they were then deceived, and are very glad that the church did not receive them." Thompson added further explanation: these men and women had not intended to "deceive the minister," but they had wanted to become church members to get closer to God because they lacked the saving grace of Christianity.[34] Indeed, it was precisely because so many black Jamaicans eagerly sought out church membership that the American ministers felt the need to make sure that they only let in the truly converted. In spite of his skepticism about the nature of the revival, Thompson must have ruled in favor of the inquirers, because in April 1851, Thompson announced that eight new members had joined the church, and there were plans for "ten or fifteen more" to join soon.[35] Cautious of the different versions of Christianity on the island, American missionaries made pains to demonstrate that Jamaican converts were truly repentant and purified from the sinfulness of slavery.

An article on the subject of inquiry meetings in the *American Missionary* described the rigorous process that the missionaries used to judge whether black Jamaicans were worthy of joining the mission churches. While he encouraged "free expression of religious feelings," Albert Richardson made sure to interrogate individually each potential convert "as to his views, experience, and manner of life." Richardson also made sure to qualify his ability to see into the souls of his flock: "Of course I can not vouch for the *truthfulness* and *genuineness* of these fragments of religious experience, yet I was careful to note down *only* such *as seemed to me* to be the honest expression of sincere hearts."[36] Richardson offered a specific example of how he knew a potential convert had chosen a new path in life. "I inquired of an aged female, who had been somewhat noted for her quarrelsome temper and fiery tongue, whether she was not likely to exhibit the same unchristian spirit and temper as formerly? She promptly replied in the negative. I asked the reason why. Said she: 'When de Lord take my heart, him mash it all up clean—all up clean, every bit!' A striking description of the process of turning a stony heart to flesh."[37] The woman's expression of faith and sentiment of renewal made an impression on Richardson; she voiced the "rebirth" so valued by the American missionaries who looked for signs that black Jamaicans had left behind the much-derided culture of slavery.

These examples of successful conversions indicate that overlap existed between the Americans and black Jamaicans, and the ministers and churches clearly appealed to some freed people. Over the course of the mission's history, the largest mission stations always had over one hundred people at Sunday services, and a steady number of church members. This evidence suggests that while many black Jamaicans did abandon missionary churches for Native Baptist congregations, this was not a universally shared ideal. People may have joined the mission churches because they were in the neighborhood, or because they liked the American minister. As later chapters show, Jamaican trustees who retained the final decision on whether or not their congregation would accept a new minister often voiced clear preferences for some American missionaries over others. For example, after arriving at Oberlin Station in 1849, Abner Olds wrote that his congregation was quite small because there had been no minister at the chapel since Stewart Renshaw left in 1845. Many people had left to join other congregations in the area. Those who had not joined other churches voted to accept Olds as their minister, but this move did not stop them from challenging his views, particularly concerning temperance. "You are righteous too much," and "your religion is too stuck up," he reported the

Oberlin Station church members telling him, even as he reassured the AMA that as far as he could tell, all of these church members abstained from drink.[38] At least some black Jamaicans saw the mission churches as their own institutions, believing that they could have some influence over their church's tenets.

Another possible reason for black Jamaicans to join the American churches is that they offered a chance for social advancement, whether through education or from being associated with a church viewed as respectable. After slavery, some freed people embraced marriage rituals and some aspects of Anglo-American gender roles. For example, evidence suggests that the mission's ideas of female respectability made the churches attractive to some freed women who sought autonomy from abusive or unfaithful husbands. Late in the mission's history, the ministers compiled annotated lists of church members, and it is telling that for the existing records for Charles Venning's Chesterfield station and at Oberlin, several women's names were accompanied with a note describing their husbands' misdeeds. Fifty-five-year-old Urania Campbell had been a member at Chesterfield since 1844, and Venning noted that "her husband has left her and is living in open adultery." Forty-year-old Letitia Bernard and forty-year-old Lydia Simms remained church members even though their husbands were excommunicated.[39]

By the end of the 1850s, the majority of church members were older married couples, or widows and widowers, and the young church members mostly consisted of children who had grown up in the mission. But the examples of women who found refuge in the church community demonstrates that the churches could also serve as havens for women with unhappy marriages, or perhaps the mission churches had led them to leave their husbands.[40] One can imagine that Urania Campbell saw her husband's choice to live with another woman as a painful reproach, a desertion, or perhaps a relief if he had been overbearing and the two frequently quarreled. Whatever the case, she had not backed away from the church that condemned her husband's actions; Letitia Bernard and Lydia Simms similarly remained loyal to the minister who excommunicated their spouses. The mission likely offered these women a community, and the women might have chosen this community because they were otherwise alone or because they preferred it. Individuals make choices about their lives based on their specific circumstances as well as the broader social and cultural context to which they belong, which means that any generalization about gendered behavior, religious beliefs, marital choices, and sexual practices must be seen as a generalization rather than an absolute.

In spite of having stable membership numbers, the ministers' letters drew sharp critiques of other churches in Jamaica and of the sinful masses who apparently spent their time trying to infiltrate the American churches. Revivals and church growth, such as the postcholera conversions at Thompson's Eliot church, were often soon followed by regretful stories of backsliding, excommunications, and disgruntled ex–church members forming breakaway churches. One missionary described his job as that of a "sifter" and declared his intention to "clear away the rubbish which has been gathering during the joyful days which followed emancipation," perhaps a remark aimed at the island's Baptist churches.[41] In 1851, the newly arrived Albert Richardson reflected on the different meaning of church membership for Jamaicans and for the Americans. He wrote, "There is a prevailing desire, among the colored people here, *to get into the church*. They have been taught to believe, that it is almost the gate of heaven; and there is a sort of feeling that if they can only get into it and enjoy its ordinances, they shall be safe."[42] In consideration of a frequently quoted biblical verse in missionary circles, one missionary meditated that while "Ethiopia is stretching forth her hand to God" and "India is raising her voice for the gospel," they often "'stretch out their hands,' and 'raise their voices' for what they suppose is the gospel but when the self-denying religion of Christ is presented they will turn away with disappointment and hatred in their hearts."[43] Black Jamaicans, it seemed, preferred their own understanding of Christianity, and the American ministers simply could not understand why formerly enslaved people would remain committed to a faith connected to slavery.

The religiosity of Jamaica struck Heman Hall, and he commented that this distinguished Jamaica from other mission fields. "Everyone is already religious," he reported. The quality of the religion was more in doubt. "Ministers dying of Delirium Tremens, and ministers baptizing and receiving to the communion those whom they know are drunkards and fornicators ... All can find preaching that suits their taste, and they can live as they please and attend chapel where their life will be no reproach to them."[44] The American ministers focused a great deal on the proliferation of black-led churches, referred to universally as Native Baptist churches by the American missionaries, and these churches' failure to uphold church discipline. When an American minister expelled a sinner from his church, that person could join a wide array of other churches, effectively rendering the punishment moot. Unlike the black churches in Ohio where Oberlin seminary students volunteered and preached, the Native Baptists did not seek out white allies or share the Americans' religious culture. Hall protested that "those who attend our chapels are reproached for doing so. It is said to them, 'Your Yankee ministers will not let you drink rum, etc. etc.'" Hall's frustration came from the fact that there were twenty-five chapels within five miles of Providence Station, and that while "a few" of these were trustworthy, most preached "a gospel that promises men eternal life while it leaves them in drunkenness and fornication."[45] Henry Evarts similarly identified the lack of church discipline in Native Baptist churches as a major challenge to the American mission's goals. A nearby black Baptist minister had just baptized three men excommunicated from Evarts's Brainerd church, and he wrote, "No inquiries were made about them or their standing in our church. This running away is very common."[46] Evarts also accused the Native Baptists of using "prejudice against or rather in favor of, color" so that they could "draw the people away from white ministers."[47]

The recurring angst over the lack of church discipline in Native Baptist churches and their recruitment methods prompted the missionaries to write extensively about what they saw to be the core problem with religion in Jamaica: so many people declared themselves to be Christians, yet the missionaries could see no signs of Christian behavior. One of the first missionaries to the island, Ralph Tyler, had written in 1842 that while "one hundred of my people at Devon Pen were members of a Baptist Church" he was unable to "see any evidence of one among them being a christian."[48] Six years later, Seth Wolcott pointed out that while "the first sight discovers a plenty of religion . . . a closer inspection discloses the solemn fact that there is but little vital godliness . . . I utter no slander when I say that it is quite common for professing christians to be both intemperate and licentious."[49] While the Americans fixated on sexuality and drinking, they also found fault with theology, particularly adult baptism and the promise to wipe away sins of the flesh. Seth Wolcott accused English and black Baptists alike of tricking their church members to believe "that by immersion heaven is certain however vicious the life."[50] If a church had no policies of exclusion or excommunication, then the church had no disciplinary measures to punish sinners. Churches like these had corrupted the meaning of Christianity in Jamaica, making it impossibly hard for the Americans to tell if potential converts fit an Oberlin standard of Christianity.

Because a black Jamaican's claim to be a Christian meant little in their minds, the American missionaries focused their attentions on sinful behavior. While they disapproved of stealing, lying, and intemperance, they were most vocal and most upset with what they considered to be unrestrained sexuality. Heretical religious beliefs and sexual licentiousness went hand in hand, in the missionaries' minds. In particular, accusations of sexual impropriety became a chief line of attack against the Native Baptists. These black ministers were not only corrupting Christianity, the missionaries complained, but their failure to enforce church discipline condoned illicit sexuality. In a published article on Jamaica, former missionary Stewart Renshaw accused Native Baptist ministers of being "always ignorant, and often grossly licentious, brutal men" who used their position of power to exercise "an iron despotism over the bodies and souls of their classes."[51] Henry Evarts complained more specifically about the black leaders in charge of the large Native Baptist church that had been built very close to his Brainerd Station. In contrast to being moral beacons for their congregation, Evarts described the church leaders as "shrewd and cunning men" able to "descend to the superstitions and low prejudices and intrigues of the people."[52] Black ministers competing with the Americans for church members could be attacked as those who, by not enforcing strict church discipline, promoted premarital sex, adultery, and other transgressions to the American idea of the Christian family.

The missionaries typically attributed black Jamaicans' inability to understand sinful behavior to their "childlike" willfulness; they were, as missionary Abner Olds put it, mere "babes in Christ" requiring "simple milk." On the other hand, when attacking the black Baptist ministers and leaders, the Americans characterized these men as overly masculine and threatening figures, on par with tyrannical white southern planters or Mormon polygamists.[53] In language that bore a striking resemblance to abolitionist attacks on slaveholders and antipolygamy propaganda, the American missionaries accused black Baptist leaders of being abusive and adulterous. In the case of one Baptist deacon, Henry Evarts wrote that "more than once his wife has come, bruised and bleeding, to complain to me of his abuses.

It has long been a current report that he has been keeping and supporting another woman beside his wife." For Evarts, the most irksome part of this situation was that the deacon's congregation continued to support him: "all of these things were well known about him when he was received to the church and put in office."[54] The missionaries proved the illegitimacy of the Native Baptists most convincingly to a home audience by their "uncivilized" gendered behavior. Native Baptism, they believed, was the religion of slavery, rehashing the old systems of concubinage and rape as a means of control, while their American Christian faith was the religion of a new order of freedom.

The American missionaries avowed their dedication to strict church discipline, but in some of their letters, they revealed their awareness of the diversity of their mission churches. After all, black Jamaicans who belonged to the American churches did not come to the churches as newborn souls, as the Americans claimed. The mission churches all elected black deacons and in several of the mission stations, Jamaican trustees, and not the American minister, had the final say on matters related to the missionaries' pay and the mission property. In order to remain at a mission station, the American minister had to maintain good relations with the leaders of his church and with the congregation. In the following examples, American ministers were made aware of the limitations of church discipline and, to some degree, of their authority over their mission churches.

In the mid-1850s, missionary Heman Hall discovered, or at least was forced to acknowledge, that many in his congregation still believed in Baptist doctrines of adult baptism. Hall preached on the subject of infant baptism two Sundays in a row, and as he neared the end of his second sermon on the subject, one of the church's black deacons "got up and flew into a violent passion and raved at the top of his voice . . . 'What kind of a gospel is this! What nonsense is this that minister has preached for two Sundays. I don't want such a gospel as this. I won't have such a gospel. I will leave the church before I will have such a gospel! Minister think we are all fools. Minister is going to make us all jackasses.'" The deacon walked out, continuing his protestations in the yard outside, even as a number of the church members went out to try and calm him down. The morning's events startled Hall, who had until this point considered the deacon "a deeply spiritual man."[55] In his interpretation of events, Hall thought that the deacon's anger erupted out of a conflict between the man's "considerable intelligence" and his emotional connection to Baptist ideas of adult baptism. According to Hall, the deacon's "intellect had been convinced by the truths that were presented while he set his will against it." In other words, the deacon's mind knew that the doctrine on baptism preached by Hall was true religion, but his "will"—his feelings, his heart—could not accept what his intellect had adopted.[56] This characterization illustrates how the missionaries conceptualized the deep-seated presence of creole culture: even if they could educate and convert willing black Jamaicans, the ministers had to be prepared for backsliding.

Taken from a different perspective, it seems plausible that this deacon, along with other church members, believed that an unspoken agreement existed in the mission church: the minister would refrain from denouncing theological doctrines as unchristian for the sake of the community's harmonious existence. After losing a number of church members to the deacon's new church, Hall blamed "the more ignorant part" of his congregation for taking "offence" when he preached on "views differing from their baptist notions." Hall clearly understood that his congregation contained men and women still loyal to aspects of Baptist teachings. Apparently, Hall wrote, "they thought it was not proper that I should *preach* on that subject, and this led them to sympathize with that deacon." As for the deacon, he was excommunicated from the church, and he left Providence Station to form his own congregation.[57] Hall lost some credibility with his congregation after the confrontation with the deacon at the Providence chapel, and not long after, he and his family relocated to Brainerd Station, an indication that he no longer fit in with his former church community. While Heman Hall portrayed the deacon's mutiny as an example of ignorance and savage willfulness, the story also revealed the fragility of Hall's own authority over his church. The missionaries had to make compromises with their congregations if they were to have any church members, and when they broke unspoken agreements as Hall did when he preached on the subject of baptism, the black church members revoked their vote of confidence for their minister.

The events had a lasting effect on Heman Hall and his attitude toward his next mission church. He wrote of his new congregation, "When they say 'they left their soul all to God,' I am left to feel that perhaps they know in their own souls what true faith is and perhaps they do not know anything about it."[58] Unsure of whether or not his converts were saved, or if they even understood salvation in the same terms as he did, Hall laid bare the dilemma facing all of the American missionaries in Jamaica. In spite of constructing neat categories like sinner and saved, heathen and converted, the reality of religion on the island defied simple binaries. As much as the missionaries might have cast the Native Baptists as antagonistic to their civilizing mission, the American churches were in part made up of the very same men and women who still practiced ritual meals, adult baptism, and probably other Afro-Christian or Christian Myalist rites.

Other members of the American mission also found that their churches were not nearly so pure as they imagined. Missionary Abner Olds found many of his potential converts to be still fully engaged in the rituals associated with creole religion. Olds had been stationed at Oberlin Station from 1848 until 1852, at which time he was invited by a landowner to form a church and school on the estate of Golden Vale. On one scouting trip to investigate the post, Olds visited a prayer meeting led by the existing Native Baptist congregation on the estate. He scoffed at the leader of the church for being illiterate and wrote incredulously that this minister encouraged his followers to fast twice a week, meaning that they did not go to work on those days. Further, on two nights every week, he wrote, "They sit up and sing all night." In spite of his dismissive tone toward Native Baptist practices, Olds proved himself to be something of an anthropologist when it came to these matters. He attended one of these night services and wrote a description of the proceedings: "At these meetings numbers of the women are in the habit of having what they call the 'convince,' which consists in falling on the ground, rolling over and tossing their arms, and shrieking out dismal cries; the congregation the meanwhile encouraged, raise still louder their voices in singing!" According to Olds, not only was the Native Baptist an ignorant man incapable of providing a modern education for the estate's children, the religious rituals prevented the laborers from their work. Toward the end of the letter, Olds noted regretfully "that they had not yet attained the idea that their religion was to affect their daily lives;—to make them better men."[59] Christianity was intimately connected to certain labor habits and morals tied to "manliness," and Native Baptists and Myal practices worked against these goals of the civilizing mission.

After he and his wife had moved to Golden Vale, Olds visited one of his prayer groups when they apparently had not been expecting him. Olds described in great detail the scene, indicating that he neither interrupted it nor absented himself from the "heathen" rite. The Jamaicans were assembled around two tables covered in white cloths, and each person had a white bowl upon a white plate. An herbal tea was served in the bowls, flavored with milk and sugar, and each person had bread to break into the tea. All of the people were dressed in white, and as Olds entered, the leader was leading the congregation in saying grace. The call-and-response service surprised Olds because it seemed all of the people knew the responses by heart. Interestingly, while Olds introduced the rite as yet another "superstition," he found himself liking parts of the service, particularly the exhortations pronounced by the leader at the end of the service that he thought were "very good." Another missionary who had witnessed and described an almost identical ritual meal ended his later account with the closing remarks spoken by the leader at the end of the service: "'You done with the world now? No tief? No lie? No backbite? No whoremonger? You have peace with all your broders and sisters?'"[60] The service thus concluded with a moral code not all that different from the one taught by the missionaries. The rite's complexity impressed Olds, yet he mused "that it were better for them not to know any thing of Christianity" instead of having an "imperfect knowledge of [it] . . . commingled with gross superstition." The good that the two missionaries found in the ritual meal were the elements they interpreted as Christian, and the other aspects they viewed as heathen corruptions. The pluralist faith of the Jamaicans enabled them to attend Olds's prayer meetings at the same time as they maintained their own practices, and this pluralism routinely evoked anxiety in the minds of the missionaries.[61]

For some of the American ministers, their time in Jamaica directed them to a less dogmatic interpretation of Christianity. Like the Baptist missionary Thomas Abbott who had told Nancy Prince that he allowed any interested Jamaican into his church, Abner Olds also developed a more expansive interpretation of what counted as Christian orthodoxy. He began to differentiate cultural practices from religious belief. After being on the island nearly four years, Olds wrote about a recent revelation that he admitted might appear "heterodox" to those at home. At one time, he wrote, he had "verily thought that a heathen or a semibarbarian *converted* would be almost immediately possessed of the habits, manners, and amiabilities of a christian in civilized lands." His experiences in Jamaica had changed his mind concerning instantaneous transformation, and he cautiously expressed his feeling, no matter how it may appear to others, "that a man may become a christian and yet be what might be termed a half naked barbarian." Conversion, Olds implied, did not necessarily entail a radical change of outward behavior. Indeed, this prototypical convert would be changed in "moral bearings" if not in habits. The outward appearances would come slowly, because even after a man "lives for a new end . . . he may not at all think that christian propriety requires that he should cover the nakedness of his back even though he be at work among men, women, and children!"[62] Perhaps the outward signs of modest clothes and a gendered division of labor along the lines of northern ideals were not the only signal of conversion. Olds did not go so far as to declare these "civilizing" advancements unnecessary but remarked that they would come in time.

Ultimately, Afro-Christianity and creole religion had rituals and beliefs that the American ministers could interpret as vaguely Christian, and at various points in the mission men like Abner Olds, along with some others, recognized that Christianity might exist in a different form than their American version of the faith. Abner Olds's move to becoming less interested in the outward trappings of faith, however, was less common than the changes undergone by other ministers, including Loren Thompson, Seth Wolcott, Heman Hall, and Albert Richardson. These men overwhelmingly remained committed to the idea that Native Baptists and black Jamaicans were susceptible to "corrupt" Christianity, and as a result, they needed more supervision to keep from going astray. In contrast to the American missionaries' religious education in the United States, black Jamaicans' more pluralist religious roots had better prepared them for the compromises necessary for the missionary encounter. They could, as Heman Hall's deacon had done, join the American churches and benefit from them without casting off all of their personal religious beliefs.

The perfectionist brand of evangelicalism of the Americans, on the other hand, made the mission almost impossible. Christian perfectionism had led the missionaries to abolitionism in the U.S. North, and it had made them interested in helping freed people in Jamaica, but it was of little use in practice in a missionary setting. Confronted with black Jamaicans who did not seem committed to the rules of church discipline, the Americans grew more attached to discipline as a means of controlling potential converts and church members, even as they fretted over the "childlike" behavior of their congregations. This impulse did not come out of a sense of biological racial superiority, even as it reflected the rhetoric of many proslavery partisans. Instead it grew out of a genuine, albeit racialized, concern to save the souls of freed people whom they believed were being led astray by black Baptists. While this might have worked with the mission's evangelical goals, it could only harm the abolitionist mission's political goals to present to an American audience "civilized" and independent freedmen. Church discipline and missionary authority also existed at ideological odds with certain strains of radicalism within the antislavery movement. For some in the mission, as the next chapter details, tensions between the civilizing mission and antiauthoritarianism could not be held in balance.

4 From Spiritual Liberty to Sexual License

In May 1850, a black Jamaican named Thomas Livingston wrote to George Whipple, the foreign corresponding secretary of the American Missionary Association, to inform him of the changes that had recently taken place at the Eliot Station's school. The forty-seven-year-old Livingston had become a shopkeeper after emancipation in 1838, and he had belonged to the Jamaica Mission's Eliot Church since the early 1840s. He reported to Whipple that the newest teacher at Eliot School, an American woman named Urania Hunt, "was not the person for this place," and Livingston told Whipple that the board had hired a black Jamaican man to take her place. In his letter, Livingston reflected on the larger context for the trustees' decision. In the past, he recounted, "The school was intierly under the control of the Minister and we had no voise in the school." While apprehensive at first, by July 1850, the minister at Eliot, Loren Thompson, fully supported the actions of the Eliot trustees. Thompson told George Whipple that the recent events were "a very important step in the advance of freedom" and remarked, "The people at Brainerd and Hermitage have taken the same stand." For Thompson, these events signaled the advance of "Manhood under the genial influences of a pure Christianity," and he proclaimed, "Let pure freedom be preached, the freedom that the Son of God gives" so that the "signs of life" might emerge from the "dry and crushed ruins of Slavery."[1]

What made Loren Thompson, the same man who once declared that very few freed people were "able to judge what a good school is," decide that he should hand over Eliot to them?[2] Why did Thomas Livingston choose this particular moment to seize control over the school when he and other Jamaican men had a long list of grievances against Thompson's way of doing things? For the entirety of 1850, the white members of the Jamaica Mission battled over the meaning of Christian liberty and its place in a missionary context, and their disputes created a power vacuum that allowed black Jamaicans to step in and take on leadership roles so that the mission's schools and churches would not collapse.

The mission stations in Jamaica were more than a space for encounters between black Jamaicans and white Americans, and this chapter examines how internecine disputes over theology and the place of white women erupted in the mission context to almost bring down the civilizing mission. In 1849, a missionary named John Hyde began to float ideas that had become popular in the postrevival burned-over district in New York. Hyde believed that the outward practices of Christianity, such as rituals and church discipline, distracted God's people from true spirituality.[3] He asserted that men and women, blacks and whites were all equally endowed with God's spirit, and he preached to anyone who would listen that God resided within each individual's soul. In other words, when Christians followed their instincts, they followed God's will and achieved spiritual liberty. Hyde believed that the hierarchies and rules of the mission were impediments to salvation, and he managed to convince most of the other missionaries that he was on the right path. For the missionaries to try to "civilize" black Jamaicans was pointless if black Jamaicans, like white Americans, had God within them. According to Hyde, true Christians and free Christians, the all-important factor in this particular abolitionist civilizing mission, followed the dictates of their inner conscience, and for the missionaries to impose their lifestyles on the Jamaicans was working against Christianity and against the principles of abolitionism.

Hyde's biggest critic was one of the mission's single women schoolteachers, Mary Dean. She questioned Hyde's theology and morals, and emphasized that men like him had absolutely no place in a mission. How would the "civilized" white Americans ever convince black Jamaicans to adopt the right kind of Christianity if they espoused unorthodox ideas themselves? The mission's men rebuffed Dean's critiques of Hyde and instead defended his rights to religion and speech. In doing so, the American ministers maintained gender hierarchies even as their support for religious liberty directed them to see the racial dimensions of the civilizing mission in a new light. Hyde's downfall came when he took his spiritual inclinations a step too far. In late 1850, it became known that he had claimed another minister's wife as his own "spiritual wife." The Jamaicans at the mission station where the adulterous couple lived voted out their errant minister, and his one-time supporters in the mission quickly recognized the error of their ways. The rapid, albeit temporary, dissolution of the mission's underlying principles and the subsequent outburst of sexual experimentation among some of the missionaries revealed how easily the abolitionist ideals of freedom and independent manhood could upset the mission's attempt to establish Christian liberty in Jamaica.[4]

In 1849, two young women left Illinois for Jamaica to serve as the first single women schoolteachers in the mission. Mary Dean and Catherine Strobie had graduated from the Oberlin-inspired Mission Institute in Quincy, Illinois. Strobie, assigned to Eliot Station, met and married a British missionary not long after her arrival, while her classmate, Mary Dean, would have a different fate. Dean was stationed at Oberlin where John Hyde and his wife had been living. During and after their time together, Dean complained that neither of the Hydes did much work, and she added that John Hyde rarely led the household in family prayer and often expressed "peculiar views."[5] The Hydes moved to another mission station after a few months, and Mary Dean greeted the new missionaries at Oberlin, Abner and Ann Olds, with much relief. Mary Dean liked the couple, and both husband and wife quickly allied themselves with Dean when she began to publicly denounce John Hyde as a danger to the mission's goals.

When the AMA asked John Hyde to respond to some of the complaints they had received about him, he couched his religious views in a language of religious liberty and individual freedom, one familiar and appealing to evangelical abolitionists. Hyde traced his religious history, writing that after his first conversion experience, his soul had grown cold. He tried outward practices as a way to cleanse his soul anew, and he followed a restrictive diet, read "spiritual books," and attended "to every duty," yet he still "felt a bondage" that he could not break. For Hyde, the institutions and practices of Protestant Christianity restricted his soul and prevented him from opening up to God. In his letters he invoked a meaningful metaphor for the antislavery AMA: his spiritual journey had been a movement from "bondage" to rituals to the "freedom" of the spirit.[6]

Hyde's spiritual journey had begun to change before he left for Jamaica. In New York an unnamed advisor had told Hyde that he was guilty of "making a Christ of religious duties" rather than knowing the true Christ. After over a year in Jamaica, Hyde wrote, his spirituality had grown deeper, and he had escaped from this "inward bondage." He wrote, "God has cut me loose from every dependence, but Christ for salvation," and he believed that he had achieved total independence. Hyde found that "I now find my mind constantly exercised in the things of God . . . without any effort on my part against my natural inclinations." He interpreted his "natural inclinations" to be the things that God desired him to do, and these things no longer included family prayer and saying grace before meals: "for more than a year past, God has not given me liberty to do it (as it seems to me) and in giving it up, I am satisfied that I have followed the leadings of God's Spirit." Hyde concluded with a sorrowful comment on the spiritual failings of his fellow missionaries in Jamaica: "God has opened my eyes to see the truth" and "it is painful to me, to see those who are laboring in this island for the conversion of men, appear so well satisfied with outward appearances." His fellow ministers had "not advanced very far in Christian experiences," and their "want of discernment" was what led them to be so critical of his own more developed spiritual views.[7]

Hyde's personal conversion narrative drew on a familiar antebellum evangelical language of bondage and freedom, but given that he was a missionary to emancipated people in Jamaica under the employ of the first abolitionist missionary organization, his choice of terminology was particularly interesting. First, Hyde denounced authority. While antiauthoritarianism had been a part of Finney's revivals, the Lane Rebellion, and abolitionist critiques of southern slaveholders, Hyde's antipathy to authority increased while in Jamaica. Unlike other ministers who had embraced their role as patriarchal ministers committed to church discipline, Hyde questioned these practices, and would continue to do so in the coming months. Second, his usage of commonplace evangelical metaphors of bondage and freedom took on new meaning in emancipated Jamaica. Surrounded by emancipated people and former planters, all in a colony dependent on Great Britain, "freedom" gained new depths of meaning than it had had in the antebellum North. Finally, it is interesting that Hyde chose to lash out against "outward appearances" in his letter to the AMA. Unable to tell for sure if a Jamaican had genuinely converted, the ministers instead looked for signs of moral fitness in how they lived their lives. While other ministers had from time to time questioned this practice, as we saw Abner Olds do in the last chapter, Hyde condemned his colleagues for considering these insignificant details.

Mary Dean's biggest problem with John Hyde was that he was a missionary. While he might profess these heterodox views at home where he could be contained, in already licentious Jamaica, his views could get out of control. Further, as a white missionary, he had a duty to represent the interests of the AMA, and Dean believed that he had drifted far from orthodox Christianity. The most irritating thing about Hyde for Mary Dean, however, was that her fellow missionaries refused to say anything against him. With the exception of her housemate Abner Olds, all of the ministers considered Hyde to be "a proper teacher." Dean felt that a distinction should be drawn between those who were acceptable Christians and those who were suitable for mission work: "I have known some Catholics and Mormons whom I verily believe were Christians," but it did not follow that "it would be right and proper to send them forth as gospel missionaries." Missionaries to foreign places needed to represent the right sort of Christianity: orthodox evangelical Protestantism. She emphasized that when teachers were sent to "a heathen land" the society sending them should "*know what doctrines they teach*." In Mary Dean's opinion, such expressions of religious liberty might be allowed for people in the United States, but this sort of religious message had no place in a mission where church discipline and ministerial authority were needed.[8]

In spite of having the support of Abner Olds, Dean had little success in getting the other missionaries—Henry Evarts, Seth Wolcott, and Loren

Thompson—to agree with her assessment of Hyde. The ministers all gave Hyde the benefit of the doubt, and they resisted limiting his activities. In contrast, they strongly resented Mary Dean's outspokenness on the Hyde matter. One missionary even told her directly that she "had better not write so much" for she was a "lone little girl." Indeed, Dean's disposition had been a source of aggravation since her arrival in Jamaica. In a letter penned about six months after her arrival, Seth Wolcott wrote, "I fear Sis. Dean has not quite command enough of herself, and is rather too much disposed to find too many Nazareths, out of which no good can come, to make herself so useful and happy as she might be." Dean met with not only Wolcott's disapproval, as Loren Thompson and Henry Evarts also commented in their annual reports of 1849 on the difficulty she seemed to be having fitting into the mission family.[9]

Rather than submitting to the ministers' authority as religious leaders and fathers in the mission family, Dean refused to stop her attacks on John Hyde. She justified herself by invoking her intellectual qualifications as well as her responsibility as a woman to serve as a moral beacon and a protector of the mission family. To remind George Whipple of her educational background, she named Samuel May, Charles Finney, David Nelson, and Asa Mahan as her religious and spiritual guides, and "more than that all I have been *searching* the *scriptures* myself to see if those things were so."[10] Charles Finney, revivalist and Oberlin faculty member, and Asa Mahan, the president of Oberlin, both occupied privileged places in the evangelical abolitionist community, and further, both men were personal friends of George Whipple as he had worked at Oberlin before moving to New York to become the AMA corresponding secretary. More than simply taking these men at their word, Dean had conscientiously crafted her own hermeneutics to assure herself that the writings of the most prominent antislavery evangelicals were correct. She thus felt quite confident in her abilities to judge the religious views of Hyde, and she had found them to be destructive to the broader goals of the mission and could not understand why other ministers failed to recognize his error.

Dean also felt that, as a woman, she had a duty to guard the morality of the mission family. Following the ideology of domesticity that saw women as the moral centers of their families and the protectors of virtue, Dean extended her reach beyond the private or home sphere, that had no real correlation in Jamaica, to incorporate the entire mission family as her own. This matched the rhetoric of women's special place as missionaries and schoolteachers that filled the articles and books penned by supporters of female education, including missionary theorist Mary Lyon and domesticity's greatest promoter, Catharine Beecher. At Lyon's Mount Holyoke Female Seminary, future missionary wives and teachers learned that while men were to be the evangelists of Christian faith, women missionaries were charged with keeping their men safe from "going native" and also had a duty to model Christian motherhood and to teach female converts how to comport themselves as Christian ladies.[11] Thus, in addition to arguing from a theological point of view, Dean wrote from the perspective of a white woman interested in modeling the Christian home and preserving the Christian family, especially since the mission family's purity had high stakes for the civilizing project. While Catharine Beecher and other northern domestic writers spread the idea that American women had a particular work to perform in preserving the nation's racial and moral purity, this was more than theoretical for Dean in Jamaica. Dean thought of herself not only as a woman with moral duties but as a white woman civilizer, and as such, she believed she held important power.[12]

This stance became especially clear in Dean's critique of Hyde. She mentioned only tangentially that Hyde "has openly said he did not believe in the divinity of Christ," but she spent a half page detailing his frequent declaration that "his soul abhors the idea of family prayer." Even as a single woman, family prayer was a particularly sensitive subject for Dean, as she wrote: "it is *family religion* that has saved me from the depths of ignorance and vice, as low as any [black Jamaicans] I have come to teach. And shall I see the family altar broken down and say nothing[?]" Family prayer had been central to Mary Dean's own salvation from sin, and it was even more important in Jamaica. When a family joined together for a daily prayer service, as was expected from evangelicals at home but especially from those abroad, they turned the hearth into a chapel and united parents and children into a congregation of sorts, and outwardly demonstrated that the home was dedicated to the preservation of morality and Christian virtue. In neglecting family prayer, Hyde demonstrated to Dean that he was ill suited for modeling Christian manhood to black Jamaicans. Family prayer, Dean insisted, also protected the mission household from the incursion of "heathen" practices, just as church discipline attempted to keep the churches pure. As a woman, Dean felt called to defend the sanctity of the Christian household, and when Hyde neglected family prayer, he not only set a bad example but he also let down his guard in a society that she felt to be mired in corruption.[13]

Yet the mission men's hierarchal sense of order precluded domesticity from taking on the same degree of authority that it had in many northern evangelical circles, and indeed, in other missionary contexts.[14] When Dean came to Jamaica in 1849, she did not find a female auxiliary society of some kind created by the missionary wives, nor did she find herself in charge of a female school or some other relatively autonomous position. Dean's use of domestic and gendered religious language also ran up against the ministers' assertions of evangelical manhood that had been established in the 1830s. Just as Oberlin in the 1830s had circumscribed women's roles even as it proved revolutionary in its coeducational and interracial nature, so did the Jamaica Mission limit white women's activities. Moreover, the ministers felt that Mary Dean's attacks worked as an unwarranted attempt to limit John Hyde's independence, and their criticism of Dean echoed the earlier complaints of Lane Rebels against the board of trustees at Lane Seminary. The mission's men were so dismissive of Dean in their letters to the AMA because they feared that she might induce the mission board to take a more proactive role at monitoring their activities, which would be an unconscionable limitation of freedom in their minds.

The Executive Committee in New York took Dean's worries seriously, but when corresponding secretary George Whipple began to inquire about Hyde in letters to the other missionaries in Jamaica, he received a startling response. Rather than seeing Hyde's unorthodoxy as problematic, the majority of the other missionaries jumped to Hyde's defense. They invoked two central reasons to explain their support of Hyde, even as some acknowledged the peculiarity of his views. First, the missionaries fiercely defended their own autonomy and expressed concern that the AMA was trying to govern them from afar. The ministers in Jamaica had no intentions of relinquishing their independence to an authority thousands of miles from the mission field that had little understanding of the day-to-day challenges of missionary work. Second, the ministers blamed the whole controversy on an overly judgmental Mary Dean. The ministers' commitment to their own independence as well as their disapproval of Dean's attempts to assert any authority would remain significant factors that allowed the brewing storm surrounding Hyde to build in strength.

The growing animosity between Mary Dean and the Olds family on one side, and John Hyde and the other ministers on the other, reached a new level in January 1850 with the arrival of another single woman schoolteacher named Urania Hunt. Hunt was expected to replace Dean's classmate Catherine Strobie at the Eliot School. She had been recruited by two of the missionary couples—Henry and Lucy Evarts and Loren and Nancy Thompson—during the missionaries' sabbatical in the United States. The Evartses and Thompsons returned to Jamaica with Urania Hunt as well as Lucy Evarts's brother, Heman Hall, and his new wife, Sophronia Brooks Hall.[15] The three married couples and Hunt all survived the rough voyage to Jamaica, but something along the way upset Urania Hunt. In addition to three uncomfortable weeks at sea, Hunt apparently had fought with Nancy Thompson over a matter of significance. The dispute proved serious enough for Hunt to postpone her move to the Thompsons' Eliot Station, where she was expected to teach, and she temporarily moved in with Mary Dean and Abner and Ann Olds at Oberlin Station instead.[16]

In the mission family in 1850, then, were Seth and Mary Wolcott at Union Station, Loren and Nancy Thompson at Eliot, Abner and Ann Olds at Oberlin, and Henry and Lucy Evarts at Brainerd. The mission also included John Hyde and his wife, Heman and Sophronia Hall, and Charles Venning and his wife, along with the two teachers, Mary Dean and Urania Hunt. The mission family was more than metaphorical, as Ann Olds and Sophronia Hall were sisters, and Lucy Evarts was Heman Hall's older sister. Urania Hunt and Mary Dean were exceptional as unmarried women, and the two moved from being close friends as housemates at Oberlin to sworn enemies by the end of January 1850. Hunt had become a devout supporter of John Hyde, while Dean remained his most persistent critic. As single women, Dean and Hunt occupied marginal places in the mission family since neither had a husband or father to speak for her in the mission's meeting, and because they received the smallest salaries by far, they depended upon the support of others for their livelihood on the island. In the coming year, the two women who might otherwise have stayed on the fringe of the mission, quietly writing letters home about their schoolchildren, instead ignited a firestorm that almost tore apart the Jamaica Mission.

Initially, Hunt believed that God had sent her to Jamaica to serve as a "peace maker [between Hyde and Dean] for which naught but the grace I have received since I came here had power to prepare me." Her initial opposition to Hyde had faded, and she now wholeheartedly observed his religious views after the two held an intense twenty-four-hour discussion: the most "exciting conversation I have held with any individual." With Hyde's help, Hunt became cognizant of her own "spiritual infancy," and now informed of Hyde's "way of faith," she felt "impelled by the inestimable grace I had received to make an effort to impart knowledge of the way" to others, in spite of the fact that she "was held back by those who had received less or received it so long before that they loved less." In Hunt's opinion, Dean and the others who did not understand John Hyde were deemed inferior to his supporters who had risen to a new level of faith.[17]

Hunt's "conversion" into a "Hydeite" (as Dean referred to his allies) distressed both Mary Dean and Abner Olds, the minister at Oberlin under whose nose all of this spiritual enlightenment took place. Now blessed with Urania Hunt's support, Hyde became bolder and more vocal about his beliefs, and the pair became constant companions, moving between mission stations as they saw fit. Dean and Olds both complained about how Hunt and Hyde would travel together on the Sabbath, not for the purpose of attending church services but "to seek their own pleasure." Olds also noted that on one Sunday when Hunt was staying at Oberlin, "she was exceedingly rude." He continued, "I was awakened from my sleep in the morning by her hallooing to Dr. H. in another room and saying that Miss Dean had broken the Sabbath . . . In all these things she was not only not rebuked, but manifestly encouraged by Dr. H." The pair, it appeared, were intent on making Dean's life miserable, for she was their primary critic in the mission. Writing about these events later, Hunt defended her actions by claiming that since Mary Dean misrepresented Hyde to the AMA on purpose, she was left with no recourse but to treat Dean with "indifference or ridicule." To be sure, Mary Dean did blame the AMA for sending the two errant missionaries, noting that the organization foolishly wasted money for "two laborers each to tear down what the others had built up." Further, Dean had to spend time correcting the two of them since it was her duty "to oppose all the teachings of Dr. H. and Miss H. just as much as I do the errors and wickedness of the people."[18]

What might Urania Hunt have gained by supporting John Hyde, when it meant breaking her allegiance with Mary Dean? Hunt's three-week sea voyage to Jamaica had resulted in a traumatic break with the Thompsons, and she had no escape from them after arriving in Jamaica as she was stationed in their mission house. As a single young woman, she would be expected to serve as a deferential assistant to Nancy Thompson, helping with housework, child care, and other domestic duties, all added on top of her four-day-a-week teaching schedule. She probably found little sympathy in the rooms of Mary Dean, as Dean generally prided herself on her own ethic of unceasing labor. Hyde's charismatic personality along with his need to gain allies made him a perfect match for a woman feeling homesick and out of place. Further, as Abner Olds's account of their antics unwittingly revealed, Hyde supported Hunt's actions within the mission, offering her a vote of confidence that the other members of the mission did not. Whether or not Hunt was actually mentally insane, as the ministers would later claim, her rapid adoption of Hyde's religious views and her quick attachment to a married man likely happened in part because of the sense of power she gained by befriending Hyde. Like Mary Dean, Hunt found herself at odds with some of the mission's ministers, but she had found a dedicated advocate in John Hyde.

With the exception of Abner Olds, the mission's ministers continued to stand by John Hyde in the early months of 1850, even as they grew increasingly irritated with both Mary Dean and Urania Hunt, whom they saw as the source of the mission's problems. Hunt's erratic behavior proved most difficult for Loren Thompson, the minister at Eliot Station where Hunt had been assigned as a teacher. After her short stay at Oberlin, Hunt had moved to take up her work at the Eliot School. This stint was short-lived, and in early April, Hunt moved out of Thompson's mission house to live with Thomas Livingston, the deacon whose letter began this chapter. While it is unclear how much Livingston had to do with Urania Hunt's choice to take up residence in his house, Loren Thompson was bewildered by her decision, and noted that she had created "a good deal of inquiry among the people." Hunt had remained near Eliot, if not at Thompson's house, so that she could have a better chance to influence the church members and her former students, and Thompson soon found himself up against an attempted coup as Hunt and Hyde tried to turn the church's members against him. According to Loren Thompson, Hunt spread reports far and wide that Thompson was deceptive, and when people asked her for proof, she claimed cryptically that his deceitful ways were visible only to her spirit, a comment that led Thompson to think she was mentally unwell. Urania Hunt also allegedly schemed to get Thompson fired and John Hyde ordained and hired by having Thomas Livingston write to the AMA. In retrospect, Thompson later remarked that the only reason that his congregation had not abandoned the church once their ears had been "filled with her unjust and slanderous talk" was because of his established reputation in the community.[19]

An elaboration on Loren Thompson's standing at Eliot Station gives some insight into his relationship with Thomas Livingston as well as the more general currents of how Jamaicans perceived the American missionaries. Some years before this incident, missionary Stewart Renshaw and his family departed Jamaica for the United States, and the family took with them two girls—the daughters of Thomas Livingston. Renshaw's intention was that the girls would help care for his own children on the voyage back to the States, and then he would educate them at Oberlin or some other interracial institute. Renshaw asked Theodore Weld if his school in New Jersey would take some black Jamaican children, likely the two Livingston girls, and he was denied his request. Weld feared that "the contact of children brought up in slavery is, almost of necessity, pollution."[20] Meanwhile, the absence of the girls stirred a great deal of conversation among their friends and family at Eliot who believed that Renshaw had taken them for the purpose of selling them into slavery in the United States. This belief indicates that the abolitionist stance of the American missionaries was not always so clear in the minds of black Jamaicans who recognized the United States as a slaveholding country, a continuing problem that a later missionary observed in the 1860s.[21]

The problem was resolved when one of the girls, named Angelina, grown up and married to an African American (presumably), returned to Jamaica in 1850 along with the Thompsons, Evartses, Halls, and Hunt. She and her husband eventually served as teachers in the mission, but at the time of their return, they were most valuable to the missionaries in that they proved the ministers to be honest brokers. Thompson wrote about this at length in early 1850. In one letter he saw potential in the fact that in leaving the island and then returning, in addition to bringing back Thomas Livingston's child, he had made new inroads with the church members at Eliot. He wrote, "My going home and returning, bringing with us Mr. Livingston's Daughter have settled questions, which in many minds have for a long time been doubtful . . . Our people had been told, by evil designing persons, that we were fooling them—that we did not intend to come back, etc. etc."[22] His return to the island salvaged his reputation and left him in a position of strength so that when Urania Hunt tried to overthrow him, he managed to maintain his position as the minister of Eliot Church.

The battle for control at Eliot continued, even if Thompson had regained his church members' trust. One Sunday while Thompson was away, Hyde and Hunt together led the church service in which they preached their religious views along with their intense dislike of Thompson. The content of Hunt's message was so inflammatory that Thompson spent no space complaining about the fact that Urania Hunt, a woman, had preached in his church. According to Thompson, Urania Hunt preached a sermon that exhorted the couple's belief that "God's Spirit was alike in all, in the children as in the Adults, in the Sinner and the Saint, and our duty was to follow this spirit." Further, the couple denounced the civilizing mission by using the same racialized metaphors of the family used by the missionaries. "Children," Hunt told the black congregation, "must not be controlled as it would be interfering with the Spirit's teaching."[23] In the antiauthoritarian gospel of Hunt and Hyde, they not only opposed the social order of the missionaries that firmly differentiated between the civilized and the heathen, the teacher and the students, but they condemned it as anti-God. The couple saw the missionaries' paternalism to be dictating God's will to others rather than allowing the spirit of God to work freely without interference. The actions of the two led the other missionaries to call a missionwide meeting on the last day of April.

On April 30, all of the missionaries convened at Eliot Station to discuss the allegedly separate issues of Urania Hunt and John Hyde, yet the meeting's debates centered on the behavior of the two single women: Mary Dean and Urania Hunt. Going into the meeting, most of the missionaries believed Urania Hunt to be a problem, but only Mary Dean and Abner Olds connected her erratic actions to the influence of John Hyde. Indeed, for most members of the mission, the issue was not whether or not Hyde should be expelled from the island, but what position he should hold since he felt God called him to perform some labor other than carpentry, the task to which he had originally been assigned. In seeking to regain control over the threatening chaos, the mission's men thought that they needed to chastise the two women at the heart of the problem, the two women who represented the extremes on either side of Christian liberty—the "atheism of liberty" espoused by Urania Hunt and the "despotism of institutions" that Dean tried to enforce.[24] The ministers' negative reaction to Hunt and Dean alike, and their indifference toward Hyde, showed the ministers' gendered way of interpreting who could express what notions of freedom. When a woman preached a gospel of liberation, as did Hunt, or critiqued the religious beliefs of one of the mission's men, as did Dean, it was seen as indicative of a mental illness. Yet Hyde's views—or perhaps his way of expressing them—was seen to be in accordance with Christian belief or, at the very least, worthy of support from his colleagues. In the end, the meeting had two main results. First, the Olds-Dean faction that opposed John Hyde gained another supporter: Heman Hall. The two men's votes were not enough to counter the decision by the mission to appoint Hyde to the position of "missionary evangelist." The other major decision of the ministers was the unanimous vote to send Urania Hunt back to the United States. The meeting thus concluded with the lines between the two factions now explicit, and with Hyde elevated to a new position and Urania Hunt tentatively scheduled to leave the mission.[25]

In early May, a flurry of letters left the island for New York reporting on the meeting and its aftermath. These letters demonstrated the changing attitudes of many of the mission's men, and they also revealed the mounting hostility between some missionaries and contained accusations of inquisitorial personalities on one hand and unorthodox licentiousness on the other. While Dean, Olds, and Hall maintained the old policies of church discipline, even when it applied to a white man, the ministers who supported Hyde drifted away from their complaints about black licentiousness and instead amplified their calls for increased personal and spiritual freedom. Despotism and the narrow-minded attacks of Dean and Olds, they argued, were a grave threat to the ideals of abolitionism and the spirit of God. This quest for greater spiritual freedom, however, was gendered because neither Urania Hunt nor Mary Dean seemed to merit any similarly licensed freedom from the ministers' authority.

Judging from the May round of correspondence, Seth Wolcott and Henry Evarts had clearly adopted Hyde's ideas of faith and spirituality. Both Wolcott and Evarts witnessed a new spiritual movement aimed at ending the rules and regulations that humans placed on God's spirit. Their conversions can perhaps be explained by Hyde's evidentially charismatic and persuasive character, hints of which emerged in a series of letters from Julius Beardslee. A former member of the Jamaica Mission who had moved to Kingston in 1846, Beardslee had been kept apprised of the recent controversies. At first he outright condemned Hyde's theological position, writing that it was absurd and dangerous to believe that "conscience is just Christ within and that if an individual, even in the darkness of *heathenism*, follows the dictates of his conscience, he will assuredly be saved." Yet Beardslee's deep disgust of Hyde's views evaporated after he had spent several days in the company of Evarts and Hyde. In his second letter, sent less than a month after the first, Beardslee confessed, "I have not been in a right state of mind—I have had a zeal for God, but not according to knowledge. The Lord has graciously opened my eyes to some of my own defects, and I have seen enough to convince me that I am not in a state to judge others." The men of the mission felt quite certain that they were righteously defending their independence and that of the people whom they had come to save.[26]

The missionary who struggled the most during these months was Loren Thompson. In early May, Thompson not only dealt with the mission business of Hyde's and Hunt's positions, but he also had to manage the change in leadership taking place at Eliot School. As to the issue of Hyde, Thompson wanted to change his vote upon further reconsideration, and while he supported Hyde's independence, he also did not think that it was his duty to contribute to his financial support. Thompson also expressed his doubts about Hyde in relation to the mission family. Hyde seemed to want to "be left free to do or not to do, go or not to go, stay or not to stay, etc. just as he feels inclined," and when Hyde found that others disagreed with his plan for ministry, he judged them "as acting hypocritically or deceitfully" rather than as truly committed to Christian liberty.[27]

Thompson's disagreements with Hyde and Hunt also reflected the fact that Urania Hunt's sudden refusal to teach at the Eliot School had upset many of his church members. This controversy sheds light on the complicated transformation that the ministers had to undergo as they moved from being abolitionists to civilizing missionaries. Hunt complained that Loren Thompson was too controlling over the school and the teacher's work, a complaint that might have been shared by Mary Dean, who also chafed when ministers felt that they knew best. Thompson attempted to assuage Hunt's concerns by telling her that "I acknowledged that I had always held this position in the view of the people and took the first opportunity to correct the matter among them and assured her that I desire her to act as freely and uncontrolled in her deportment as I did in mine." Yet Thompson's attempts to reach a compromise did not go far enough, in Hunt's opinion, and she quit her post with this as her reasoning. In the resulting vacuum, Thomas Livingston had stepped up along with a set of church-appointed trustees, and Thompson observed that "the people feel like having school trustees appointed who shall have the general management and control of the school" rather than relying on the missionaries.[28] Chastised by Hunt and Hyde's harsh condemnations, Thompson felt that maybe he had been too controlling in the past, and he was optimistic about what might come of the new experiment of a Jamaican-controlled school.

While missionary teachers Mary Dean and Heman Hall recoiled at Hyde's ideas about education, his disciple, Urania Hunt, and Brainerd's teacher, Charles Venning, had embraced them for their own schools. Before leaving Eliot altogether, Hunt justified her abandonment of corporal punishment by her religious beliefs as she told Mary Dean that "she would not punish one of her scholars for she would *not flog God* and God was really in every one of them." Charles Venning, the teacher at Brainerd School, also found Hyde's approach to education quite convincing. He turned his school over to Jamaican trustees as well, and when asked why, he echoed Hyde's views: "The Providence of God seems to indicate that the time is past for the people to be carried." Now "they must learn to walk, they will stumble and fall and cry but such discipline is necessary if they are ever to be men." According to Venning and the other disciples of John Hyde, the Jamaicans no longer needed to be treated as perpetual children in the Christian family. The "discipline" required was not that of a watchful parent, but the discipline of becoming independent. Interestingly, while Venning and the others saw the fault in their paternalist need for control, they did not stop thinking about the Jamaicans as children; they merely changed their parental approach. When the missionary teachers gave up their authority in the school, it reflected less a recognition that Jamaicans were equals and more a proof of the missionaries' own religious ideas. Whether they were forcefully indoctrinating black children like Mary Dean or willfully choosing not to teach anyone like Venning, neither took the thoughts and feelings of the black Jamaicans into consideration.[29]

Since the upheavals in leadership at the Eliot School in May, it became apparent that the antiauthority positions of Hyde and Hunt had a practical effect on the mission schools. Like Thompson's realization that he may have been overbearing in his control over Hunt at the Eliot School, other ministers who supported Hyde spoke out against the patriarchal stance they had previously taken in the mission family. The schools' programs of material progress and socialization dictated by white missionaries seemed to Hyde and his followers to be in contradiction with the liberating goal of the Christian mission. By putting an end to the imbalances of power found in the classroom, however, the missionaries were going back on promises made to black Jamaicans by abandoning the educational services they provided to the children enrolled in their schools, a point made in Livingston's letter. Aside from the element of religious indoctrination in the mission schools, the American teachers also taught reading, writing, and math, essential tools black Jamaicans would need if they were to succeed as small farmers in a country where whites faced few consequences for cheating former slaves on land sales, leases, and other business transactions. However, Hyde's personal quest for spiritual freedom had little to do with the needs and wants of black Jamaican parents. Hyde's teaching philosophy held that education could not be forced on children unwilling to attend school. He told one missionary that "we are not to teach the children, until they see the value of knowledge, and come and beg to be instructed."[30] Hyde's followers either turned their schools over to black teachers (or perhaps were taken over by black teachers when the Americans stopped showing up), or closed their schools altogether.

We can only imagine the dread with which George Whipple received these letters from the people whom he had handpicked to evangelize Jamaica. In adopting extreme interpretations of Christian liberty, they not only attacked the AMA's authority over the mission but threatened to undo the work that the AMA had set out to do in Jamaica: to show the people in the United States that freed people could become just like hardworking white Protestants. As a result of the discord coming from his missionaries, George Whipple requested that the missionaries reconvene to reconcile their differences, although he privately hoped that they would collectively decide to dismiss Hyde, whose behavior, to the outsider, seemed obviously counterproductive.[31] Whipple likely hesitated to issue a direct dismissal from New York because it would only confirm the ministers' suspicions that the AMA was attempting to regulate the spiritual beliefs of its missionaries. In spite of his repeated criticism of missionary societies of all kinds, Hyde had not found it necessary to stop taking a salary from the AMA. Hyde declared that he would continue taking "the devil's money" in order to do as he wished, a problem even for Hyde's supporter Seth Wolcott, who wrote Whipple several times about Hyde's failure to perform any helpful sort of work.[32]

The second missionwide meeting convened in June, and it provided an arena for a dramatic confrontation between Abner Olds and Heman Hall on the one side and the remaining missionaries on the other. John Hyde went so far as to attack Olds directly by calling him a hypocrite and told him that his "spirit would preeminently fit [him] to be a leader of the inquisitorial lands."[33] Hyde's charisma and his outright dismissal of the likes of Mary Dean and Abner Olds rallied his supporters even more, and any attempts by Olds and Hall to counter Hyde's views were met with hostile accusations. Ultimately the meeting concluded with Hyde regaining the support of the wavering Loren Thompson. Perhaps the most startling occurrence at the gathering occurred after Olds, Thompson, and Hall had left to return to their mission stations. Hyde's most outspoken defenders, Seth Wolcott and Henry Evarts, decided to ordain John Hyde.

As a new wave of spirituality encouraged Hyde's followers to abandon their paternalist positions as schoolteachers and ministers, they also began to rebel against religious and social conventions in their own families. In April, the Hydes and Urania Hunt had moved to Brainerd Station to live with Henry and Lucy Evarts. In the early summer months of 1850, all of the missionaries except for Heman Hall and Abner Olds had stopped holding regular family prayer and church services, and even more alarming to the orthodox few, the residents of Brainerd Station had started to question the institution of marriage. The established gender roles of father-missionary and father-husband quickly dissolved in the new liberated spirit of Hyde's teachings, which created an avenue of a form of free love. If God was within, after all, then following an urge to have extramarital sex was following God's will. In the religious turn taken at Brainerd Station, husbands could not try to control the "spiritual" inclinations of their wives, nor could wives expect their husbands to remain faithful to their marriage vows.

The first hints that something improper was occurring at Brainerd came from Heman Hall, the younger brother of Lucy Evarts. In late June, a couple of weeks after the last rancorous mission meeting, Lucy asked her brother to aid her husband Henry during his spiritual crisis. Hall recorded his trip to Brainerd in two letters. The first dodged specific details and spoke generally of "a strange state of things" on the island, probably because Hall felt uncomfortable about stating his observations that reflected poorly on his sister and his brother-in-law. The second letter, however, written a week later, went into considerably more detail. Hall wrote that when he had been called to his brother-in-law's bedside, Urania Hunt had joined him. She got into bed with Evarts, and "was there most of the evening with no other person in the room and no light in the room." Hall also reported that Hunt spoke "of 'going in a-swimming' in company with Dr. Hyde and wife . . . all together and all entirely naked." Significantly, Hall reported that the missionaries did not keep their new sexual openness for themselves alone, but that they had also advised a Jamaican woman that she could live with a man other than her husband if she wished, because "we do not know what the Spirit will require us—that it will not lead us to commit fornication in heart, though it may outwardly." For themselves and for the Jamaicans to whom they preached, Hyde and Evarts separated outward behavior from inward spirituality, so one's material life did not reflect negatively on one's soul.[34]

While the missionaries had all thought that Evarts and Hyde had only tolerated Urania Hunt because of her delicate mental state, this situation changed when Evarts announced to his colleagues that Hunt had been "sent here by God as she has been made instrumental in bringing my mind up to many precious things in the gospel." Hunt was a "prophetess," misunderstood by those who had yet to become "spiritually minded." Again, Evarts spoke about a spiritual hierarchy, and those lagging were not the "uncivilized" black Jamaicans but the overly legalistic Mary Dean and Abner Olds. Like some strains of perfectionism in the United States, Hyde and Evarts had adopted the theology that true Christians were above church discipline and laws, for they had achieved a higher truth. Also, like the emerging Spiritualist movement, they focused their attentions on the spiritual power of a young woman. They believed that proof of their advanced faith could be found in their own aversion to the rules that they had formerly accepted; Dean and Olds had simply not yet realized this more elevated level of spirituality.[35]

Evarts's spiritual crisis led him to resign from the AMA. In his resignation letter, the same letter in which he extolled Urania Hunt's spiritual wisdom, he wrote that he believed that missionaries should not take money from societies but should instead work for their income, because "in this way the spirit which leads us to our work would be made more evident to those for whom we labor than it now is." Further, Evarts wrote that accepting the society's funds meant that the missionary was bound to certain beliefs endorsed by the society, leading to a "real impossibility of enjoying perfect liberty of conscience." Evarts believed that the missionary organization's structure and his own accountability to the people who paid his salary were limiting his own liberty to do God's work. It was unwise, he wrote, "for any of us to place ourselves under temptation to dictate others, or to be dictated beyond the liberty of the Gospel." It was his goal to test the Gospel's power, so to speak, by taking the bold step of relying on God to provide for "the wants of his people" instead of relying on a "human arm." In these statements of faith, Evarts asserted his new understanding of the full implications of freedom and liberty, namely that as missionaries, taking orders from a society in New York and then passing along their content to the black Jamaicans, the missionaries were themselves constraining the freedom of the people they sought to liberate. Evarts represented his newfound faith as a source of manly independence, the exact sentiment missionaries had wanted to cultivate in the souls of formerly enslaved black Jamaican men.[36]

While Evarts spoke only about the higher and more spiritual pursuits he sought to attain through following a purer gospel of liberty at Brainerd, a later account offered by Loren Thompson went into more detail about the scandalous nature of the situation first described by Heman Hall. Speaking about Urania Hunt's insanity, Thompson noted that Evarts had at first allowed for Hunt's questionable behavior because of her delicate mental state. He wrote,

> She would before the family (and in the presence of strangers,) sit down at his feet, lay her head in his lap, and ask him to stroke her hair. She would throw herself upon his bed at night—put her arms around his neck, kiss him, and freely talk about sexual emotions, making a distinction between Emotion & Passions, she would do the same to Dr. Hyde, would go with him to the river to bath. And in a state of nudity do so. These things I suppose they only tolerate on the ground of her insanity. But when such conduct was regarded as the natural fruits of the Spirit, and that persons in a highly Spiritual state would naturally be led to do such things and that Miss Hunt's madness was but the madness of *Paul*, it put a new feature upon such conduct.[37]

While Thompson had believed that Hyde and Evarts were merely humoring Hunt so as not to worsen her mental condition, he changed his mind when he heard that the two declared her to be struck by God's spirit as Paul had been on the road to Damascus. Seth Wolcott also found Hunt to be the root cause of what was taking place at Brainerd. He recounted a conversation in which "she frankly acknowledged . . . that she felt free, (free by the Spirit of God, so I understood) to enjoy sexual intercourse with any man who had the *same liberty* with herself—it would then be a spiritual intercourse—approved of God."[38] Proclaimed a prophetess with a direct connection to God, she found a way to get at least some men of the mission to pay her proper attention, unlike Mary Dean, whose protests continually were pushed to the side. Like the Spiritualist mediums who were contemporaneously attracting attention in central New York, Urania Hunt used her alleged spiritual gifts and her sexuality to gain a degree of power in the mission.

Hunt's spiritual authority was not uncontested in the Jamaica Mission, and the ministers finally convinced her to return to the United States for the sake of her health. If Hunt was not insane, Loren Thompson wrote, "I can but regard her as notoriously wicked—this may seem uncharitable, yet it is the only construction that I can put upon her conduct."[39] The ministers had to reconsider matters when even after Hunt's departure, the sexual antics at Brainerd continued. John Hyde declared Lucy Evarts to be his spiritual wife, and he went about building a very different kind of family hierarchy at the Brainerd mission station. Wolcott, Thompson, and most of the other ministers had, to varying degrees, believed that Hyde had a right to express and act on his religious beliefs and that to put restrictions on him would be a limitation of his freedom. Now they came to the realization that the goings-on at Brainerd and in the Evarts, Hyde, and Venning families reflected something far beyond an expression of Christian liberty.

In August, Loren Thompson and his wife went to stay with the Wolcott family for a few weeks to help with the labor-intensive process of milling the year's crop of sugar cane grown by the farmers around Union Station. Thompson described the recent events as tests of faith, and cited biblical passages addressing "trials" put forth by God for the faithful, and remarked, "For trials we feel grateful to God. We have in all good conscience endeavored to exercise ourselves by these trials."[40] The apologetic members of the Jamaica Mission attributed their lapse of judgment to a test of faith that they had ultimately passed, to misunderstandings, and to their distrust of the reliability of Hyde's early critic, Mary Dean. In their letters written in the late summer and fall of 1850, they blended these explanations for why they had tolerated Hyde for so long.

Seth Wolcott explained that he had found Dean's condemnation of Hyde so offensive that he had been pushed into Hyde's camp only through his opposition to Dean. His distrust of Dean's judgment had even led him to doubt the first reports of sexual infidelity at Brainerd. To him it seemed "false and calumnious" and written in a spirit that seemed "to say 'Away with him. Crucify him, crucify him.'" But after learning, as did Thompson, of the actual circumstances at Brainerd, he realized that there was more to the story than false allegations. More metaphysically, Wolcott felt that while Evarts and Hyde still professed to be working for God, "It seems to me that Satan as an angel of light holds them just there—right up to God, since he can hold them no where else, yet filling them with lies fashioned after the similitude of God's truth." This rather stunning image of Satan's directing his servants to speak evil in a godly language shows the degree of confusion Wolcott suffered at having one of his best friends turn to practices that he could not understand. Far from being an independent actor, Evarts had been Satan's instrument. Yet Wolcott also recognized that Evarts's points about being accountable to God instead of to human authorities or organizations like the AMA *sounded* like orthodoxy, even if it was not. He lamented his friend's decision to leave the mission as well as Evarts's feeling that one who becomes a true disciple of Christ "will of necessity bring upon one the absolute hatred of the church and the world universal." Wolcott mourned the loss of his friend and their increasingly irreconcilable differences, but at the end of the summer in 1850, he and the other missionaries still knew only part of what was happening at Brainerd.[41] Thompson, Wolcott, Julius Beardslee, and eventually the teacher at Brainerd, Charles Venning, all returned to the fold of the AMA with a renewed dedication to the family order.

Thompson also cleared up any doubts that the AMA might have harbored about his involvement with Hyde and Evarts by praising the practice of family prayer. He wrote that while he had refrained from having family prayer for a time, he now understood it to be "a duty, naturally growing out of the family relations, and he who lives in his family without it, deprives himself of a heavenly privilege, and violates a law of social order."[42] Thompson's reaffirmation shows that the ministers were also aware of the connections between the gendered family and the larger social (and racial) order of the mission. Yet Thompson as well as Mary Dean had it reversed: the collapse of the family order at Brainerd came after, not before, Hyde's initial questioning of the civilizing mission. His critique of racial and religious hierarchies led to the partial end of gender hierarchies at Brainerd, not the other way around, even as Hyde's use of familial language applied to both.

The repentant ministers now faced the task of bringing the situation under control. The Evarts family still hosted the Hydes at Brainerd, and in the fall of 1850, the Brainerd church members voted them out and asked the AMA for a replacement. As custodians of the mission's property, the Brainerd trustees evicted the couples from the mission house as well. In response, Evarts and Hyde decided to leave the mission because the church members were "unwilling to receive the truth." Lacking any place to go, the couples stayed at Brainerd as long as they legally could, even after they were officially dismissed from the AMA in October 1850, for being "antinomian perfectionists." Loren Thompson wrote in December 1850 that Hyde and Evarts had responded in kind, and had "cast out" the rest of the mission, "ex-communicated [us] because we sanction the action of the society in casting them off and because we remain connected with it and preach not their gospel."[43]

The missionaries also criticized Henry Evarts for failing in his patriarchal responsibilities in his household. Not only had he allowed his wife to be enthralled by Hyde, but he also stood by as all kinds of disorderly and abusive behavior took place at Brainerd. Echoing earlier missionary condemnations of Native Baptist ministers, Thompson reported that John Hyde "beats Mrs. Hyde as he would a child." Further, in a biblical analogy to the patriarch Abraham's two wives, Mrs. Hyde had reportedly started to think of herself as "Hagar while Mrs. Evarts is the Sarah." Henry Evarts, on the other hand, had no place in this family, allowing Hyde to be "the 'sole monarch' of all that was Mr. Evarts," and even the children of Lucy and Henry had taken Hyde's last name. Thompson also was disturbed to find that Evarts had ceded his place at the head of the table to John Hyde. If the ritual of the seating order at the table represented the family order of sex and age, then Hyde had symbolically claimed the father's role. Hyde and Evarts had, in different ways, failed to uphold the Christian family and their fatherly roles at the head of their individual families. Hyde's critique of authority had inserted itself into the most intimate relationships, and in the context of his beliefs, Evarts had no authority over his wife Lucy. Notably, Hyde had a more difficult time applying his radical individualism to his wife's person as he apparently beat her.[44]

The new family and social order among the men and women at Brainerd became even more troubling when it was learned in March 1851 that John Hyde and Lucy Evarts had rejected their marriages in favor of living together as husband and wife. Mrs. Hyde and Henry Evarts had not yet followed suit, for, Wolcott wrote, "when I was there 'the spirit' had not yet given them liberty." Wolcott was baffled: "These persons seem to have got into such spiritual liberty and light that they are quite without reproof. They talk and act like mad people. Their perversion of common sense, reason, and the word of God is beyond description. The people have all left these teachers alone in their glory—quite horrified at such developments." Wolcott praised the black Jamaicans for shunning the civilized "teachers," illustrating just how much the situation in Jamaica had changed from less than a year earlier when the missionaries' letters were filled with the depravity of black Jamaicans. Now the problem they faced was not the wantonness of the black Jamaicans, but the uncontrollable and reprehensible behavior of their own white, American, and supposedly civilized colleagues.[45]

Another problem for the missionaries concerned the Hyde and Evarts children. There were five Evarts children, all under the age of ten, and several young Hydes at Brainerd who had little parental control. While the missionaries were used to complaining about black Jamaican families and the inattentiveness of Jamaican parents, they now had to figure out some way to deal with their own white children. The breakdown of the family structure and the proper fulfillment of motherly and fatherly duties by the two couples seemed worse than the sexual improprieties, and Brainerd had become a place entirely unsuitable for children. In May, when Albert Richardson and his family arrived to take over Brainerd, the AMA began the legal process of eviction for the Hydes and Evartses. Richardson visited Brainerd before the two couples departed, and he witnessed John Hyde having "illicit intercourse with Mrs. Evarts in broad daylight, *before the family and with his doors wide open.*" What once had been accusations leveled against the Native Baptists had now become the popular gossip about the American missionaries, and just as the missionaries had once feared the negative home influences on black children, they now faced the same problem with their white former colleagues. By June 1851, the foursome and their children moved to thatched huts about nineteen miles from Brainerd and, according to Heman Hall, "They are earning nothing, and are spending in a prodigal manner what little they have. . . . They seem to think that God will take care of them, and that it would be a dishonor to God for them not to live well." Hyde's earlier interest in collecting shells for display and jewelry ("conchology" as the others called it) that had occupied his time when he was supposed to be working for the mission had become the method by which the two couples supported themselves.[46]

The ideas behind Hyde's religious views resonated with the beliefs of Oneida perfectionism as well as the evolving metaphysics of Theodore Weld, a decidedly more traditional man, in spite of his marriage to a woman's rights activist, who argued with Lewis Tappan in the mid-1840s over the tenets of evangelicalism. In an 1844 speech by Weld called "Truth's Hindrances," he declared that "whatever the problems . . . men must confront that inner voice that spoke Truth, no matter how faint, and follow its dictates."[47] Yet clearly in Jamaica, these ideas operated in a different social and religious context. They fit with the protests of black Jamaicans resisting white ministerial authority, and in Jamaica, this radical interpretation of freedom became a tool for the dismantling of the civilizing mission. True freedom, they argued, meant that there should be no "civilized" and "savage," Christian and heathen, but all were equally endowed with God's light. They might have listened to the Jamaicans in their congregations who at this time were asking for greater control in the schools and churches and have taken these requests to heart, even though it seems that many Jamaicans pressing for greater control, like Thomas Livingston, were doing it out of a dislike of the unpredictability of the Americans. The errant missionaries might also have felt liberated from convention by leaving the strictly ordered northern church community for Jamaica.

With the arrival of Albert Richardson, and the reorganization of Brainerd, the missionaries turned their focus away from the Hydes and Evartses and began to plan out new mission stations to look to the future of the mission. In the summer of 1851, Mary Dean decided to return to the United States for a year, perhaps due in part to the bad blood that had developed between her and the other missionaries. Meanwhile, Heman Hall was eventually able to get some of the Evarts children away from their parents, and he, Wolcott, and Olds adopted three of the five children.[48] The new spiritual marriage of Hyde and Lucy Evarts temporarily dissolved in late 1851, and Richardson wrote in January 1852 that Hyde had rejected Lucy Evarts from his bed after she became pregnant with his child. Now able to joke about the situation since the Hydes and Evartses had removed themselves from the mission property, Richardson found this to be "a most impressive comment upon the spiritual nature of their intercourse!" He predicted that their situation would only end in ruin and switched tones to describe the ongoing licentiousness in his own church: "Three of the most promising women in our congregation have been seduced within a few months . . . The ch[urch] has taken a very decided stand, and we hope by lord's help, to stay the tide of Licentiousness and create a healthy public sentiment on this subject." The gospel of liberty preached at Brainerd no longer meant a relaxation of church discipline and social regulation, particularly of Jamaican sexuality. The critique of the civilizing mission launched by John Hyde had become irrelevant as he and his friends lived increasingly erratic lives.[49]

While rumors of the Hyde affair trickled back to the United States through personal letters of the missionaries as well as leaks from the AMA officers, the mission remarkably continued undamaged. Few of its financial supporters withdrew their money, a point perhaps related in part to the growing numbers of abolitionists in the United States after the 1850 passage of the Fugitive Slave Act and the 1852 publication of *Uncle Tom's Cabin*. The AMA assured its supporters that the mission remained in good standing among Jamaicans "white and colored" in spite of the American "fear that the unhappy errors of some formerly connected with it would weaken, if not destroy, its influence." More than simply existing, the mission was expanding, an *American Missionary* article excitedly reported. "Applications are being made for the opening of new stations, three of which the mission deems of such importance that they have requested the attention of the Executive Committee to them."[50]

When Mary Dean returned to Jamaica in 1852, many of her new students and their families had been under the instruction of John Hyde. Dean explained her opposition to Hyde as a perpetual battle of wills, and she had no intention of giving up the battle for souls. She and Hyde were "antagonists," she wrote, "and have been ever since we met. He for Satan. I for God." All of the deprivations she suffered at Chesterfield would be worth it, she asserted, and she prayed that she would live long enough "to be the means of converting one more soul than he destroys," hoping that the last soul "could be the Dr. himself."[51] Caught between the patriarchal ministers like Seth Wolcott on the one hand and the spiritual libertines like Hyde on the other, Mary Dean continued to uphold her staunch evangelical faith and her opposition to biblical hypocrisy whether it came from the direction of Hyde or Wolcott and the others whose losses of faith she had witnessed.

The situation between John Hyde and his legal wife sheds light on the nature of their relationship and the awkward position his wife took on when her husband had left her for his "spiritual wife," Lucy Evarts. In May 1852 Hyde's wife left her husband while pregnant with his child to return to New York with their children. John Hyde showed up in Kingston a day after she had sailed, quite upset at his wife's defiance of his will; ironically her desire for freedom was not viewed as legitimate by her husband.[52] She eventually sought a divorce from Hyde, a rare event in the 1850s, but she remained in epistolary contact with him and gave birth to his child in

December 1852. During the winter of 1853, she began corresponding with Urania Hunt, who had been living with her parents in Elmira, New York. Hunt initiated the correspondence, writing to Mrs. Hyde that John had asked her to retrieve his youngest son and take him back to Jamaica.[53] Mrs. Hyde had absolutely no intentions of sending one of her children to Jamaica, especially not in the care of Urania Hunt. But her ex-husband's attempt to claim the child left her with a growing ambivalence about having divorced her husband. John wrote letters to her in which he equated her decision to divorce him with her failure to remain a devout Christian. She confessed to George Whipple that her husband had interpreted her "unwillingness to return to him as an unwillingness to suffer persecution for righteousness sake." According to John Hyde, by staying in New York she was "yielding to the temptations offered by relatives and the world." Hyde's words to his ex-wife placed her in a state of spiritual confusion, and she wrote to Whipple that she had "been so long harassed and driven about by every wind of doctrine" that she had decided to close her heart to religion for the time being. She continued to receive letters from Hyde, and she hoped to answer them "in the way that will secure the best good to him," although she did not plan on ever rejoining him in Jamaica.[54] When Mrs. Hyde paid Urania Hunt a visit at her New York home, she found a woman with quite different intentions. Writing about Hunt, Mrs. Hyde noted that Urania was "deranged, though not insane." She also observed that Hunt's family had little tolerance for her "peculiarities" and that the young woman wanted to return to Jamaica and John Hyde with whom she would be "appreciated."[55]

In 1853, Urania Hunt got her wish and did indeed return to Jamaica in order to live with John Hyde and Lucy and Henry Evarts, but the foursome did not last long. Soon after Hunt's return, in September 1853, Henry Evarts was killed when a cow attacked him, although the details of his death were quite suspicious, and it was implied that he might have been murdered. Urania Hunt died less than a year later, in February 1854, after falling ill at Hyde's house, and it was widely believed that he had poisoned her either on purpose or by mistake when he tried to treat her for the illness. Hyde and Lucy Evarts quickly disposed of her corpse before there could be an autopsy, and Hyde was put in jail for six months for burying her without an inquest.[56] Hyde and Lucy Evarts, however, remained together in spite of their brief separation, and they had at least two children together. It was reported that the eldest died in 1856, and soon after, her brother Heman reported that she "gave" her second eldest son by Henry Evarts, George, to Seth Wolcott. The other four Evarts children were distributed among family members in the United States, and their youngest child, a boy named Samuel who was born in August 1849, was adopted by Abner Olds and his wife. Lucy Evarts and John Hyde eventually returned to the United States at the end of the 1850s. No new news of the couple appeared in the archives after 1858, but their saga would be retold as many of the people who visited or worked for the Jamaica Mission had known Henry and Lucy Evarts as students at Oberlin. In the retellings, the ministers tended to leave out their once-favorable attitudes toward John Hyde.[57]

The unexpected result of the sex scandal, however, was that black Jamaican church members, if not single white women, gained a greater foothold in the mission's governing structure. The black deacons at Brainerd remained more powerful than their counterparts in other mission churches, and black schoolteachers grew more common after the precedent of John Campbell's employment at Eliot Station. The ministers' shifting views perhaps proved to Jamaicans the inherent transient nature of the white Americans and prompted them to take greater charge over the AMA institutions. The experiences of Mary Dean and Urania Hunt showed that the mission's men were susceptible to arguments on behalf of religious freedom even as they resisted the requests of white women for greater autonomy and independence within the mission family. In the end, of course, the collapse of the marriages and gender order at Brainerd finally made the mission's men see Hyde's views as counterproductive to the goals of their civilizing mission.

5 Cultivating Land, Cultivating Families

During the upheavals of 1850, the Jamaica Mission's participants experienced firsthand and in dramatic form the social disorder they feared might happen if freedom went unchecked. The profligate John Hyde and his followers had taught a sobering lesson about the need for vigilance when it came to family bonds and sexuality, and in the wake of the Hyde fiasco, the missionaries reinvigorated their efforts to uphold the Christian family as it applied to themselves and to black Jamaicans. As we have seen, anxiety about black families and sexuality existed before the sex scandal, and the American missionaries had frequently used gender practices as a way to evaluate potential converts and to attack Native Baptist ministers. This was not unique to the Jamaica Mission, as Anglo-American missionaries throughout the world identified the domestic sphere as a way to judge a people's "civilization" and as a targeted area for moral reform and racial uplift.[1] For their part, the missionaries in Jamaica invoked an abolitionist tactic to solve the problem of the persistence of slave culture that they believed to be the cause of Jamaican licentiousness: black landownership. Landownership would be a financial boon for black men, and it would make it more likely for them to marry, therefore decreasing the number of unwed mothers and the incidence of cohabitation. Laboring on their own land, black men would develop feelings of manly independence, the missionaries believed, and they would provide for their wives and children. Children could go to school, and women could tend to their homes and families and engage in moral reform activities to help cultivate public morality.[2] The transformation of black Jamaican families would begin with landownership. Indeed, as Amos Phelps, the mission's American sponsor, proclaimed during a visit to Jamaica in 1847, landownership would be a civilizing force, and it would create "a feeling of independence, and make them act like men."[3]

In the late 1840s, the American missionaries and the American supporters of the mission schemed to raise money in order to help black Jamaican church members purchase their own land. The circumstances of turmoil over the instability and uncertainty of wage labor and the fact that bankrupt estates opened up new opportunities for black landownership joined with the ministers' beliefs in the linkage between landownership, gender, and Christian liberty. As Amos Phelps suggested, landownership would inspire manliness, and the missionaries hoped that Christian homes would follow. While many ex-slaves agreed with the Americans on the need for landownership, they connected land with family life in an entirely different way. As slaves, black Jamaicans had claimed ownership over the cottages and provision grounds they had built and developed, and in passing down what they considered their property, they solidified kinship lines in a society that denied them rights to self-ownership, marriage, and property.[4] After 1838, family land continued to represent the wholeness of the family, but freed people did not treat ownership rights in the same way as Europeans and Americans, nor did their family arrangements always line up with the expectations of Anglo-American missionaries. Relations between mothers and children, or brothers and sisters, could be stronger than the bonds of marriage, and it remained common and acceptable for women to have children outside marriage, and for men to live apart from their children.[5]

When efforts to support black landownership failed to produce the results that the American missionaries expected, they shifted their focus away from arguments in favor of black men's independence and instead looked for other ways to influence Jamaican home life. The heralded solution came in the form of a manual-labor school that would board its students, therefore isolating young people from the island's pernicious culture while also inculcating the habits and practices of a Christian family. Although the idea of some kind of boarding school had been a subject of discussion for some years, in 1854, Seth Wolcott bought a thrown-up sugar estate, Richmond, and set about making grandiose plans. The bulk of the estate would be divided up into small plots of land to sell and rent to respectable black families, while the estate's buildings would be converted into dormitories and classrooms for a manual-labor school. With the students all becoming members of the Wolcott family, the school would serve as a model of industry and morality for all of the estate's tenants to observe and follow. In Richmond, the American mission turned away from the more American-inspired plan to support black independence from any kind of dependency and instead created a version of the Baptist free village where black Jamaicans had to live according to the missionaries' terms and rules.[6]

The clash between the American and British views of what black people needed after slavery came to the forefront during Amos Phelps's visit to Jamaica in 1847. The one-time coordinator of the West India Mission Committee in Boston, Phelps had traveled to Jamaica for his health, but he also reported to Lewis Tappan about the state of the missionaries who now belonged to the American Missionary Association. Phelps bristled at what he perceived to be the prevailing sentiment among British missionaries: their belief that the "emancipated are really inferior in nature, etc., and that a guardianship should be exercised over them."[7] Landownership, he contended, was essential to the formation of manly men, and in his letters to Lewis Tappan, many of which were reprinted in the *American Missionary* and in the D.C.-based *National Era*, Phelps waxed poetic on the subject. The British had gone about emancipation in the wrong way, and an American example was needed to prove that ex-slaves could thrive in a free society. Phelps went so far as to claim that this political objective rivaled the mission's religious purposes, arguing that besides the obvious goal of "the salvation of the people, the great object and value of an American mission here, is to work out the experiment of freedom on New England and American principles, in distinction from West Indian and British."[8]

Phelps believed that the American missionaries offered a different kind of freedom. The British had, for example, financially compensated slaveholders but had done little to support freedmen in terms of money or infrastructure. Lewis Tappan and Amos Phelps agreed that paying off the old masters represented the imperial government's tacit approval of slavery and refusal to reeducate the master class. Phelps found that the island's planters had shown little remorse for owning slaves, and he described white Jamaicans as "slave-scolding, brow-beating, domineering, as far as possible, as in olden times," and complained that whites demonstrated the "master spirit" fused with "the spirit of British aristocracy." Indeed, he believed that the British had never intended "the emancipated [to be] anything more than a low English peasantry."[9] English prejudices of race and class and the planters' financial interests to keep the freed people attached to their estates as dependent, low-wage workers countered the ideals of emancipation. A similar complaint was made at the First of August celebration at Oberlin a few years earlier in 1845. "The real difficulty," one speaker told the audience, "is that the spirit of slavery still lives, and is as rife as ever in man's obdurate heart . . . We shall see yet that our cause must embrace the entire abolition of all servile relations and conditions, and the thorough admission of equal rights and privileges for all the sons and daughters of the wide family of man . . . We must come to treat them as brethren, and sustain their rights as we do our own, and in fact, hold them as a cherished portion of universal humanity."[10]

In contrasting his plan for how Americans should approach emancipation with how the British had handled the West Indies, Amos Phelps thought primarily about the mission's relation to American abolitionism, rather than the goals of a civilizing mission. In his attempt to counteract the negative reports of Jamaican emancipation appearing in the press at home, Phelps asserted that all of those reports of Jamaica's problems could be ascribed to the character of Englishmen, and the way the British had overseen emancipation, rather than to emancipation itself. Yet Phelps's support for greater black independence and the call for equal rights that earned praise in the pages of the *Oberlin Evangelist* increasingly seemed like flights of fantasy to some of the American missionaries in Jamaica. In the same way that sexual licentiousness had made the Americans tighten the rules of church discipline in their churches, it also gradually shifted the justifications that the missionaries made for black landownership. Land was less an issue of black independence because black men, like all men, deserved equal rights, and more a way to tame and control what the missionaries considered to be unrestrained sexuality. If Christian liberty rather than out-of-control license was to prosper in Jamaica, black men must own land and build strong families who would create a culture of public morality emanating from the private sphere.

During the mission's early years, many of the black Jamaicans who joined the American churches still lived on estate land rather than owning their own property. The American ministers complained about the wage-rent system in which planters had begun to charge very high rents for land that freed people claimed as their own. Writing in 1839, Theodore Weld's friend Charles Stuart commented on the strong attachment that freed people had to the cottages and provision grounds they had built up during slavery. He wrote that many freed people believed that the Queen "had given their cottages, grounds, and fruit trees to them . . . for their cottages had almost all been built by themselves with little or no expence [sic] to their masters. The fruit trees had been planted and nurtured by their labour only, and even under slavery had been partially admitted to belong to them; and their grounds were mostly mountain lands, used for no other purpose by their masters."[11] By charging more rent than an individual earned in wages, black women and children were forced back into wage-labor jobs, and faced with planters' reassertion of control over their families' labor, many black people left their familial homes to find land somewhere else.

Like many British missionaries, the Americans also strongly disapproved of the planters' policies that kept freed people in poverty and dependency. In the mission's first years, David Ingraham wrote about the scant wages that laborers received, and the high rent they were forced to pay, a situation that resulted in frequent labor strikes. The missionaries would have agreed with the Anglican missionary Benjamin Luckock, who published a history of Jamaica in the 1840s. Although freed people had been willing to work for wages, the principles of free labor simply did not exist in a society when "the master so held everything in his own hands, as to regulate, at his own will, the rate both of rent and wages." Luckock, like Amos Phelps and the American missionaries, saw the flight from the estates in the early 1840s as a move toward Christian civilization rather than a reversion to barbarism. On "freeholds of their own," the ex-slaves could live out "the Scriptural picture of sitting down under their own vine and fig-tree, none daring to make them afraid."[12] The American missionaries praised landownership and small freeholders as the best possible framework for Jamaican society. Practically, it would give them a stable population and a welcome relief from the problem of collapsing estates and migrating church members.

The American ministers also endowed landownership with the power to transform dependent slaves into independent men, a goal that was at the heart of their civilizing mission. Just as they had attributed their religious difficulties to the "superstitions" emanating from the Native Baptists, a problem that could in many ways be linked back to the overly open policies of British missionary churches, they laid blame for the persistence of slavelike dependency at the feet of wage labor. They castigated wage labor, at least as it existed in Jamaica, as an imperfect form of freedom and a barrier to the goals of the Jamaica Mission. One missionary proposed that for Jamaica to thrive as a free society, it "is a necessity that the people should be the responsible cultivators of the staple exports of the Island, and intelligent persons must become the manufactures and exporters of the same." Wage labor, on the other hand, failed to instill any sense of ownership, and it led "to indolence, unfaithfulness, and wasteful habits," and consequently "must be abandoned." When freed people labored for others rather than for themselves, they continued "pernicious habits, so prejudicial to morals as well as to the temporal prosperity of all classes of the inhabitants of Jamaica." Indeed, the only solution to the economic and moral crisis that the missionaries found on the island would be "for every laborer in the fields to become a laborer *for himself*, that he may reap the benefits of his industry, or bear the evils of his indolence and wastefulness." Through landownership and self-sufficient labor, black Jamaican men could finally purge the "debasing influences of slavery" that "prevent manly and noble actions."[13]

The missionaries' loathing of dependency reflected their own sensibilities as much as it did their goals for the civilizing mission. In the early 1840s, the Oberlin ministers had hoped to form a self-supporting mission, but this had not come to pass. Later, Seth Wolcott expressed a sense of failure about his need to constantly request loans from the AMA, and he wrote to George Whipple that he would prefer to "earn my bread by the sweat of my face! But I don't know that I could sweat much more than I do already if I should try." For the ministers like Wolcott who had been educated at Oberlin where manual labor had become a character-building component of the curriculum, the inability to make ends meet in Jamaica proved a constant disappointment. While they could raise much of their own food on the land attached to the mission stations, the ministers still did not get enough money from their church members to strike out on their own, independent from the AMA's support. Some Jamaicans questioned why they needed to support the ministers since they assumed "rich people are giving us money to be used for their benefit." Others simply could not afford to spare money: "the wants of this people are very great and increasing," Wolcott acknowledged, and perhaps alluding to the declining British missions in Jamaica, he asked, "Others are forsaking them and who will take them up?"[14] In their efforts to secure land for black Jamaicans, the ministers also expected to produce more generous donors to their chapels and schools.

Loren Thompson proved one of the most proactive Americans when it came to landownership, and his mission station's location gave him an opportunity to act. His interest in land illustrated his own views of its importance to the mission as well as his willingness to respond to the demands of church members. The Eliot church members had informed Thompson of their ongoing problems with the area's planters, and he agreed that the estate owners were being unfair. Thompson informed the AMA that the estates around Eliot Station were "combinations," and the owners had agreed among themselves to pay lower wages, effectively forcing laborers "either to go without money or work for what the Estates may chose [sic] to give them." Indeed, Thompson's chapel was located on the Charlottenburgh Estate, and the annual crop accounts show that Charlottenburgh and its neighboring properties had long-standing business relationships. Attorney Henry Westmorland supervised Charlottenburgh as well as Llanrumney Estate, the animal pens, Montrose and Flint River, and Richmond Estate, and he had the power to set the wage rates for workers on all of these plantations. A worker seeking greater wages would have had to travel some distance to reach another employer's land. In this neighborhood, proprietors had lowered wages while charging freed people the same amount for rent on their provision grounds and houses—£1 per acre.[15]

On a separate sheet that lengthened his letter, Thompson offered a longer treatise on the need for black landownership: "I wish now to say a few things as to the importance of the people's being freeholders. Hitherto, they have got on pretty well all things considered, in leasing land, but such is the present condition of affairs in Jamaica that the sooner the people can procure little homes for themselves the better." Thompson declared that his church members "do not wish to lease, another month even, their land. They wish to purchase it." The annual crop account for Charlottenburgh contained a note about the sale of ten acres of land in 1848, indicating that Thompson indeed raised enough money to accomplish his goal.[16] While Thompson listened to his church members and represented their wishes to the AMA, he also noted the added benefits that would result when they purchased land. His church members wanted land, but they *needed* "little homes" if they were to begin to become civilized Christians. In the next year, Thompson attributed a new spirit of morality at Eliot to black landownership, happily reporting that the new landowners showed signs of developing the "public sentiment against *public* crimes—such as lying, dishonesty, fornication, and drunkenness."[17]

Like Amos Phelps, Loren Thompson subscribed to the notion that black independence from white landowners best contributed to the goals of the civilizing mission. While the missionaries remained committed to black landownership, they were disappointed when even black freeholders continued to engage in "licentious" behavior, or perhaps more accurately, did not adequately condemn instances of immorality in their community. Most often, the ministers complained that black Jamaicans did not take marriage seriously, and it became clear that fostering manly independence through landownership had not been enough to spark the development of the ideology of domesticity among black Jamaicans.

As Nancy Cott, Sarah Gordon, and Amy Dru Stanley have shown, nineteenth-century Americans invested a great deal of importance in the sanctity of the marriage contract and in the critical role of marriage in upholding Christian liberty in a free society.[18] Although like any ideology, separate spheres had both critics and supporters—and, further, did not always reflect reality—it lay close to the heart of northern reform and missionary work. Northern reformers believed that marriage tamed men's sexual appetites, and wives' influences and affections pushed men to act in a more moral way. The American Board required all ministers destined for foreign mission fields to marry, not only because the missionary wife would keep her husband from "going native," but also because the missionary marriage modeled civilized gender roles to heathens, and it provided an extra laborer, the missionary wife.[19] Separate spheres fit less comfortably with abolitionism. Even as antislavery activists used separate spheres ideology to attack southern slaveholders, women's rights proponents within the abolitionist movement drew on the same rhetoric to poke holes in the legal statutes governing marriage.[20] Indeed, the AMA missionaries did not always agree on what was meant by a proper marriage, a point proved rather dramatically when John Hyde took a "spiritual wife." As the next chapter discusses in more detail, a less scandalous but more long-lasting transformation of separate spheres ideology was under way in the U.S. North during the 1840s and 1850s, and this transformation would begin to make inroads in the Jamaica Mission.

While the missionaries may have had increasingly different ideas about marriage and family life in the latter years of the mission, they could all agree that unwed mothers and premarital sex were incompatible with Christian liberty. Premarital sex robbed women of the sexual purity so essential for true womanhood, and there seemed to be no sense of public outrage with young people who had sex before marriage. American missionary Stewart Renshaw found marriages in Jamaica to be lacking romantic love. He observed few couples who had united because of a love match, and instead he observed that most marriages took place because of economic necessity and the customary sexual division of labor: "a woman wants some one to 'dig her yams,' the man, some one to 'boil his pot,' and wash his clothes."[21] To Renshaw, these economic considerations did not lead to the bonds of tenderness and affection that would make them loyal to one another and that would set them up to be good parents. Renshaw did not comment on the fact that companionate marriage had only recently become the fashion in the United States. In Jamaica, the missionaries attributed widespread adultery to these so-called marriages of convenience. At Union Station, Seth Wolcott wrote, "The sentiment prevails extensively, that a married man may have as many sweethearts as he pleases."[22] Heman Hall had excommunicated two church members for adultery in 1852, and the *American Missionary* editorialized that Hall's trials derived from the "terribly corrupt state of public morals" on the island, as well as the "legacy of woe and crime that slavery has left to its victims."[23]

As they realized that landownership had not done the trick, the ministers continued to use church discipline as a means to punish young people who had sex and children before marriage, even though "the sin is so common, that a young woman who enters the marriage state without having first become a mother, is regarded as possessing *uncommon virtue*."[24] Not all Jamaicans felt this way, however, and Heman Hall noted that "one of our most prominent members turned away his oldest daughter" for becoming pregnant before marrying. This was not without pain on the part of the father: "He is a good man and feels it deeply. The pains he has taken to instruct his family would be a worthy example in any community."[25] The diversity found in Hall's church speaks to what other historians have argued about gender roles in post-emancipation Jamaica. While some freed people continued to live according to the definition of respectability that had existed during slavery, others had embraced the Americans' moral codes. In this particular letter, the missionary's praise for the Jamaican father left no space for the young woman's version of events, perhaps pointing to the fact that when black Jamaicans adopted the family model of Anglo-American missionaries, it was black women who had the most to lose.[26]

Another problem the American ministers encountered in their mission churches was the widespread connection between marriage and church membership as linked rituals, a belief that probably stemmed from the fact that all of the island's Christian missionaries, including the African American Baptists, emphasized the importance of marriage. After relocating to his new mission station on the Golden Vale Estate, Abner Olds found many of his inquirers thought that marriage was the prerequisite for church membership, and he had a hard time "making the people understand that religion does not consist in the performance of a few ceremonies." Olds recognized that this was in part the fault of missionaries: "The duty of marriage has been much urged by some, until many think that living in the married state is about the sum of all that God requires." As an example of what this meant for his work, Olds summed up a recent conversation with an inquirer. When Olds asked whether or not he was married, the potential church member answered: "'O, yes!' . . . 'I am all ready to draw to table! (to come to the communion)." Olds added that black Jamaicans viewed marriage as "constituting an evidence that they are in favor with God."[27]

Missionary Charles Venning dealt with the related question of whether to allow unmarried Jamaicans to be received into the church. In one reflective letter, he mused that it might be better if his church followed the island's customs, and only allowed young people into the church after they passed through a phase of "sowing their wild oats." He wrote derisively of the generation that had been born into freedom, arguing that they had been "stimulated by extreme notions of freedom, and restrained but little from vice especially the vice of licentiousness."[28] Less than a year after Venning expressed his misgivings about young Jamaicans, he excommunicated several in his church for premarital sex. These young people had threatened "all our hopes concerning this people" by hurting his church's reputation in the neighborhood. An embarrassed Venning wrote that one Native Baptist minister had offered his condolences for the recent turmoil and "professed to be shocked at the conduct of our folks."[29] In good missionary form, Venning located the root of the problem in the customs of the Native Baptist churches, which taught young inquirers to avoid starting "a religious life *until they were married*," a stance that permitted young people to "live in sin for as long a time as may be," and then after getting married they could join the church with all of their sins forgiven. The problem for Venning was that he could not admit unmarried people into the church for fear of their behavior, and yet in doing so, he was going along with the Native Baptist practices that he found so problematic. He worried about what this meant for his church and, more generally, for the young people of Jamaica and the future of the mission that had invested its work in reaching out to the younger generation. "Satan," he wrote, "has been for these years hastening them on fast in the broad way to destruction."[30]

The solution to the ongoing licentiousness that the missionaries struggled to defeat in their mission churches and in Jamaican society came in the form of a defunct sugar estate in St Mary. With funding from the AMA and American investors, Seth Wolcott purchased Richmond Estate in 1854, and he announced that the Richmond project would be the mission's saving grace. The AMA required "more than a recited catechism to save Jamaica," and they had to "produce the fruits, as well as teach the doctrines of righteousness."[31] The plan was to divide a majority of the 1,090-acre estate into small plots of land to be sold to Jamaican freeholders. The remaining 100 acres and all of the buildings would house a manual-labor boarding school aimed at isolating black children from their unwholesome surroundings. At Richmond, the families living on the estate and the students boarding with the Wolcott family would not only have land and homes but they would also be under the constant supervision of Seth Wolcott and his missionary associates. Richmond answered the complaints of the missionaries who believed that Jamaican homes failed to inculcate children with moral bearings. As one schoolteacher wrote, "I have always noticed that after a vacation the children are much harder to govern . . . They are not much benefited by the influence of home."[32] Richmond provided a way for the missionaries to build an American space in Jamaica, one immune to the culture of slavery that they had not been able to keep out of the mission's churches. Richmond would, of course, not be immune to the encounters and unexpected turns that had taken place in all of the mission stations.

To raise money for the estate, the missionaries launched a publicity campaign in Jamaica and in the United States, but they initially lacked support from the AMA. Lewis Tappan expressed grave concern about the endeavor, in large part because the missionaries' requests to buy Richmond came just as several of the ministers had fallen into debt because of failed speculation on a copper mine on the island.[33] With the urging of Abner Olds and Albert Richardson, Tappan agreed to give five hundred dollars to Wolcott for the purchase of the estate, a small portion of the twenty-five hundred dollars Wolcott owed for the estate, and a great deal less than the ten thousand dollars he had requested for establishing a trust for the project.[34] Already returned to the United States, Olds and Richardson recruited investors interested in aiding Jamaican freed people, and the two men along with Seth Wolcott wrote glowing reports of the estate's potential.[35] Richmond's terrain was mountainous, and two hundred acres of the estate had been and could be used for growing sugar cane, with the rest of the land being mostly pasture for the plow animals and provision grounds that had been used by the slaves for growing their own food. Seth Wolcott noted that the estate had "extensive and flourishing cocoanut groves" and a water-powered sugar mill that was "first rate." The estate's steep terrain required that most of the land be hand-plowed, as animals could not safely navigate the inclines, but Abner Olds testified that the soil was ideal for growing coffee, arrowroot, yams, and plantains, crops that the missionaries envisioned exporting for sale to friends of antislavery in the United States in addition to selling at the island's markets.[36] There were also a number of buildings on the property: two houses, one large and one small, that had been occupied by the estate's attorney and overseer, a grand house in a state of severe disrepair, as well as the sugar works and a distillery.[37] It brought the teetotaling missionaries great satisfaction that the "Old Still" would be transformed into the school's rooms and a dormitory. Loren Thompson agreed, writing favorably about how the "Richmond enterprise" was "converting [the] Richmond *Rum* and *Sugar* Establishment into *halls* of *industry* and *learning*."[38]

The Richmond Estate never became worth the fifty thousand dollars at which it had once been valued, and it was more of a utopian fantasy than an "eloquent model for future American action," according to Lewis Tappan's biographer, Bertram Wyatt-Brown.[39] Indeed, when evaluated as a moneymaking enterprise or for how quickly Jamaicans bought the freeholds, Richmond did not live up to the expectations of the AMA and Seth Wolcott. In 1858, Wolcott wrote that most of the "more enterprising" black Jamaicans had "purchased lands long ago," a point that the English abolitionist Joseph Sturge had made to Lewis Tappan. The freed people who still rented land "have too little the spirit of farmers to own anything of importance." Wolcott also noted "that not a little pains has been taken to persuade the poor people, naturally suspicious enough, that they better look out for some 'yankee trick.'"[40] In August 1859, five years after Wolcott acquired Richmond, only sixteen individuals had bought land on the estate, although the estate had many renters.[41]

While the landownership component of Richmond disappointed the AMA, Richmond's school became the central focus of the Jamaica Mission in the 1850s and 1860s. During his visit to Jamaica in 1847, Amos Phelps had proposed that the missionaries' primary goal should be to support black landownership as the best means to change Jamaican gender roles: "the first thing is to have the people become the proprietors of the soil—to buy up the land wherever they can, in little properties of their own, and put up their little houses and get their other little comforts around them. Nothing will give them a feeling of independence and make them act like men sooner than this."[42] At Richmond Estate, the plan to sell land had failed, and the missionaries had put the bulk of their efforts toward the Richmond Industrial and Normal School instead. Believing that Jamaican homes preserved rather than combated licentiousness, more drastic measures were needed, and this involved inserting missionary influence directly into the home life of black Jamaicans. This was not a new idea for the mission's women, and especially for the single women schoolteachers. Mary Dean visited her students' parents in their homes. She traveled along mountain paths with her "map of the world" that she would unfurl to "show them the difference between educated and uneducated nations and tell them the sure consequences of letting their children grow up in ignorance."[43] As a boarding school, Richmond seemed a much better solution to Dean, who wrote that it would be a "fenced city."[44]

Before purchasing the Richmond Estate, the missionaries had already been thinking about how they would construct a manual-labor school on the island. Ruth E. Carpenter, a visiting "voluntary missionary" from Oberlin, was interested in investing her husband's money in an educational endeavor. From Jamaica, she wrote to George Whipple that she found the children on the island to be "bright and teachable if taken early" and "kept away from evil influences." The mission's existing common schools were not entirely useless, but she thought it "almost impossible to educate a child surrounded by heathen influence more than one half of the day so as to make him an upright earnest worker for others." Carpenter, like the missionaries, felt that the only way to change a society was to affect the means of socialization of its children. In enrolling Jamaicans in a boarding school, they would not only be isolated from bad influences but they would also "be taken care of . . . and considered as a family." Seth Wolcott agreed wholeheartedly with Carpenter's idea, writing, "Mrs. Carpenter's plan for schools [is] quite like the one I have long cherished—a family school. I could get any desirable number of children from ten to sixteen years old given me as my own children." Wolcott and Carpenter perceived no difficulty in finding students for their school, assuming, of course, that Jamaican parents were willing to give over their children.[45]

If a manual-labor school succeeded, the profits could be reinvested in other institutions, and it would answer a need. Wolcott wrote in early 1854 that there were "calls in every direction to establish schools and many of them are urgent. I met a man this morning from a thickly settled neighborhood some 5 miles from here, where they have had an apology for a school which is now given up. The people want a school." Without it, he worried, "a hundred children are here left to run worse than wild."[46] More schools in Jamaica would also help the cause of abolitionism in the United States. Recognizing that many in the North had been disappointed by the progress of emancipation in the West Indies, Carpenter avowed that with manual labor schools in place, "Jamaica would not as now disappoint those who were looking to see the Africans rise." The missionaries planned to remake Jamaican society one child at a time.[47] The AMA's treasurer Lewis

Tappan agreed, even after his earlier approbation about the Richmond project. Tappan wrote to Wolcott, "What sanguine hopes we had 17 years ago," when Jamaican emancipation had occurred. These hopes had since "been battered in various ways." In Richmond, he saw a new beginning, one which would prove that "the emancipated" could be improved in their "social, moral, religious, and industrial capacities," and this would be "a very effective blow at American slavery."[48]

After returning to the United States, Mrs. Carpenter and her husband failed to hold up their end of the bargain, leaving Seth Wolcott in debt.[49] To help mitigate his financial woes, Wolcott and Tappan together sold stock certificates to interested investors in the United States for joint ownership of one hundred acres of land at Richmond.[50] The board of trustees overseeing the land included George Henderson, a Kingston attorney, and Thomas Oughton, also an attorney and the son of the Baptist missionary Samuel Oughton.[51] This alliance bears further discussion. At the time of Richmond's purchase, Thomas Oughton had been in the United States and was preparing to return to Kingston, along with his new wife, a young woman named Maria Hicks who had been a schoolteacher in the Jamaica Mission. Bound to the Americans through ties of marriage, the Oughtons would remain closely linked to the Jamaica Mission for decades. For Jamaican history, however, it is Thomas's father, Samuel, who is the more famous figure. In 1854, at the same time as Wolcott investigated and purchased Richmond, Samuel Oughton confronted an angry congregation at his East Queen Street church in Kingston. The Baptist Missionary Society had given the church's trustees ownership of the church property, and after most of those church leaders had died, the congregation wanted to make sure the property remained in their hands since they felt that their money had paid for the church. Oughton disagreed with the new arrangements, and a number of black leaders tried to occupy the property. After the initial skirmish, Oughton addressed his congregation with the utmost paternalist sentiments: "I pity you, you poor ignorant people," he was reported to say.[52] The dissent grew over the next several months, ultimately resulting in riots during which Oughton's antagonists attacked his house. The police intervened, arresting fifty-three people and securing Oughton's authority over the church property.[53]

The elder Oughton also composed a lecture on the benefits of the civilizing influence of consumption and capitalism, and his belief that black

Jamaicans would advance when, as historian Catherine Hall puts it, they had "artificial wants, the material possessions around which a proper domestic life could be organised."⁵⁴ Richmond's proprietor and headmaster Seth Wolcott partially agreed, and he made the case that Richmond would be a school interested in uplift. But Wolcott maintained his Oberlin sensibilities as well, and he had no interest in forming a middle class more interested in consumption than in hard work. Located in the rural mountains rather than in the more urbane Kingston, Richmond would not make "great scholars, but good men, good citizens," Wolcott declared, and he would stand by this for the remainder of his life. Wolcott proposed that the school should not be "designed for *g-e-n-t-l-e-men* and *l-a-d-i-e-s* but for the people, to educate *men* and *women* and good citizens." The "pattern" for the school was to be the "New England family with all its domestic and other influences," as Oberlin had been to the missionaries, rather than an elite institution for the island's more privileged pupils.⁵⁵

During its first full year, the school enrolled twenty-three students, and Mary Dean served as the school's teacher. In 1856, Wolcott (the "principal" of Richmond) and Mary Dean (the "assistant") circulated an advertisement about Richmond for those interested in supporting it around the island. The notice informed its readers that Richmond had been "designed to furnish to children and youth of all classes, the means of a thorough, practical, English education, adapted to the wants of common life. It aims to educate the masses—to secure to them the highest practicable intelligence." As at the Oneida Institute and at the original plans for Oberlin, the manual-labor component of the school was meant to "enable the poor to obtain knowledge," and also "to promote physical as well as mental industry." Unlike the American manual-labor institutes, however, Wolcott also emphasized that the school would be a family. Richmond had "a family at its head of which a large portion of the pupils will be members." This enabled the school to meet "a most urgent want, a desirable home and healthful family influences." As cholera epidemics in 1851 and 1854 had left many children orphaned, the circular also noted that the school was especially open to orphaned children who would "be considered and treated much as adopted or indentured children." Wolcott apparently saw little difference in the terms "adopted" and "indentured," implying that the children attending the Richmond School would be expected to pay their way through their labor within the family and on the institution's farm.⁵⁶

Given its mission to the island's poor, funding the school remained a constant preoccupation. Richmond, along with the mission's other schools, accepted small grants from the Jamaican government beginning in 1856. Since emancipation, the colonial government and officials in England had discussed the importance of funding education for the masses, but little money was devoted to this cause. By the mid-1840s, the Assembly created a board of education and £1000 was allocated to aiding schools operated by religious parties. A report in 1847 took issue with the "excessively religious orientation" of many schools, and it also required that schools receiving funding from the state provide some kind of manual-labor component to their curricula. As a point of comparison, the Baptist missions refused the government money at this point, arguing that the manual-labor requirement was an attempt to reinstate forced labor on the island.[57] The Americans, having a strongly positive personal attachment to the benefits of manual labor, eagerly accepted funding for their schools. In November 1856, Wolcott explained that he had recruited some potential supporters in Jamaica, and "now we are besieging hard the legislature." The American missionaries were, in two weeks, to present a "petition before the House of Assembly to adopt a general plan of education and *especially* for a *special* grant to Richmond."[58] The new men he had invited to join Richmond Estate's board of trustees included Richard Hill, a colored assemblyman who himself believed that "family habits" were needed to go along with religion.[59]

By August 1857, the enrollment had increased to 36 students, and "32 of the above are members of my family," Wolcott wrote.[60] Wolcott reiterated the school's purpose and its difference from more expensive and exclusive schools on the island, and he also demonstrated how closely he was aligned with the views of the government, perhaps even shaping those views. He wrote, "Our course is thoroughly unflinchingly industrial, designed to meet the wants of the mass—to develop a self-dependent and hence independent manhood."[61] While the student body was almost half young women, Wolcott centered his attention on his task of teaching young men to behave as "proper" men. Indeed, his wife and an unmarried schoolteacher, Sarah Upson, tended to the "domestic duties" of the large family, while also instructing "the least advanced." Wolcott acknowledged that at Richmond, the children were subjected to discipline that was "much severer in many respects, though more rational than" what they were used to. At any rate, he wrote, "They are not sufficiently annoyed by it to make them willing to leave us." In fact, he observed, "Most of our older pupils seem inclined to prolong their stay much beyond our anticipations."[62] At Richmond, Wolcott created the family order he found lacking in Jamaican homes. Where church discipline and independent freeholders had failed to transform Jamaican gender ideology, the confines of the family at Richmond had somewhat better results. Not until the aftermath of the Morant Bay Rebellion in October 1865 would the school be shaken when Wolcott was forced to expel a number of students. Whether the students were influenced by Wolcott's discipline, the family order, or, perhaps most likely, knowing that there were few educational opportunities available to them, only a few students were ejected from Richmond during the school's history. Many of the students, both men and women, went on to serve as deacons and teachers at the other mission stations.

The AMA's goal to reform Jamaican family life through black landownership unfolded in a way that Amos Phelps could not have foreseen during his visit to the island in 1847. At that earlier stage in the mission's history, landownership and the religious work of the mission were of equal importance. For Phelps and for the missionaries who were coming to Jamaica from American manual-labor schools, the experience of owning land and becoming a self-sufficient farmer was a transformative experience, imbuing a man with material wealth and a feeling of independence. Over time, however, it appeared to the missionaries that landowning Jamaicans, even those who married and had families, were not progressing along the ladder of civilization as expected. The persistence of "licentiousness" proved that landownership and church discipline would not lead to the public morality required in a Christian civilization.

Richmond presented an opportunity to support black landownership without sacrificing ministerial authority. While this venture did not entirely pan out, the industrial school on the estate became one of the most important parts of the Jamaica Mission. The boarding school at Richmond was seen as a way to combat the negative influences of Jamaican home life while also offering a chance to cultivate American-style family values in young Jamaicans. Although the missionaries agreed on the important need to introduce these children to "civilized" behavior, the methods to be used in this effort were always in contention. As the next chapter shows, the Richmond model of strict discipline would come into direct conflict with a more sentimental education promoted by younger missionaries and female missionaries who had decidedly different ideas about how the most intimate part of the civilizing mission should be conducted.

Almost ninety years after Seth Wolcott bought Richmond, in January 1941, Miss Mary Adella Wolcott appealed to the colonial government in Jamaica on behalf of the estate. She felt "emboldened" to write to the governor, Sir Arthur Richards, because he had lately expressed interest in helping the poor farmers in the parish of St. Mary, Richmond's home. Miss Wolcott asked if the government would consider buying Richmond so that it "could finally go back to help the parish and the people and the Island—objects Grandfather Wolcott had in mind when he bought it back about 1855." She recounted a history of the estate, as it had been told to her by her father, Henry B. Wolcott. After purchasing the one-thousand-acre estate,

> Grandfather sold off small lots to the people—or rather gave, they only paying for title deed if that. At that period the poorer people could hardly get any land—land in this parish was cut up into big estates. So Richmond was probably one of the very first land settlements. Grandfather (Rev. Seth Taylor Wolcott) and Grandmother Wolcott also ran an industrial school for 14 years here, successfully training 300 young people, descendants of whom are still living useful busy lives, showing that much depends on early training.

When her father took over Richmond in 1872 after Seth Wolcott's death, he had focused more on his political pursuits than on the land. Educated at Oberlin College, like his parents, but interested in politics instead of the pursuit of agriculture or missionary work, Henry Wolcott had been a disinterested manager, and the estate had become deeply indebted. His daughter was a poet, and Mary Adella Wolcott proved to be more of a dreamer than a businesswoman. She wished that she could use the land to build "an industrial school, a baby Tuskegee . . . There are so many lovely things I would do!" Suffice it to say, the government had little interest in her utopian schemes. One document in the stack of correspondence noted that Miss Wolcott was an "eccentric," and a nice letter turning down her offer should be sent.[63] The Richmond School served as a bridge between the manual-labor schools of the 1820s and 1830s and the industrial-education plans for southern blacks after the Civil War, but clearly it was Booker T. Washington's vision of racial uplift at Tuskegee that had become better known.[64]

Part Three

In 1858, Lewis Tappan, the AMA's treasurer, voiced his growing frustration with the Jamaica Mission and its ministers. After conversing with a recently returned Mary Dean, Tappan met with an outgoing missionary to share his concerns about the field. The graying abolitionist confided to Bigelow Penfield, a twenty-four-year-old Oberlin graduate, about his dissatisfaction with "the course pursued by most of the missionaries," and he also spoke "of the need to revolutionize the whole concern."[1] Without question, Mary Dean's feminine civilizing mission had clashed with the mission's patriarchal family order, but she was not the only person to complain about the older ministers and their practices. Penfield and his wife, Sarah, both a generation younger than Loren Thompson and Seth Wolcott, would also find the mission family order and the ministers' methods to be old-fashioned and counterproductive to the AMA's goals. The final two chapters turn to the growing distance between the Jamaica Mission and evangelical abolitionists in the United States.

Although a young man, Penfield had an impressive pedigree connecting him to Oberlin's history. His stepfather, Henry Cowles, was one of the school's longest-serving professors and the editor of the *Oberlin Evangelist*. Cowles's first wife, Alice Welch Cowles, had been the first head of the school's Female Department, and she had organized the Oberlin Female Moral Reform Society.[2] After her death in 1843, Henry married the widowed Minerva Penfield, Bigelow's mother. Minerva also engaged in moral reform work, and in the 1850s, she and her daughter, Josephine Penfield Bateman, were central figures in Ohio's temperance movement, even though Henry Cowles still disapproved of women speaking in public.[3] Minerva also served on Oberlin's Ladies Board, a group consisting mostly of faculty wives charged with the responsibility of overseeing the "moral character of young women of the student body."[4] After the radical leadership of Asa Mahan in the 1830s, Oberlin's succeeding presidents, Charles Finney and James Fairchild, had moderated the school's politics, but the Cowles-Penfield family remained on the abolitionist and moral-reform vanguard.[5] In 1848, Henry Ward Beecher had famously aided in the rescue of two slave girls, Mary and Emily Edmondson, and his sister, the novelist Harriet Beecher Stowe, sent them to live with the Cowles family at Oberlin. Bigelow was no stranger to an interracial household when he moved to Jamaica.[6] Penfield's nineteen-year-old wife, Sarah Ingraham Penfield, had a different kind of connection to the Jamaica Mission's work. Her father, David Ingraham, had been the first Oberlin missionary in Jamaica, and Sarah had been born on the island in 1839. The couple found much wanting in the Jamaica Mission. Bigelow Penfield wrote six months after arriving, "Mr. Wolcott is scarcely a missionary at all, and I believe he does not expect to draw a salary much longer. I fear that Brother Thompson, with his strong bias and his mind not eminently logical, will be the greatest obstacle in the needed reformation."[7] The mission stations that had hosted encounters between Jamaicans and Americans, the Oberlin ministers and British missionaries, heterodox and orthodox Christians, and masculine and feminine interpretations of the civilizing mission now served as the site for a clash between two different generations.

A major source of the generational divide in the Jamaica Mission involved gender ideology and the relationship of gender to the civilizing mission. Between the mission's beginning in 1839 and the arrival of the Penfields in 1858, the gender ideology of evangelical abolitionists in the United States had shifted considerably. In the 1830s and early 1840s, the "woman question" had split radical abolitionists. Oberlin's administrators had generally sided with the more conservative views of Lewis Tappan and the American and Foreign Anti-Slavery Society, rather than the women's rights position of William Lloyd Garrison and his Boston-based followers. The dividing line between these two distinct factions became increasingly blurred in the late 1840s and 1850s. At Oberlin, female students broke down some of the rules that had characterized the school in its first decade. One student, the future suffragist Antoinette Brown, recalled a conversation with Charles Finney in 1848 in which she convinced him to allow female students to speak about their religious experiences in front of all of their classmates, male and female. Professor John Morgan, a one-time Lane Rebel, allowed Brown to fully participate in the school's literary society. She told Lucy Stone that he had promised her that "he would not critticise [sic] me any more severely than he would if I were a gentleman." Brown's mention of Bigelow Penfield's older sister, Josephine, as a friend about to be married and relocated to Haiti as a missionary suggests that at least one of the Penfields associated with the emergence of the early women's rights movement at Oberlin.[8] Indeed, when Josephine's husband Richard Cushman died in Haiti in 1849, Lucy Stone was sad for her friend's sorrows, and noted that the twenty-year-old Josephine performed the funeral by herself. "Josephine is a noble girl, and has the elements of real greatness, and now that she is free, she may make something."[9] Oberlin produced several important women's rights activists in the late 1840s, and historian Robert Fletcher observed that the school's women often sat on the vanguard while Oberlin's men remained more suspect of the women's movement.[10]

Even white abolitionist women who did not approve of woman suffrage managed to expand the definition of the women's sphere in the 1850s. Abolitionist women organized clubs, held bazaars, coordinated letter-writing campaigns and petitions, and penned books and articles. The Fugitive Slave Act's passage in 1850 riled up a new wave of white abolitionists, and bloodshed in Kansas in 1854 had also recruited new white northerners to join the abolitionist cause. Women also became more engaged in abolitionist politics during the presidential election of 1856. Jesse Benton Frémont, a woman who had disobeyed her slaveholding father to follow her heart and marry an abolitionist, attracted the support of northern men and women alike when her husband, John, ran as the first Republican presidential candidate in 1856. By the 1850s, the broader view of women's moral authority that went along with a more flexible ideology of domesticity in the North had become a weapon in the arsenal attacking southern patriarchy. Unlike northern homes, governed by selfless and morally pure mothers, white slaveholders ruled over southern households, commanding their wives and children, sexually violating slave women, and corrupting the family hearth.[11]

Although the missionary men in Jamaica probably admired the feminized and matriarchal domestic scenes presented in popular fiction like Harriet Beecher Stowe's *Uncle Tom's Cabin* (1852), they made little room for white women to have more authority in their own mission families. As early as 1849, Mary Dean had tested the missionary men on their willingness to accept her as a colleague and as an equal, at least when it came to certain moral matters. Like evangelical white women in the United States in the 1840s, Dean did not seek equality, in terms of her salary or voting rights in the mission, but she did want her concerns about the religious and moral standards of the mission addressed. The mission's men saw Dean's accusations as insubordination, and they accused her of unladylike and unchristian behavior. Of course, while they focused on Dean as the troublemaker, Hyde systematically dismantled all of the hierarchies that the mission had built, proving himself to be the real threat to the ministers' authority. This ongoing friction between Dean and the ministers anticipated the later conflicts that would occur when a younger generation of missionaries arrived in Jamaica with their different ideas about the Christian family.

The question of gender in the Jamaica Mission concerned more than the gender hierarchy the ministers drew on to organize themselves. As the Hyde case showed, the patriarchal order of the white missionary family and the racial hierarchy of the civilizing mission could not be separated. Gender and the practice of domesticity shaped the "civilizing" work in the mission households, and as gender ideology changed in the North, conflicts between women and men and older and younger missionaries arose in the Jamaica Mission. The older ministers' domestic practices emphasized the hierarchy of the patriarchal household, and Seth Wolcott embodied this with his black and white family at Richmond. While the mission's older men had come of age at a time of transition, and they had questioned religious authorities when they proclaimed their commitment to immediate abolitionism, they remained tethered to hierarchical and deferential social relations, and they drew on this when they structured their mission households. In Jamaica, the ministers never feared for their personal safety, but they expressed profound anxiety about the loosened society left behind after emancipation and the widespread licentiousness of Jamaica. In much the same way as John Shipherd had dreamed of Oberlin as a covenant town, meant to bring moral order to frontier whites, the Oberlin ministers in Jamaica wanted to remedy disorderly Jamaican families, a lack of comity among churches on matters of discipline, and rum drinking through discipline in their mission stations. Yet when they referred to the black children in their households as "servants" or shut down black deacons who had theological disputes with their sermons, while endorsing their fellow missionaries' heterodoxy, we can see how the gendered hierarchy of the mission family became increasingly racialized. To many of the mission's women and to the younger generation of missionary couples, the older American ministers in Jamaica seemed more in tune with paternalistic southern slaveholders than radical abolitionists.

The mission's single women, and those who married while in Jamaica, proved to have a somewhat different approach to domesticity, one that also resonated with the gender ideology of the younger generation of missionaries who came to Jamaica in the late 1850s. The mission's women schoolteachers and the younger missionary women believed that racial uplift and "civilizing" was work best done through maternal influence and sentimental attachments. It was better for black and white members of the mission family to share the same food around the same table, for example, and for white women to keep close watch over the young people under their care. In embracing the authority they gained as white women tasked with the work of the civilizing mission, many of these women grew bolder in their demands for autonomy within the mission family. Yet as the mission as a whole began to focus more intently on the family as a civilizing force, as evidenced at Richmond, the ministers closely scrutinized the domestic practices of every missionary. The missionary women who disliked strict discipline and hierarchy and who favored forming sentimental attachments to black children found themselves at odds with some of the older ministers.[12]

It should be emphasized that neither the mission's women nor younger missionary couples proved more egalitarian than the older ministers when it came to racial and religious differences. If anything, their methods intruded far more into Jamaicans' private lives. Yet the affectionate ties cultivated in the more feminized mission households unintentionally fostered ambiguities about the dividing lines between civilized and savage that had long defined the missionary enterprise. Two anecdotes from the Penfields illustrate the growing weaknesses in the racial and religious hierarchies of the mission. Faced with a new minister, Bigelow Penfield, in 1858, the church members at Oberlin Station called him the "young youth," and they regularly offered him advice, a practice that his wife, Sarah Penfield, found irritating. It was "a trial . . . to have them always telling us how other missionaries have done, evidently expecting we will do the same."[13] Bigelow may have been the missionary sent to teach black Jamaicans how to be civilized, but he soon found that he was on the receiving end of a great deal of advice from black Jamaican church leaders.

Black Jamaicans also made Sarah Penfield question her position in the mission, an internal conflict made evident in two strikingly different accounts she wrote about meeting the woman who cared for her as an infant. In a private letter about her visit to Shortwood, the estate where she had been born when her father was a missionary in Jamaica, Penfield wrote that "my old nurse took me to a little chamber where I was born and made me eat of some cake like what she used to make for father and drink the lemon drink he loved—called me her own daughter and told me many things about my parents and myself."[14] The second time Penfield wrote about this incident, it was for a published article in the *Advocate and Family Guardian*, and this public version of events omitted the intimate exchange recounted in her letter. Instead it portrayed a caricature of "Grandma Burton" speaking in creole and startling Penfield with her outburst when she realized her identity: "'He!' she screams and claps her hands, so sharply I start involuntarily. 'He, me missus! God too good! I never spect this!'"[15] The tender and domestic encounter found in Penfield's earlier private account was absent in her public narrative, which placed her at a distance from her former nurse. There was no shared meal, the two did not enter a "little chamber," and it seems unlikely that Grandma Burton had any knowledge to impart. In the personal letter Penfield identified herself as a child compared to the older woman, who was a source of knowledge about her family and childhood. In contrast, the published article implied a different relationship in which Sarah exemplified the civilized womanhood she had been sent to teach the unladylike Grandma Burton.

Sarah and Bigelow Penfield were not the only missionaries who faced uncertainties about their work. Although nothing as dramatic as the Hyde scandal took place in the 1860s, small fissures grew into rifts between different factions in the Jamaica Mission, and the Civil War and American emancipation forced the missionaries to question their purpose. Marked by a revival, the Civil War, and the Morant Bay Rebellion, the 1860s initiated a reconfiguration of the Jamaica Mission, one that eventually ended with the withdrawal of AMA support. By the early 1870s, only three Americans remained in Jamaica, and almost all of the mission's churches and schools were under the supervision of black Jamaicans.

6 Civilizing Domesticity

The Jamaica Mission is remarkable for the number of single women it employed in the decades before the Civil War. Twelve single women schoolteachers worked for the Jamaica Mission, while the much larger American Board, founded over thirty years before the AMA, had only employed thirty single women by 1860.[1] The AMA's Oberlin roots as well as its abolitionist politics made it more open to female missionaries, particularly when it came to single women as moral stewards. Young white women had been among the first volunteers to teach in black schools in the United States in the 1830s, and they similarly relished the opportunity to serve God through teaching freed people in Jamaica. Therefore, while few letters exist from missionary wives, making it difficult to compare the abolitionist women in Jamaica with Patricia Grimshaw's missionaries in Hawaii, or Joan Jacobs Brumberg's study of Adoniram Judson's several wives in Burma, the Jamaica Mission calls attention to single women missionaries and their ideas about the civilizing mission as well as their place in the mission family.[2]

The single women schoolteachers who joined the mission almost always lived with a minister and his wife, and they were expected to act the part of daughters in the mission family. For some women, this was an ideal arrangement, while others wanted greater independence. Maria Hicks was a perfect example of the ideal missionary daughter. In her first letter to the AMA after getting to Jamaica, she noted that Mary Dean would be "away off at Chesterfield by herself." In contrast, Hicks was to live with the Way family at Oberlin, and she remarked that "Bro. and Sister Way treat me with parental kindness, aiding me much in my labors." Whereas some of the missionary women felt constrained by the mission family, Hicks appreciated the Ways, and she also asked George Whipple for advice. She wrote that she had read "Paul's excellent epistle to Peter" many times, but she still awaited "Whipple's letter of instructions to Maria."[3] Maria Hicks, like a number of other unmarried missionary women, would not remain unattached for long, and she married Thomas Oughton, a son of a British missionary and an attorney in Kingston.

The expectations for married women in the mission were less well defined. Were missionary wives to be helpmeets for their husbands, or were they to conduct their own missionary work, as teachers? Unlike the single women, they would receive no payment for their work. The paucity of letters from missionary wives adds to the challenge of explaining how these women understood their role in the mission. From what little evidence exists, it appears that like the unmarried schoolteachers, missionary wives had a variety of views on their duties. The majority of the mission's wives focused on their duties within their household. They wrote few letters to the AMA, and their husbands, the heads of the households, represented their interests. This was in spite of the fact that many of the women had been quite involved in reform activities at Oberlin. Lucy Evarts, for one, had been a senior at Oberlin when she faced down a group of white vigilantes who tried to thwart her efforts to teach at a black school in Pike County, Ohio. What is most striking about women in the Jamaica Mission are the absences. That these college-educated women who had been active in moral reform and abolitionism at Oberlin did not establish a women's organization in Jamaica, as women did in other mission fields, raises questions.[4] Did the women focus more on teaching at their mission stations and caring for the many dependents in their households than on improving society more generally? Did the distance between the mission stations and the hard-to-navigate terrain limit their access to one another? Or was it the racial and gendered hierarchies of the mission family that circumscribed the role white women would play in the mission? From the ministers' letters, it seems that few married women in the 1840s and early 1850s attempted to expand their role in the mission, with the exception of Lucy Evarts's unorthodox decision to become John Hyde's "spiritual wife." But this silence changed in the late 1850s when Sarah Ingraham Penfield joined the Jamaica Mission. She and her husband came to the island with a sense of entitlement as members of two of Oberlin's first families, and they held back little when they found fault with their colleagues. The Penfields' marriage and their more modern ideas about how to run their household drew the disapproval of many of the mission's older men, who also thought that the younger Penfields should obey their older and more experienced colleagues. Moreover, Sarah Ingraham Penfield's private letters have been preserved, offering insight into how she and other women in the mission viewed their work and the ministers.

Missionary work forced into the open a variety of conflicts among evangelical abolitionists. This chapter follows the experiences of single women and married women as they translated the ideology of domesticity into a feminine civilizing mission, and it shows the various moves they made to find a satisfactory place in the gendered hierarchy of the mission family. Second, this chapter takes on the question of the relationship between race and the ideology of domesticity. As Amy Kaplan has argued, separate spheres and domesticity were more than gender ideologies articulating male and female difference.[5] Purveyors of domesticity also charged white Protestant women with the duty to protect the national character, and to act as "civilizing" influences on their own families as well as the racial and religious others within the United States. Domesticity positioned white women alongside white men in the political responsibility of caring for the nation's well-being. The male and female missionaries in Jamaica also saw the kinship between domesticity and the civilizing mission, even if they did not always agree on how domesticity should be employed.

For many of the single women in Jamaica, the mission provided a matchmaking service. This trend began with one of the first two unmarried female missionaries to Jamaica, Catherine Strobie, who wed a British Baptist minister and resigned her post as a teacher at Eliot's school. Her replacement, Urania Hunt, did not work out as planned, as we saw in chapter 4, but two years later, a new single woman joined Loren Thompson's family to assist his wife, Nancy, at the Eliot school. With twenty-six students at the end of the term in July 1852, the Oberlin native Sarah Blakeley was happy with her work at Eliot, writing that her labors helped to save "these priceless jewels." Her students seemed "as bright and apt to learn" as students she had taught in the United States, but their creole language often prevented them from understanding "very many of the English terms" she used. Blakeley's situation with the Thompsons was, at least by her reports, going very well, and she praised their kindness. She had no difficulty, at least in her letters to the missionary association, fitting into her expected place in the mission family and in her role as an assistant to Nancy Thompson. Blakeley's time at Eliot ended after a year, however, because she married a fellow teacher in the mission, an Oberlin graduate who had been her shipmate on the voyage from the United States.[6]

After marrying Addison Moffat in December 1852, Addison and Sarah moved to Mount Pleasant, where Addison had his school. Hinting at some unresolved tensions concerning their decision to marry, Sarah felt the need to reiterate her commitment to missionary work. She had not acted "selfishly" in choosing to marry Addison, she wrote, but had followed the path she believed would glorify God.[7] The other missionaries agreed, although not without a hint of resentment. As Loren Thompson wrote, their wedding had been attended by eighteen adults and nine children, "a happy band of brothers and sisters convened together to bear testimony to the constitution of a new family." He continued, "We all rejoice in the *new family* though *we* are left again without a teacher."[8] The Moffat-Blakeley marriage pleased Thompson in that it created another family to serve as a positive model for Jamaicans, even though it took away his teacher. Overall, the missionary men were far more comfortable with having Sarah become a missionary wife than in keeping her as a single woman schoolteacher. As a married woman, she had a clearly defined place in the mission family, and the marriage also enhanced the status of her husband, Addison, in the minds of the other ministers for he now had a dependent wife.

Sarah Blakeley Moffat's marriage and eventual motherhood did not mean that she had lost interest in her work as a missionary. Unlike the women who moved to Jamaica as ministers' wives, Sarah Moffat, perhaps because of her former status as a missionary employee, continued to update George Whipple and the AMA's New York office on her school's progress. These letters from her new station reflected a different voice than the communications of the mission's men. For example, the minister Seth Wolcott requested that a minister be stationed at the Providence School, making the case that an older man would have more authority and would provide the "thorough discipline, not of children only, but of parents also" required. While "a common teacher may discipline his school indoors . . . he cannot discipline the parents. Ministerial authority is demanded here."[9] Another missionary complained about the "superstitions, soul-destroying notions" that were "instilled into the minds of this deluded people."[10] Unlike the men in Jamaica who fretted about the manliness of black Jamaicans and their tendencies towards "licentious" behavior in the new climate of freedom, Sarah Moffat, like many white women missionaries, concerned herself with sentimental ties. Further, her letters continued to depict Jamaica in a romantic light, speaking to her appreciation of the emotional qualities of black Jamaican religious life, the same aspect that many northern women favored in evangelical faith. She told George Whipple that the "prayers and remarks" of "uncultivated minds" during prayer meetings "benefited and strengthened" her, and "their expressions, though coarse and unrefined, are often full of sound practical truth, and affect my heart."[11] The mission's men found the "unrefined" quality of black Jamaicans irritating and demonstrative of a lack of education and theological rigor, whereas Sarah Blakeley Moffat found the "uncultivated minds" to be empowering.

The so-called primitive qualities Sarah Blakeley Moffat observed in black Jamaicans that elevated her own sense of spirituality did not mean that she ignored the "civilizing" work required of her, however, and she invoked the language of domesticity to define her place in the civilizing mission. Moffat believed that her domestic gifts as a white woman allowed her to mold young black Jamaicans into civilized Christians. She declared that "all the little avenues to their hearts" must be watched "lest the roots of selfishness and deceit and theft obtain a hold."[12] While she certainly sought control over her students, as did the white ministers, Moffat wrote about this in a different way than the mission's men, who spoke of the need for discipline in their churches. Like growing numbers of women in the

United States, she used a more psychological form of discipline than did the mission's men. The softer discipline of Sarah Blakeley Moffat and other women in the Jamaica Mission echoed the advice of Catharine Beecher in her popular manual concerning domestic matters, originally published in the early 1840s. Beecher recommended that her readers "govern" their children by following a "medium course": neither "a stern, unsympathizing maintenance of parental authority" nor an indulgent position from which the parent lacks the "right to command."[13] Seeing her missionary work as a domesticating influence, Sarah Blakeley Moffat approached her black Jamaican students, but also their parents, as she would children.

While Sarah Blakeley Moffat largely conformed with the ministers' views of acceptable domestic behavior, some women in the mission found confining the limitations placed upon them. One teacher, Mary Howe, was sent home after less than a year when she complained about the ministers' controlling temperaments. Howe had worked as a teacher for many years among the Seneca near Buffalo, New York, and she consequently had experience in missionary work and also was nearer to the ministers' age than many of the other single women teachers. During her brief time in Jamaica, Howe proved to be difficult. She refused to ride on horseback, delaying her passage to Eliot, her assigned school. After two weeks at Brainerd, she wrote to Loren Thompson, the minister at Eliot, declaring her intention to return to the United States because she was "both homesick and heartsick at the thought of remaining." Thompson told his superiors in New York that Howe was disgusted by the black students she was supposed to teach, and she had apparently been warned by friends against working for the abolitionist AMA before she even left the United States.[14]

In spite of Howe's obvious eccentricities, the way in which the ministers discussed her reveals much about what they valued in their single women schoolteachers. Loren Thompson was preoccupied with the fact that Howe wanted nothing to do with the "mission family," and her position that if she had known the circumstances in Jamaica she would "never have come." Thompson wrote, "We as a mission are as one family" and Howe "likes independency (i.e.) to do as she chooses and none to controll [sic] her, and the fact that she must be under some controll here, as we all are one to another, greatly distresses her."[15] Independence might be expected of the American men and hoped to be cultivated in the black men, but for an unmarried missionary woman it was perceived as a direct threat to the "mission family." A more suitable candidate for the mission would be a "faithful help-meet," wrote Albert Richardson.[16] Richardson meant that the teachers sent by the AMA relieved the ministers and their wives from the time-consuming responsibility of teaching school.[17] As God had created Eve as a "helpmeet" for Adam, then the teachers, whether male or female, performed the womanly work of educating and civilizing Jamaican children while the men of the mission tended to their soul-saving labor. Sarah Blakeley Moffat abided by this family order, exercising her feminine civilizing mission without challenging the mission's men, but Mary Howe rejected it entirely.

Sarah Blakeley Moffat's life choices and attitudes represented the feminine civilizing mission most compatible with the ministers' ideas, and Howe (and her predecessor, Urania Hunt) the least. Mary Dean's application of domesticity to the civilizing mission was something in between. She sought authority over the white ministers on the island as well as the black Jamaicans, and she held them both to the same standards, a point that often put her at odds with the mission's men. Dean arrived in Jamaica in 1848 from Quincy, Illinois, where she left behind her widowed mother and frequently ill sister to whom she always sent a portion of her salary. Her return to the United States in 1851 for a year, and then again permanently in 1857, came about only in part because of her problems with the missionaries and her health, but also out of a sense of responsibility she felt toward her family, particularly as her mother became older and more frail.[18] Dean had attended the coeducational and abolitionist Mission Institute in Quincy where she had been a classmate of Catherine Strobie, the young woman who married soon after arriving in Jamaica in 1848. In his letter about the two women to George Whipple, the school's headmaster, Elijah Griswold, wrote that Catherine Strobie would likely "take better care of her self than Mary Dean" because Dean was "very apt to neglect herself for the benefit of others." Dean had a "superior mind" and "much feeling" compared to Strobie, who had a more "strict moral principle." Strobie's marriage took her away from Jamaica in 1849, but Mary Dean remained in the mission until 1857.[19]

In 1852, Mary Dean returned to Jamaica after spending a year in the United States, and the ministers relocated her from her one-time post at Oberlin Station to a more remote location, much to the irritation of her former pupils. Indeed, it was not uncommon for black Jamaicans to ask specifically for Mary Dean to serve as the teacher.[20] Her new school, Chesterfield, was isolated from the mission stations, and one of the ministers told her later out of spite that she had been sent there because the ministers had thought that she "was fit only to live alone."[21] More diplomatically, the *American Missionary* testified to "her knowledge of this people, and her experience in teaching among them," a prerequisite for Chesterfield since "the teacher there will be three miles away from the missionary family—will be obliged to live by herself, and hence be deprived of that frequent counsel and assistance which a new-comer might need." Albert Richardson added, "There *ought* to be a male teacher at Chesterfield . . . The people have bought land, and are thickly settled around it, and they want a good man to live and labor among them."[22] Apparently a combination of the ministers' personal antipathy and trust of Dean allowed her the privilege they rarely allowed other single women in the mission, who were expected to act like daughters and assistants within a minister's home.

Dean's sense of righteousness grew during her time in the mission. Living on her own, as would a male missionary, she adopted black children into her household. From her work as a white woman who had converted domesticity into the duties of a civilizing missionary, she became even more interested in independence than she had been during her first tour of duty in Jamaica. In 1855, she gave up her autonomy to teach at Wolcott's Richmond School; predictably, she disliked losing the independence she had gained at Chesterfield and at her other most recent post, Rock River. After a little over a year, her conflicts with its principal, missionary Seth Wolcott, made it impossible for her to continue to live with his family. In January 1857 she resigned from Richmond and retreated to the home of another teacher, Charles Venning, and his family until March 1857 when she returned to the United States for good.

The ministers in Jamaica resented Mary Dean's criticism, but in her letters to the AMA, she encapsulated her harsh evaluations in the language of domesticity. Sometimes emphasizing her self-sacrificing work for the betterment of others, Dean played the role of a woman who had learned to deal with extreme hardships without complaint. She easily took on the roles of daughter and sister, pleading with the AMA to listen to her side of the story, and it appears that her methods worked. Dean was the only female missionary in Jamaica who directly corresponded with Lewis Tappan, and the letters indicate that the two had a mutual respect for each other.

Tappan praised Dean's sentimental poems, which she sent to him regularly, and he personally managed Dean's requests for money to be sent to her mother. Tappan and his wife kept Dean up to date with the latest books, newspapers, and religious tracts that she needed in her classroom, and Tappan often confided in Dean about the mission's business.[23] Tappan even concluded a letter to Seth Wolcott with the note that he should "remember us to Miss Dean. She is a missionary worth having."[24]

Their letters also contain a level of familiarity not seen in other missionaries' letters to Lewis Tappan. Writing in 1855, Tappan exclaimed, "Dr. Hyde! What a scoundrel Dr. H. proves to be! I never saw him, but recollected that his testimonials were ample. He deceived many and probably himself." Later in the letter, he confessed that when he learned that some of the ministers had speculated on copper in Jamaica, this had "disheartened me more with respect to the Jamaica Mission than anything that has ever occurred."[25] In her correspondence with George Whipple and Tappan, Mary Dean also drew on the power of female moral authority. As a pious woman, a member of the more moral sex, Dean claimed to be following her Christian duty when she informed on the behavior of her fellow missionaries. Her unceasing attention to others' moral lapses was more than a reflection of American domesticity, and it also derived from her position as a white civilizer. Moral righteousness was even more necessary in Jamaica than it was in the United States, she frequently reminded the AMA's officers. Well-connected and savvy about how to manipulate the ideology of domesticity to serve her ends in the mission, Mary Dean and her battles with her fellow missionaries illustrated the divergence between gender in the Jamaica Mission and the gender ideology of the evangelical abolitionists in the North.

Finding herself at remote Chesterfield after returning to Jamaica in 1852, Mary Dean was quick to point out the disparity between the wages paid to men and women in the mission. At Chesterfield, Mary Dean had few domestic comforts, and she had only her salary for support. There was a "nice new house," but it was "without a stone, chair, or an article of furniture." She persevered: "This is just what I am used to. I have always had to provide fuel, light, furniture, and for all the expenses of housekeeping out of woman's wages, which has sometimes made pretty close corners."[26] Indeed, her recent yearlong stay in the United States had been the cause of much anxiety as her teaching jobs had not paid her enough money to accumulate any savings that she might have given to her mother and sister or kept for herself.[27] Dean questioned her salary even as she assured George Whipple that she did not mean to claim equality with men. Her letter continued, "I am not complaining or speaking on the subject of women's rights but stating facts."[28] This was not the first time that Dean skirted the controversial women's rights platform adopted by her more radical abolitionist sisters in 1848. During her sabbatical in the States in 1851, she had visited churches and ladies' organizations in Illinois, Wisconsin, and Iowa to raise money for the mission, but she assured George Whipple that she was not herself giving speeches: "Don't suppose I intend to speak in public on the stage. I have engaged tongues more eloquent to speak for me while I . . . speak individually with my hearers."[29] Dean addressed the issue that had been highly divisive in the abolitionist movement at the beginning of the 1830s when Angelina and Sarah Grimké created a storm of controversy when they lectured to audiences containing both men and women. Yet even as Mary Dean shrugged off her interest in women's rights, she still drew Whipple's attention to the sexual inequalities in the mission. While not a man, Dean was willing and eager to speak on behalf of the Jamaica Mission to raise much-needed money, even though she would probably not benefit directly from her efforts.

While Dean's position as a woman in the mission family left her at a disadvantage financially, it also granted her a degree of freedom through which she could directly criticize decisions being made by the ministers in Jamaica and the mission board in New York. In a letter to Lewis Tappan, she wrote,

> by the by, I have always heard, yes for many years and it has been the talk, that 'Mr. Tappan is very rich,' and maybe he would be willing to give a small sum from his vast treasures to the poor in Jamaica. $5000, yes, he would scarcely miss it, and oh what a multitude of ignorant children it would educate. But who is to ask for it? If it be a crime who will bear the blame of it?[30]

Tappan's response reminded Dean that while he seemed rich to her, given the expenses of living in New York City, he did not have so much as five thousand dollars to donate to the mission cause. Perhaps feeling chastened, Tappan felt compelled to explain that for the past "five years, I have devoted my time to the antislavery and missionary cause, gratuitously, supporting my family in this expensive place, and giving to various objects."³¹ Unlike the missionary men who loathed asking for money from the AMA, Dean, as a woman, carried none of the burdens of self-sufficiency and manly independence. Although turned down for her request, the fact that she asked for money showed how gender ideology shaped the ways men and women approached their relationship with the AMA.

Dean's letters also veiled strong criticisms of her fellow missionaries in the softer language of feminine weakness. In one she begged Whipple "to have patience with me but this once while I pour out my complaints," and in another, she wrote, "I will take the place of a servant, only allow me to speak my grievances."³² Mary Dean also made more specific complaints about particular missionaries in spite of her awareness that it did not "look very amiable for young ladies to be always finding fault." Dean could not contain her dissatisfaction with "false brethren and sisters."³³ A minister would never have abdicated his independent manhood in such a way, yet for Dean this type of pleading was quite useful. As a woman, Dean had no vote in the mission's decisions, and writing to Whipple and Tappan was the only means of getting her voice heard. On one occasion when the ministers had discussed sending her back to the United States, she appealed to Whipple for assistance. She began by calling herself a "great baby" who had required care when she had first returned to New York from Jamaica in 1851, and she reminisced about Whipple's "angelic" voice and words that still brought a "sudden shower of tears" to her eyes. From sentiment to assertion, Dean quickly turned to protest the plans of the ministers, telling Whipple that she would die before leaving her post if she were to be replaced by "heretic or drowsy do-nothing souls."³⁴ Women in the mission were also not above Dean's criticism, as she reported on Mary Howe's "strange views and conduct" and asked why the AMA had not investigated her more thoroughly during Howe's stay in New York City.³⁵

Mary Dean used domesticity to balance her roles as submissive woman and moral critic in her relations with the Executive Committee and the mission's men, and domesticity also informed Dean's matriarchal relationship to the black Jamaican children adopted into her household. She took pride in the practical skills that enabled her to survive in an empty house at some distance from her fellow missionaries, at both Chesterfield and Rock River. It appears the decision to move had not been hers; she wrote to Whipple that "the Brethren removed me to Rock River," and described the difficulties of the school's location. The school had eight acres but on such steep terrain that it could not be used for pasture. While she was only four miles from one of the mission's chapels, the journey over the mountainous terrain was quite dangerous, requiring her to cross several rivers and to travel along muddy and sometimes flooded roads. Further, she noted, "It was not judicious to leave my family of seven children." While she had almost one hundred students at Chesterfield, at Rock River her school contained twelve students in addition to her "own" seven children. At Rock River, she felt "like a foreigner shut up from Sabbath privileges," but as "the united voice and wisdom of the Mission has put me here, I will try what I can do."[36]

As one of the few single women missionaries in Jamaica to live separately from the other missionaries, Mary Dean could create her own household in a way that she probably never would have done in the North. As a schoolteacher in frontier towns in Illinois and Wisconsin, Dean either lived at home or she boarded with a family. In Jamaica, however, she lived as a single woman and could be both a mother and an authority figure because of the power she derived from her status as a self-declared civilizing missionary. Another missionary schoolteacher, Lucy Woodcock, a young woman who attended Oberlin and who came to teach at the Eliot School, found herself in a similar position when she was left alone at Eliot for six months in 1858. With the Thompson family away, Woodcock pronounced herself the "monarch of all I survey," and told her brother that "I shall have more cares and enough to take up my time so I shall not have any opportunity to get home."[37] Defining themselves as civilizers and white women committed to the transformative power of domesticity, Dean and Woodcock gained a sense of authority in Jamaica that they did not find at home.

Mary Dean's ally at Oberlin, Ann Brooks Olds, wrote about her missionary work in similar terms in 1849, several months after she and her husband had arrived at Oberlin Station. In a very rare letter to the AMA from a missionary wife, Ann Olds wrote because her husband was too sick to attend to his correspondence. At Oberlin, she told George Whipple, she and her husband had decided to begin a school, and because they had no one to teach, Ann volunteered her services. This apparently was not what the AMA had in mind, and Ann apologized to George Whipple when she realized "I had gone contrary to your wishes, or *at least that your wishes were opposed to the course I had taken.*" But she defended her work, writing that although Dr. Hyde thought there to be no need for a school until they received a sign from God (she denounced this as yet another sign of Hyde's "ultra" views), "I feel that we might remain idle until this and the following generations have passed into eternity before the Lord would give us any stronger manifestations of his will on the subject." Ann wrote that she would stop her work if Whipple insisted, "but I must beg you will not request me to leave those in whom I have become so much interested."[38] Ann Olds's letter shows that some missionary wives felt as Mary Dean did about the importance of their work, and like their moral reforming kindred in the United States, the act of uplifting others, in this case black Jamaican children, fed into their zeal and led to a sense of moral authority. Unfortunately, not until the end of the 1850s do we have letters from another missionary wife to compare with the single women.

Like Ann Olds's attachment to her students at Oberlin, Mary Dean also formed lasting relationships with young Jamaicans, and they corresponded with her after she returned to the United States. Dean grew close to one fourteen-year-old student at the Chesterfield School named Elizabeth Mogg. Mogg's parents had both been born into slavery, and her father, John, had become a deacon in the mission's church at Chesterfield. While he was literate, his wife Letitia was not, but the couple arranged for their daughter Elizabeth to become educated, which included sending her to live with Mary Dean.[39] Elizabeth wrote to Dean after she had returned to the United States. Writing in the effusive and affectionate style common to nineteenth-century women, Elizabeth's letter detailed her spiritual trials and desire to see Dean again. The Jamaican girl felt that there was no one to whom she could confess her sins after Dean had left, and she wrote, "My love to you is unabated," and she again longed "to have the pleasure of looking steadily into that calm, sweet face, and those eyes beaming with love."[40] Whether or not Dean reciprocated Mogg's attachment is not known, although Dean did forward the letter to George Whipple with a note indicating that this was one of the students whom she wished the AMA would support financially.[41]

Mogg's letter to Dean indicated the degree to which Mary Dean's civilizing mission differed from that of the mission's patriarchs. As a woman, Dean had to find novel ways to engage in the mission's governance, and similarly, she had developed a different mode of "parental" control over black Jamaicans. Rather than seeing herself as the stern father responsible for leading his wayward children on the right path, Mary Dean fostered bonds of affection between herself and black Jamaicans. Jamaican parents also liked her, and when she was stationed at Chesterfield in 1852, her old friends at Oberlin "were quite disappointed in not being able to secure the services of their old teacher."[42] Indeed, Dean had her own theory of missions that she believed entitled her to judge her fellow missionaries, both men and women. Dean believed that missionaries needed to be "working and practickle [sic] people." According to Dean, "Missionaries need to be amphibians and able to live in two elements equally well, for the moral atmosphere here and at home is as different as the air and water." She had become frustrated with some ministers and teachers in the mission, and declared that "If I did not think slavery the sin of sins and the quintessence of all evil, I should sometimes be tempted to go over to the American Board for I know they use every precaution against imposters."[43] At Rock River, she put into action her mission theory by acting as the mother and schoolteacher to the few children whose parents let them attend Dean's school and listen to her evangelical message. Even though she lived far from the others in the mission, she never backslid from her faith or morality. She believed that she exemplified the amphibious missionary, able to interact with black Jamaicans in a way that resulted in affectionate relationships even as she refused to cede any moral ground in terms of her faith and understanding of civilization.

In 1855, Mary Dean moved to the newly founded Richmond Normal School to serve as the "assistant" to Seth Wolcott, and the differences between how Dean and Wolcott had been conducting their mission families became clear. As would be expected based on her past experiences, Dean showed some hesitancy about giving up her autonomy to be under the Wolcott family roof. She insisted on serving as "a sort of matron" who, rather than relying on the family for room and board, asked to be paid wages by Wolcott for her labor.[44] Dean had no intention of playing the daughter to Seth and Mary Wolcott, and instead tried to negotiate a degree of independence. After a year of teaching at Richmond, Dean decided to return to the United States because her mother's health had become precarious. During the months before her departure, she found herself on the outs with her colleagues. In late 1856, Wolcott learned that Dean had been giving out small amounts of money to Jamaican children, probably those whom she had supported at Rock River and at Chesterfield. Wolcott and Heman Hall, the mission's corresponding secretary at the time, felt charitable donations to be contrary to the goals of the mission—to create independent black Jamaicans—so they agreed to withhold Dean's salary from her.

Like the later AMA missionaries to the South during the Civil War, both Wolcott and Hall heartily disapproved of giving the black Jamaicans "charity" for fear that it would perpetuate dependency.[45] Mary Dean, not surprisingly, interpreted her actions in a different way. During her time in Jamaica, Dean had regularly accepted donations from friends in the United States to supplement her salary; as she had also sent a portion of her salary back to her mother and sister in the United States, the notion of asking for and giving money was second nature to her, unlike the mission's men who loathed any kind of dependency. On the eve of her departure, Dean penned a long letter to Charles Venning justifying and explaining her actions, and detailing her frustrations with Wolcott and Hall. She told Venning that when she decided to return to the United States, she had asked Seth Wolcott to pass along fifteen dollars to two of her former students at Chesterfield. He apparently refused her request, and she felt that he "treated the matter with the same coldness."[46] In her opinion, the ministers were hypocrites, as they certainly found a "large and sure salary a very nice and convenient thing," and she was sure that they had "read in the bible the often repeated precept concerning giving to the poor."[47] Dean believed her gifts to the children to be acts of affection and kindness. "I would die for these children," she wrote to Venning. "I do think our worthy children should receive aid and I intend to get it to them and send it [to] their mt. house if none of the missionaries will give it to them."[48]

Perhaps Dean's fondness for her students came from the fact that she had formed closer bonds with them than with her fellow missionaries, whom she found controlling, unpleasant, and selfish. She apparently did not keep these views to herself. According to Heman Hall, the trouble between Dean and Wolcott grew out of Dean's "own peculiarities."[49] He wrote additionally that "she has said many things respecting Mr. and Mrs. Wolcott which were severe and cruel and untrue, things which if said under some circumstances might be a serious detriment to Richmond."[50] Neither Hall nor Wolcott ever wrote exactly what accusations were leveled, but Dean's departing letter to Venning shows her side of the conflicts between the ministers and herself. Dean felt that she was treated differently as a single woman in the mission, and the constant judgment and criticism of the mission's men had grown to be a burden that she could no longer carry.

Dean wrote freely about her long-felt grief that, as a woman, she was judged differently than her fellow male teachers. She wrote to Charles Venning, "I don't hear the brethren dictating to you what texts you shall teach in Jan. or Feb. They don't say whether your pupils shall sit or stand while reading. They leave you to make your own rules, but *I* this awful 'me' must be found fault with for *everything* I do." She continued, "If I speak it is the opinion of some that I ought to be silent. If I go out, some think I should have stayed at home. If I can't give, I am called callous, if I do, I commit almost an unpardonable offense. All my performances are misdemeanors."[51] Dean must have enjoyed her time at Chesterfield and Rock River because of the autonomy she had at the remote schools, and she found it harder to readjust to the role expected of her in the Wolcott family at Richmond. Yet in the end, Dean regretted her estrangement from the other Americans in Jamaica, and she remarked sadly that while she had been planning her departure from the island for the past six months, "Not one told me a common affectionate good by."[52] Mary Dean left Jamaica and returned to the United States by her own will, but her parting from the other missionaries was hardly on good terms. Undoubtedly, Mary Dean conveyed a quite negative picture of the mission to her friend Lewis Tappan when she returned to the United States in 1857.

As Mary Dean tried and failed to claim authority based on her status as a white woman in the Jamaica Mission of the 1850s, white women in the North met with more success in expanding the boundaries of the women's sphere. Evangelical northern women increasingly understood themselves as vital participants in the public sphere, even if they declined to endorse the more radical planks of the woman's rights platform. Further, northern women believed that the home was a powerful source for moral good, and domestic novels showed how homes and mothers could impact society more broadly. In the 1850s, abolitionists frequently referenced the importance of domesticity and maternal influences in their attacks on southern slavery. Domesticity and women had a critical role to play in the family and in society, they argued, and white southerners not only prohibited black women and men from marrying and establishing families, the dominance of patriarchy also kept white southern women from manifesting their authority over their families and homes.[53] This gradual reinterpretation of domesticity from female submissiveness to a kind of female authority appeared in the Jamaica Mission in the late 1850s as a younger generation of missionary couples arrived on the island. The missionaries' different ideas of domesticity and women's duties gave them a different perspective on the civilizing mission and on how to go about the work of racial uplift in Jamaica. The clashing ideas of domesticity between the older and younger missionaries led to disputes over the best practices for the civilizing mission.

The missionaries who raised the most commotion in the mission were Sarah Ingraham Penfield and her husband Bigelow. To put their ages in perspective, Sarah Penfield was nineteen when she moved to Jamaica with twenty-four-year-old Bigelow, and the Grimké sisters' controversial speeches and the abolitionist schism in 1840 over the "woman question" had both taken place before she was born. Unlike Mary Dean, Sarah Penfield did not write directly to the AMA with her dissatisfaction, but instead wrote to her very influential in-laws in Ohio, Henry Cowles and, especially, Bigelow's mother, Minerva Penfield Cowles. The paucity of letters from other missionary wives makes it difficult to compare Sarah Penfield to her peers, yet the fact that her protestations also appeared in the ministers' letters suggests that few other married women engaged in similar criticisms of the mission's men.

Sarah Penfield found much at fault with the daily business of the Jamaica Mission, and she was particularly sensitive to issues concerning the mission's single women. Like Mary Dean before her, she complained about the different wages for men and women, remarking that a female teacher's salary, $420, was hardly a living wage. She thought that the $110 difference between ministers' salaries and the payments made to the women teachers was too much, but "that the ministers here have seemed to countenance such a great gulf between them and the teachers."[54] Penfield similarly voiced her views that it was unfair that the missionwide meetings excluded women. According to her, the mission's corresponding secretary frequently joked "that if all the gentlemen voted for a motion and all the ladies against it, he should write home that it was an unanimous vote, and this when [the mission board] requested the ladies to vote, too." She became irritated enough to tell the secretary, Heman Hall, directly how much this remark of his bothered her, and he stopped saying it, at least in her presence. In her opinion, Sarah Penfield felt there was "far too much conservatism in the mission." Even though women were excluded from voting in the mission's meetings, Sarah's status as a married woman with a sympathetic husband allowed her to get her views on the table, and she reassured her mother-in-law that except for that one confrontation with Hall, "You may be sure I do not trouble myself to vote or say anything at the meeting except through my husband."[55]

While Penfield limited her involvement in the "public sphere" of the mission's meetings, her most persistent challenges to the older ministers came within the confines of her own home. The ministers' close attention to her household habits—and for that matter, to everyone in the mission's disciplinary measures—shows how closely linked domesticity and civilizing were for the Americans. Penfield contrasted the ideals of her family with the civilizing mission of the other missionaries, whom she felt had drifted from "the Oberlin way." Like others in the mission, the Penfields "adopted" Jamaican children into their family, and after being on the island only a few months, they found themselves with a "large family" that often left them in dire fiscal straits. Like the other missionaries, the Penfields agreed that incorporating Jamaicans into the mission family was essential, but they disagreed with how the young people should be treated. Both Penfields were "*greatly disappointed* in the missionaries" for "in no way acknowledging [their adopted children] as equals." Abner and Ann Olds and Mary Dean, now back in the United States, had been exceptions, Sarah wrote, but most of the older members of the mission—Heman Hall and Charles Starbuck, along with Wolcott and Thompson—proved "equally conservative," and she noted that "their conduct is so utterly adverse to our Oberlin training [that] it seems to us quite wrong."[56]

The younger missionaries did not differ at all in what they believed "proper" gender and family relationships to be. Sarah Penfield, like her elders, complained about the habit of young Jamaican women living with men before marrying them. Unlike the male ministers, Penfield wrote from the perspective of the woman. In an article that appeared in the New York–based *Advocate and Family Guardian*, a publication that started as the organ of the New York Female Moral Reform Society in the 1830s, she observed that "it is almost the universal practice for a girl to go and live with a man upon his simple promise to marry her." Penfield certainly disapproved, because such promises of marriage were "often more broken than kept." Sympathizing with the abandoned woman, Penfield did not harp on her licentiousness or sinfulness, as did the mission's men, but blamed the deceptive man.[57]

The Penfields also made direct attempts to intervene in domestic disputes taking place around them. Sarah Penfield recounted to her mother-in-law the story of a Jamaican mother who was attempting to punish her son physically after he stole an apple from one of Oberlin Station's trees. According to Sarah, the boy was tied up to a tree, and his mother "with a huge stick began beating him." Bigelow Penfield rushed over to the scene and "begged her to stop, and when she would not, he stepped between her and the child and pushed her back when she tried to whip past him." Sarah wrote that the woman became angry at Bigelow, and she "ordered him out of her yard. Her loud voice might have been heard half a mile as she abused him and dared him to unloose the child." In spite of the pleas of "the little fellow," Bigelow did not intervene, "thinking he had no right to." Sarah noted that she felt "very sorry for the little fellow" as he seemed "quite bright and smart." He had worked for her in the past, and she had paid him in clothing that he could wear to Sabbath School. Sarah wished that she could take the little boy away from his mother, but because they lived so close to Oberlin Station, she feared what might happen if she did.[58]

In the Penfield family, regulating children through emotion would rule over the disciplinary rod. Sarah told an aunt that being in Jamaica, "shut out as I am from almost all *other* society," she did not know how she could live without "the first warm love between husband and wife, parent and child."[59] Sarah Penfield gave birth to the couple's first child in February 1860, but during 1859 she preoccupied herself with the needs and wants of her Jamaican family. Her letters provide a window into the domestic life that characterized her house. She joked with Bigelow's sister that "you would be quite amused to see how motherly I am with my five children about me," and early in her pregnancy, Bigelow hoped she would recover from her bouts of morning sickness to take "her accustomed place at the head of domestic affairs."[60] She described one of the children, Anna, as a "noble good girl" but thought she could be more of "a leading spirit among the younger children."[61] Anna proved to be an excellent help with the Penfields' baby, but Sarah observed that she "is far more likely to be sick on washing days than any others."[62] Sarah also commented on the skin color of the children: the next oldest, Thomas, "was quite black but carries such a pleasant, happy face" and proved to be "a great help to Mr. Penfield." When school was out of session, Thomas worked steadily and saved up money so that he would have "something to start off in the world with."[63] Willie was Sarah's favorite, even though he was often in trouble. "He has a good mind and excellent memory and will make a fine scholar . . . but he is greatly inclined to indolence," she wrote, and Thomas agreed, telling Sarah that Willie "hasn't *energy* enough."[64] In the spring of 1860, Willie had left the family, and Sarah commented, "The children do far better without him."[65] The youngest two members of the Penfield household were girls, Silena and Anna's cousin, Mary. Sarah planned to take Mary back to Ohio when they returned, as she was being "sponsored" by the Columbia (Ohio) Sabbath School.[66]

The children all attended school until four in the afternoon, and then on Friday and Saturday the girls helped Sarah with the labor-intensive laundry; the boys helped tend the garden in which the Penfields grew yams and sugar cane and were in the process of planting seeds that had been sent from Ohio.[67] The Penfields also instructed the children in "unobjectionable games . . . often giving them exercises that draw out the mind as well as interest and amuse it."[68] The pleasure Sarah derived from the children and the importance she assigned to what she and her husband were doing by adopting them provided enough reason to keep them even when the cost of feeding and clothing the extra family members meant that the couple went into debt. How the children felt about the fact that they had been sent to live with the Penfields remains unanswered. In one case, Sarah noted that one of the girls in her house, Margaret Williams, was "neither bright nor smart but her grandmother is very anxious to have her learn how to do things."[69] It is clear that the girls were expected to work for their board, clothing, and food expenses, and they aided in the difficult work of keeping the house in order. Bigelow wrote to his brother that housekeeping was a battle against chiggers, ticks, lice, ants, termites, and rats that "run in troops over and through the house at night, making more noise than a parcel of school children and doing such damage as they choose."[70]

While the children were tasked with labor when not in school, they were not considered servants in the Penfield family, which became evident not long after they joined the mission. One evening, missionary Charles Starbuck joined the Penfields for dinner, and he was appalled at the Penfields' practice of allowing the Jamaican children to eat the same food with them at the same table. According to Sarah Penfield, "He went on about it at such a rate and acted so cross that it made me quite miserable and I thought perhaps we had best have the children wait when he was here." Her husband begrudgingly agreed with her, and as the couple had not yet a table large enough to fit their six children along with guests, it made practical sense. The next time Starbuck paid the Penfields a visit, the new table and linens had arrived, making it easy for everyone to fit at the same table. In spite of this (and perhaps to spite Starbuck) Sarah "set the table for all again," eliciting the expected response: "and oh, how mad he was. A *child* for acting so would have gotten a sound flogging." When the children joined the adults in the sitting room after dinner, which Sarah liked "so we may see that they use their time properly," Starbuck became even more piqued. Sarah Penfield defended her actions, noting that if the children were left to their own devices, as they were at the other stations, she would feel like she was failing in her "duty." Inviting the children to dine at the family table and to join the adults in the sitting room was a means of exercising control over them, but in a more hands-on way than the tactics used by the other missionaries, who insisted on "civilizing" through enunciating clear divisions between themselves and black Jamaicans. Even though the cost taxed the Penfields financially, they both thought it critical to their missionary work to give "them as good as we have ourselves."[71]

The issue of the dinner table did not disappear. The degree of interest taken by the missionaries over this question shows how the missionaries understood domesticity to be central to the civilizing mission. The Penfields found allies in some of their fellow missionaries, usually the younger ones whose attitudes toward "prejudice against color" was "preferable to those of the other brethren."[72] In October 1859, Bigelow got into a discussion with Heman Hall's wife, Sophronia, about the situation. He learned that her family's decision to make the children "live on yam and fish" instead of the "variety of food they use at their own table" was cheaper and enabled them to support more children, and she felt that "the children themselves would be generally better satisfied to eat by themselves than with the mission family." Also, the Halls did not want to "foster pride in the children" for fear that they might "consider themselves our equals if we allow them to share our meals."[73] To Bigelow Penfield's annoyance, Sophronia Hall also referred to the children as "servants." In a striking statement about his abolitionist colleagues, Penfield noted that the other missionaries thought that even "training of the right sort" could not change black Jamaicans' inferiority.[74] Sophronia and Heman Hall invoked a different mode of domesticity in their mission household, which contrasted with the Penfield family as well as the mission household of Mary Dean. The Halls used the domestic setting to emphasize racial and social distance rather than drawing on domesticity to work for racial integration. To borrow a phrase from Albert Hurtado's study of colonial California, the interracial mission households were filled with "intimate frontiers" that many in the mission refused to cross.[75]

In addition to showing the different ideas of domesticity and civilizing, the dispute illustrated how the older ministers felt the need to control how younger families organized their mission households. The Penfields continued running their family as they thought best, and in March 1860, only a couple of weeks after Sarah had given birth to their daughter Mary Cowles Penfield, Loren Thompson stopped in to stay with the couple on his way to Kingston. According to Sarah, who was at the time bedridden after her difficult labor, "He gave us such a talking to about our treating of the native children. He said we were losing the confidence of the rest of the mission, that we should find ourselves isolated from the rest of the mission if we persisted, and . . . that we should ruin the children."[76] Thompson had started into his speech in Sarah's "sickroom" and while Bigelow convinced him to go walk around outside to finish what he wanted to say, it still upset Sarah and she had a relapse of fever. Worried about what might happen to them within the mission, the Penfields decided that they would make the children eat separately when the other missionaries came to visit. The Penfields' allies, the Wilsons, agreed. Limited space prevented them from sharing one table, but they had their "children eat in another room but the door is open between the two and they have meat and other things as in the family," wrote Sarah Penfield, and would only do differently "when other missionaries were there."[77] In agreeing to abide by the other missionaries' rules during visits, the dispute was resolved, at least on the surface. Loren Thompson continued for many months to express his grief "about the course we are taking with our native children," which Thompson found to be "a continual rebuke" against him.[78] The missionaries, male and female, all saw the family table and the more general manner of running the mission households to be a battleground on two fronts: the fight between the white Americans over control of the mission and the need to win more black Jamaican souls for the side of civilization.

What did the missionaries see as the consequences of bad domesticity and lapses in discipline? They feared licentiousness would prevail in the households that ran on insufficient discipline. Charles Venning complained that Seth Wolcott had been too permissive in allowing immoral men to work for him at Richmond and to attend the school. In his own defense, Wolcott insisted, "We do not retain in our employ a thief; nor one living in concubinage and refusing to marry." Indeed, enforcing these rules for his laborers had "hastened several couple[s] into lawful wedlock." Although Wolcott agreed that he could not "speak of the virtue of our laborers in those higher terms of praise," he could "thank God they are no worse." To defend himself even further, Wolcott added a biting criticism of his own about the Penfields' household: "*Your* missionaries, I believe, endeavor earnestly to train their servants as they would their children. But pardon me for saying that their success as with other excellent families in producing persons of desirable social virtue has been lamentably smaller as all will testify." One of Richmond's graduates, a black Jamaican man, had been teaching at Bigelow Penfield's Brainerd Station. When the missionaries voted in favor of giving him a fixed salary, "It was out that he was about to be a father of Bro. Penfield's choice servant girl. Thus terminated his and her relations with us as missionaries." Wolcott asked, "Shall I say that this escalated from Bro. P.'s lax discipline—want of attention to the *morals* of his family—or his voluntary immoral surroundings? Never."[79] Wolcott's decades of experience as a missionary had led him to the conclusion that no amount of domestic influence, whether in the strictest missionary household or in the sentimentalized homes of the younger missionary couples, could drown out the broader immoral culture of slavery. At this late point in the mission's history, Wolcott showed signs that he had resigned himself to the fact that it was unlikely that so small and so poorly funded a mission could change the hearts and minds of very many Jamaicans. The question of civilizing tactics—of domesticity—was academic. The way that a handful of American missionaries ran their households could do little to transform Jamaican culture.

In the Jamaica Mission, the more updated domestic ideology brought to the island by Sarah Penfield and her husband conflicted with the older ideas of Loren Thompson and his colleagues. The men had never been very open to granting white women any leadership in the mission family, and when challenged by Mary Dean or the much younger missionary wife Sarah Penfield, the mission men refused to put up with challenges to their authority and their years of experience. The white women in the Jamaica Mission, however, offered a different model of the civilizing mission that reflected their attachment to the ideology of domesticity as a way to preserve liberty and social order. Like northern women committed to domesticity, many of the women missionaries in Jamaica, and the single women in particular, believed that keeping a close watch on black Jamaican souls through exercising maternal power worked more effectively than the strict disciplinary measures of the ministers.

The Jamaica Mission provides a concrete case study for how northern white women put domesticity into practice in the civilizing mission and in how they used domesticity to put themselves on the same plane as the mission's men. We can see how these two components of domestic ideology were often interrelated, although not always, as the case of Sarah Blakeley Moffat showed. For both Mary Dean and Sarah Penfield, the domestic claims that, as white women, their duty was to "domesticate" foreign elements and to keep their homes pure was inseparable from their claims to greater authority in the mission family. The antebellum instances of white women's special duties continued through at least the early twentieth century as scholars of European and American women have argued that feminists often advocated for suffrage and equality by contrasting themselves with nonwhite men, both at home and in the empire, and by emphasizing their centrality to the project of racial uplift.[80]

The ideology of domesticity, as enacted in the Jamaica Mission, also points to other conclusions. First, the women who did not use domesticity but who still sought greater power in the mission—Mary Howe and Urania Hunt—were both labeled insane and sent home. Also, even as domesticity aided in the creation of the categories of "civilized" and "uncivilized" based on gender practices and the manner of keeping house in different cultures, domesticity also drew on a sentimental discourse of feeling, love, and sympathy that allowed the mission's women to avoid talking about discipline and instead conduct the civilizing mission on different terms. While this in no way changed the power dynamic of the missionary encounter, it allowed the missionary women to create ties of affection between themselves and black Jamaicans that the older mission's men often saw as counterproductive to the mission's goals.

7. Revival, Rebellions, and Colonial Subordination

Beginning a letter in October 1865, missionary Seth Wolcott regretted the lack of "*good news!!*" to convey to the AMA. Instead all he had to offer was news that could only be called "*sad, sader* [sic]," and, Wolcott ominously wrote, "soon it will be *sadest* [sic]."[1] He felt frustrated that church membership and school attendance were in decline and that fewer people seemed to obey the ministers' commands. During a conversation with "one good brother," he had inquired, "Why do these things—God's word, which we preach, seem to have no effect with the people? *Why will they not hear us?*" According to Wolcott, the church member answered him plain and simple: "'Minister, they do hear you but they don't believe what you say.' 'They think there [sic] sins you preach about are very little things. God will never notice them. They are no great harm.'"[2] Black Jamaicans who attended the mission churches simply did not believe the ministers' threats. The Jamaicans who had hosted the Americans for decades tolerated their American neighbors and participated in the mission community, but very few had embraced the American idea of Christian civilization or the stakes of failing to uphold the morality the missionaries expected.

The larger context of Wolcott's letter puts it into a different light. Two weeks before, laborers in St. Thomas-in-the-East had stormed the courthouse in Morant Bay to protest the government's revitalized attempts to remove them from the land they claimed as their own. In the following days, the violence spread into other rural regions as frustrated workers burned estate houses and, in some instances, mission buildings. The island's colonial governor, Edward John Eyre, responded with rapid and brutal force, reported Wolcott, "ordering troops from other islands, calling on man-of-war vessels and sending troops to the Bays and important points on the coast." Additionally, Eyre declared martial law for the parishes of Surrey County, the eastern third of the island. At first relieved that the violence had not spread, days later Wolcott encountered police and others "armed to the teeth" looking for rebels who had taken refuge at Richmond. Rumors spread like wildfire, and the facts of the rebellion and the unexpected connections the American missionaries had with one of the leaders, George William Gordon, surfaced as well. Writing amid the confusion of the rebellion's aftermath and the uncertainty of what this would mean for the mission, Wolcott concluded his report with a prayer: "May God have mercy on us and stay the effusion of blood."[3]

During the weeks immediately following the Morant Bay Rebellion, the American missionaries feared for their lives. It was the first time the ministers felt endangered by the island's people rather than by diseases or inclement weather. They blamed the rebellion on Native Baptist ministers and other black leaders whom they believed spread superstitions among the masses. These men, the missionaries averred, would be the ruin of the island. The ministers wholeheartedly supported the governor's actions to put down the rioters, even when it became known that hundreds of alleged rebels had been rounded up and executed without any semblance of a trial. While many in London and the United States were shocked by Eyre's disproportionate response, the American missionaries stood their ground, telling George Whipple that he and his fellow AMA officials simply could not understand circumstances on the ground from the distance of their New York rooms. In spite of all of the missionaries' best efforts, their Christian civilization had not taken root in Jamaica, and the events at Morant Bay seemed a dark sign of the mission's future. For many missionaries on the island, including the Americans, Morant Bay represented black people's ungrateful response to the gift of emancipation.

This chapter turns to the mission's final years and the way major events like Morant Bay and the American Civil War as well as more local happenings led to the mission's slow decline. The 1860s began with an apparent boon; the excitement of a religious revival led many new converts into the mission's churches and reinvigorated the American ministers' belief in their work. The Great Revival, however, drew on Myalism as much as the evangelicalism of English and American missionaries. The revival leaders fostered black-led churches, and the Native Baptist congregations increased in numbers and popularity in early 1861. On the other hand, white missionaries' experiences in the revival led them to question whether or not they could fully erase the "heathen" relics of the freed people's African pasts.[4] Not long after the Great Revival began, war broke out in the United States. The mission used the plight of American freed people to urge their church members to become more independent and self-sufficient, arguing that these new freed people needed the AMA's money more than did the Jamaicans. Indeed, the Civil War pushed the Jamaica Mission to consider its purpose and whether or not it might not be transferred to an English society. During the war, no new ministers were sent out, and a number of those already in Jamaica left the island to return to the United States. Understaffed and underfunded, the mission employed fewer than five Americans after 1865, a sharp drop from the mission's former numbers, and the bulk of the mission's work was conducted by Jamaicans—white, brown, and black. The American mission became a Jamaican institution.

The Great Revival in Jamaica was, as historian Robert Stewart puts it, "the consolidation of the synthesis of evangelical Christianity and African religion."[5] The Myalist character of the revival was not immediately apparent to the island's white missionaries. Sarah Penfield, for example, saw it as evidence of "the power of the Lord" that she thought was being "felt in an unusual degree throughout the world in these days," and she saw it as a sign that "He will go conquering the nations of the earth until every knee shall bow and every tongue confess that Jesus is the Christ."[6] The first reports in the missionary letters remarked on religious revivals taking hold in the island's western coastal parishes, and by January 1861, Loren Thompson reported that he had held a joint meeting with a Presbyterian congregation on a Thursday, and "the house could not hold all the people that came"; on the following Sunday, "The church were [sic] more than ever in earnest and solemnly pledged to each other a more faithful life and godly work." The spirit of God, Thompson felt, had finally come to emancipated Jamaica.[7]

At the same time as religious enthusiasm grew in Jamaica, war seemed inevitable in the United States, and the *American Missionary* pointed to the revival in Jamaica as a positive light on an otherwise dark horizon. The editors did feel the need to provide a cautionary note preceding the ministers' accounts of the revival: "that it presents some strange features will be readily seen, but we think that no one, after perusing these letters, can deny that it is a genuine work of the Holy Spirit."[8] The following letters reported an increased ecumenical spirit. Loren Thompson reported that an organization named the Evangelical Alliance had planned a prayer week during which a different mission station would play host to neighboring churches each day, all united to pray "for the outpouring of the spirit on the world at large." Thompson mentioned that even members of a recently dissolved Native Baptist church "are seeking to unite with us." Thompson's colleague, Charles Starbuck, gave a report about his correspondence with a Scottish Presbyterian minister at the nearby Rose Hill mission station. The missionary, Mr. Boyd, told Starbuck about one of his congregants, "a shy, backward person" who suddenly "broke out into the most extatic [sic] strains of rejoicing that I have ever heard from a human being." Boyd had been amazed with "the clearness and purity and elevation of her thoughts ... which was all the more striking from its contrast with the broad negro *patois* which she used." Boyd's congregation was also praying for a similar spirit to reach Starbuck's Brainerd church.[9] The revival's spirit had brought a temporary end to the "sectarianism" that the American ministers so often used to explain the failures in discipline. Lax missionaries and the prevalence of Native Baptists, after all, had provided alternative churches for American converts who had been disciplined. Now, these differences seemed unimportant.

If the revival brought about a new ecumenical spirit, the ministers also emphasized how the conversions pointed to a new moral order. Perhaps anticipating criticisms of "animalistic" blacks undergoing a primitive religious experience, the ministers made sure to note how the converts turned their back on "barbaric" practices of fornication and adultery. The growing attendance at Eliot Church on Sunday morning prompted Thompson to hold an inquirers meeting that evening to give attendees the opportunity to come forward and publicly confess their past sins as the first step on the road toward forgiveness and church membership. Thompson's recorded confessions focused on sins of the flesh, the sins that the mission cared about the most. "Such confessions of sin," he wrote excitedly, "I have never heard before in Jamaica":

> One married woman confessed among other things (her husband being present,) that she had kept with *four* married men and *eight* bachelors, during which time, she had separated from her husband. Another unknown young woman confessed that she had stolen, another woman [confessed to cheating on her] husband by whom she had had two children and was soon to have a third—he being present,—also confessed to his wife and promises a new life. Another woman confessed to the sin of living in open fornication for years—her load was heavy—could live so no more, has left the man, etc. Another man confessed himself guilty of the sin of drunkenness and fornication before marriage, also lying, theft, etc., etc. More than 20 thus confessed their sins, old and young.[10]

Thompson emphasized the candor of these confessions and their public nature, since this had long been important to how the missionaries envisioned public morality and the correcting of sinful behavior. Also telling in Thompson's account is the degree to which sex, more than the other sins of drunkenness, theft, or lying, lay at the root of the confessed sins. A repudiation of an unholy gender order, as much as a host of other sins, was the best illustration for the American ministers of a truly reformed and a truly civilized soul. Indeed, in March 1861, Charles Venning wrote with the fervent hope that "this gracious visitation should result in sanctifying and elevating the people, in their family and social relations, and thus lay the foundation of all that is good in the future."[11]

At Eliot Church, Loren Thompson focused on the children in his congregation and led a revival meeting aimed specifically at these young souls. Since the early 1850s, the missionaries had been intent on reforming the "rising generation," and the revival mood seemed to have given them a chance to affect the island's youth. Of thirty-five children attending one meeting, including Thompson's daughter Lizzie, all but one "were more or less under convictions," he wrote, and "never have I witnessed such a scene." He described "so many little children all bathed in tears and some sobbing as though their hearts would break." While some of these children had Christian parents, Thompson feared for those who "are as lambs in the midst of wolves" and called on Lewis Tappan and others in the United States to pray for "these tender lambs." The most interesting child, a little girl named Naomi, had become so affected by her sense of sinfulness that she had had to leave her classroom because of her tears. This potential convert pleased Thompson, who wrote that this little girl was correcting her mother and older sister. Additionally, four "native children in our family" showed evidence of conversion, and he hoped "they have given their hearts to God."[12] While the manifestations of faith at Eliot might have been exactly what Thompson had long hoped to see, the revival moment as a whole gave rise to and reinforced Myal sects throughout the island and resulted in the dawning of a new era of Afro-Jamaican Christianity in the Zion Revival faith, one that hardly could be compared to the Congregational perfectionism the missionaries hoped would take hold.[13]

Bigelow Penfield wrote with similar expectations to his parents in Oberlin, Ohio. Penfield also noted the effect the revival had on his own spirituality. He found that "God is drawing very near my own soul and seeking to revive it," and he felt the need to confess to his mother and stepfather all the sins of his youth, telling them that if what he had done had been known at the time, "It would have been their duty to have excommunicated me." These sins ranged from not spending enough time at prayer to allowing "a mistake made in my favor [to] go uncorrected" to having a heart that "has been too often the abode of lust and impure thoughts." He asked that his letter be read aloud to everyone during a service at Oberlin's chapel so that his sins and repentance would be made known publicly. Bigelow's letter arrived along with a similar one from his wife, Sarah, who discussed her own spiritual failings and her hope to become a better Christian.[14] One of the mission's schoolteachers, Sarah Treat, also personally felt the effects of the revival. She had been with the mission for four months in May 1861, and she "thanked God ever since I came, for sending me here. He has turned me upside down by leading me to thinking instead of dreaming. I love and trust my heavenly father more than before."[15] Arriving in Jamaica during the height of the revival, Treat had the combined experience of adapting to a new place and undergoing a religious experience.

In contrast to the almost tangible religious excitement in these accounts, Seth Wolcott looked at the potential effects of the revival in more sober and material terms. In a letter written during the early stages of the Great Revival, he noted that while "there may be no general marked 'revival of religion' . . . there will be a higher order of religious development." In explaining what he meant, Wolcott elaborated that "the spirit of enterprise and industry is greatly increased . . . The people are cultivating for themselves much more largely—are supplying themselves with more and better material—are living better and everything seems tending to a higher civilization." Additionally, the earnings from the Richmond Estate's sugar crop were "over $50 weekly." Unlike his more emotional friend Loren Thompson, Seth Wolcott faced the religious enthusiasm creeping into the mission churches with a hope that order, industry, and financial growth would prevail.[16] Discipline and the family order would remain intact at Richmond, if Seth Wolcott had anything to do with it. Both Wolcott and his similarly minded colleague Heman Hall returned to the United States in the fall of 1860 and thus were not present to comment on the most fervent moments of the Great Revival. If Wolcott had been in Jamaica to witness the revival, he might have had a change of heart.

By the end of May 1861, the excitement about the revival from earlier in the year had turned into a more mixed appraisal. British missionary John Clark wrote a letter for the *American Missionary* in which he commented that while many people were "truly converted" during the recent revivals, "Satan at once began to sow his tares and they speedily sprung up. The minds of thousands of the most ignorant and superstitions of the people were filled with alarm . . . [They] gave up work and wandered about from place to place." Obeah men preyed on these wandering souls, claiming to have authority because they had been "visited by the spirit of God."[17] Bigelow Penfield was the only one of the American ministers to continue to speak highly of the revival spirit, even as the "bands" alluded to in Clark's letter appeared. His wife, Sarah Penfield, was more suspicious. Unlike the earliest days of this revival, Sarah Penfield wrote, these bands incorporated "superstitions and odd notions," including the idea that "judgment is just at hand, and interpreting the second chapter of Joel as applying to these times." Unlike the older missionaries who had experienced the Second

Great Awakening and its aftermath of Millerites, Mormons, and various other manifestations of the "burned-over district," Sarah Penfield was shocked by this turn of events. Not only did the revivalists preach about the coming day of judgment, they also claimed to be "favored with communication from the other world." Sarah reported the unfortunate news that "many of the young people who had joined the inquiry class went off to meet some of these bands and were stricken." Bigelow had fortunately "been able to keep them from most of these delusions," and "one by one we have seen them coming into the glorious liberty of the Sons of God." In an article published in the *American Missionary*, Bigelow confirmed that "there is an immense deal of evil, but as I believe, much more good in the movement," as the "sin of concubinage and fornication is being torn and broken up, root and branch, and multitudes are getting married on all sides."[18]

In early 1861, the Penfields faced a more immediate threat in the person of the former AMA missionary, Julius Beardslee. As one of the original Oberlin ministers in Jamaica, Beardslee had remained a trustee for some of the mission's schools and churches even after he left his post to become a teacher at the Mico Institute in Kingston in 1846. His "religious somersault" from Congregationalism to Campbellism and the Disciples of Christ during a visit to the United States in 1857 turned him into a direct threat to the mission.[19] The Disciples looked to create a primitive church movement that resembled the spirit-led ethos of the early church, and they also embraced adult baptism, a factor that would make Beardslee's newfound faith fit in among Jamaica's mostly Baptist population.[20] According to George Allen, an Oberlin professor who taught at Richmond for a year, Beardslee "claims to be the first man to introduce the true Gospel into Jamaica," and his lack of church discipline illustrated his real purpose to get "numbers and power on his side to effect his ends."[21] The AMA missionaries disapproved of Beardslee's religious doctrines, and they prohibited him from preaching at their churches, but this only angered him more. He informed Bigelow Penfield that he would preach regardless, "to all who wished to hear."[22]

In the wake of the revival, Beardslee had won enough support from the Oberlin church members to become the church's pastor. His success at Oberlin revealed important aspects of how the mission had conducted its work differently over time. The reason that Beardslee could take over the mission's property traced back to the original deed for the station. The usurped Penfield explained, "The deed of the station was so worded that whoever could get two thirds of the members to give him a call to become their minister, with the concurrence of two thirds of the trustees, could have lawful possession of the premises. This Mr. Beardslee obtained, and we of course were obliged to yield."[23] This sort of arrangement where the church's members and trustees had the ultimate say about whether or not they would keep one of the missionary ministers harkened back to the mission's early days. In the first decade of the mission, the American ministers served at the pleasure of the black deacons, elected trustees, and prominent church members who had sway among their peers. This setup worked well with the ministers' abolitionist beliefs to promote black self-reliance and independence, but it created situations that conflicted with the social control called on for the civilizing mission.

Over the next several years, Beardslee was a constant irritant on the fringe of the Jamaica Mission. After his success at Oberlin, he targeted the congregation at Chesterfield, where Charles Venning served as the minister. This more recent addition to the mission, however, could not be taken over by Beardslee because the black church leaders had no claim to the property as they had in the original stations. This did not stop Beardslee, who wrote a letter to Venning that "wherever the way was open" he would appear with his Campbellite message. When the AMA missionaries warned him against trespassing on their property, Beardslee reportedly told them "that if that was trespass he hoped to commit it as long as he lived."[24] With echoes of John Hyde and his desire to follow his own plan, regardless of others, Julius Beardslee's intentions to operate outside the usual courtesies concerned his former colleagues. Yet in contrast to the Hyde imbroglio of 1850, none in the mission defended Beardslee or joined his side to defend his vocation and rights to religious independence. Men like Seth Wolcott, Charles Venning, and Loren Thompson, who had been in Jamaica in 1850 and sided with Hyde for a time, had learned a lesson about the danger of unbridled independence, even when it was claimed by one of their fellow white men. For the younger cohort of missionaries, like the Penfields, Beardslee was more of a frightening figure than a fellow traveler, a relic of an older age of abolitionism and perhaps a representation of what one might become after straying from the path of religious orthodoxy, especially in a place like Jamaica.

Like other white clergy in Jamaica at the time of the Great Revival, the Americans felt deceived when it became clear that their version of Christianity was only a small part of the awakening. The revival certainly contained elements of evangelical Protestantism, but it also included spirit possession and other characteristics that fell into the missionaries' category of "superstitious heathenism." If the American mission on the island had always been marked by upswings and collapses, the period immediately following the revival brought the mission to one of its lowest ebbs. Not only were the ministers confronted with Jamaicans who had stopped listening to them, the AMA and many of the mission's American supporters had shifted their focus away from the small Jamaica Mission and toward the more immediate crisis of the Civil War and the state of ex-slaves in the American South.

The American missionaries prayed for the Union's victory in the Civil War, but they also feared for their own existence as it became clear that the AMA would be playing a major role in relief efforts for refugees and freedmen. War had begun in April 1861, and by the end of the year, the Union Army had made advances into Virginia and it had also occupied the Sea Islands off the coast of South Carolina. The Virginia slaves who fled their plantations to get behind the federal lines and those in South Carolina whose Confederate masters had fled were an instant dilemma: not yet officially free, these men, women, and children also no longer had masters. After some deliberation, the federal government declared them "contraband." The editors of the *American Missionary* expressed their dislike of this term, and they suggested that "colored refugees" be used instead. "We prefer this designation of the people who are fleeing to our camps and fleets, to that of 'Contrabands,' 'Freedmen,' or 'Vagrants,' because the first implies property in man, the second describes the ex-slaves as actually free, when their condition is otherwise, and the third indicates a degradation and status which the Refugees do not deserve."[25] The AMA leaped into action, sending a missionary to Hampton, Virginia, in September 1861, and deploying another to Port Royal, South Carolina.[26]

These two men began to lay the groundwork for the decades-long missionary efforts that the AMA would organize in the South. In New York and Boston, the AMA joined with other philanthropic organizations to recruit teachers and ministers for this work, and they ended up with a diverse collection of abolitionists and entrepreneurs, as Willie Lee Rose eloquently describes in *Rehearsal for Reconstruction*.[27] Although its participants and organizers often thought of the Port Royal experiment as the first of its kind—the first to show how a Yankee character could be planted in the hearts of contraband—the Jamaica Mission, founded on similar principles, entered its fourteenth year as a part of the AMA. The end of slavery in the United States brought a different tone to the Jamaica Mission, and additionally it gave the members of the mission a more receptive audience in the United States.

The ministers in Jamaica took advantage of American emancipation to encourage their mission churches to become more self-sufficient, the longstanding goal that had been in place since David Ingraham's first foray into missionary work. Thornton Bigelow Penfield had witnessed the home front firsthand when he returned to the United States in 1864. His wife, Sarah, had gone home some months before due to ill health, and her condition had worsened. After her death in April 1864, Penfield stopped using his middle name, Bigelow, and signed his letters with his first name, Thornton. Leaving his small daughter with his parents, a bereft Penfield returned to Jamaica and recommitted himself to missionary work. While in the United States he had met with the AMA's officers and had gleaned the changes that were in the works. For example, his church at Brainerd and the chapel at Eliot both needed new roofs, and the task of paying for these would fall on the church members. "I on my part," Penfield wrote, "laid the matter before the Congregation at Brainerd. I urged the time they had enjoyed freedom and gospel privileges and the example of the freedmen in America, etc., etc."[28] The congregation responded positively, which "surprised" Penfield, and he was even happier when donations increased.

While Penfield found that American emancipation had helped push his stations toward self-sufficiency, Seth Wolcott pointed out the more difficult side of the AMA's retrenchment from the Jamaica Mission. He felt that it was detrimental to the mission for there to be "a sense of insecurity as to the permanence both of ministers and teachers," a condition he attributed to himself and his colleagues. "We have perhaps helped to create this feeling, in our earnest efforts to induce them to rely more on themselves setting forth that the Freedmen in America would need all the resources of the AMA on their behalf."[29] The contrasting perspectives of Penfield and Wolcott probably reflected the way many of the people associated with the mission felt. On the one hand, the decreased funding from the AMA enabled "native assistants" to be appointed as teachers and, later, as ministers. Children who had come of age living in the missionary families and attending the mission schools would have steady employment where once an American teacher would have been. On the other hand, the "insecurity" pointed out by Wolcott would have raised questions about the viability of the mission with no more American support or staff. The Americans supplied schoolbooks, hymnals, and newspapers, and they had been instrumental in getting funding from the government for missionary schools.

The Americans could leave the mission and return home, but what would become of the people whom they left behind? The attachments formed in mission families could be intense, as the example of one Richmond student, Mary Ann Lamb, demonstrated. Lamb had grown up living with the Thompsons at Eliot Station, the closest church to the Richmond School. When the Thompson family left the island in 1858 to return to the United States because of their failing health, they arranged for the twenty-year-old Mary Ann to move in with the Vennings at Chesterfield where, Thompson wrote, she could assist "him as a member of *his family* and will continue to do so till we return." Lamb accompanied her former family to Kingston for their departure to New York, and according to Thompson, she "did things which we had to reprove her for." As they separated on bad terms, Lamb apologized for her behavior in a letter that Thompson received in Ohio, and he found it an exemplary case of how useful family ties were to the civilizing mission.[30]

Lamb's letter also hints at her own internal conflicts of being torn between her Jamaican family and the mission family, and the complicated position for children raised in the mission households. In her letter, Lamb apologized to the Thompsons, writing that after she left Kingston, "I felt crushed and that I would sink beneath my own wickedness, it was such a burden to me." Whatever she had done in Kingston—perhaps drinking rum with friends or maybe rebuking the Thompsons for leaving her—Lamb considered disobeying Thompson's wishes for her future. She thought about staying at "home" or with her mother who lived near Brainerd Station, instead of going to the Venning family at Chesterfield. Lamb then had a sudden change of heart, going from "total darkness" to seeking "Christ in earnest, and I hope, with humble broken heart." In spite of overcoming this particular trial, Lamb expressed the same sentiments often voiced by evangelicals: "Although I am among Christians I feel so fearful all the time, I am in the world, just like a little boat on the mighty deep, knowing not where and when a storm of sin and temptation may be coming from." Yet her spiritual trials and backsliding incident had only strengthened her faith, and Lamb declared her intentions to prepare to become a missionary for Africa.[31] The declining interest that the AMA showed in the Jamaica Mission drove the ministers to try and create self-sufficiency, but at times, their attempts to distance themselves from the world they had helped to create came as a betrayal to people who had sacrificed their role in the community at large to join the mission.

Emancipation in the United States not only changed the dynamics of the mission in Jamaica, but it also renewed interest in the AMA's work since the missionaries could be firsthand witnesses of the workings of emancipation. The members of the Jamaica Mission realized their importance, and they found themselves in a slightly different light as the question of immediate emancipation was now really on the table. From the war's beginning, the *American Missionary* advocated for immediate emancipation. In June 1861, the newspaper ran an article noting that "whenever immediate emancipation has taken place it has been attended with peaceful and prosperous results. This had been fully demonstrated in the West Indies."[32] Other American journalists took up this question as well.[33] Indeed, they had their own "proof" in the form of missionaries in Jamaica, although the ministers brought forth quite different interpretations of emancipation. For some older missionaries who had come of age during the 1830s, black independence had been emancipation's greatest goal; the younger members of the mission, however, tended to emphasize the compliant nature of blacks who were easily led and governed.

In response to a request for information about the Jamaica Mission, Loren Thompson wrote a letter to a church in Newark, New Jersey, and the minister read it aloud to his congregation. Thompson affirmed that "there can be no doubt as to the beneficial results of emancipation to the mass of the people." Not only had the process been relatively smooth, he insisted that most of the reported problems of emancipation in Jamaica had come from "the bad management of the planters immediately after emancipation, and the want of capital." Now, however, "The slanders heaped upon this land by the enemies of the colored man will soon pass into oblivion." The religious excitement of the revival, "the increased domestic comforts, and the increase of exports and imports" all bode well for Jamaica's future. Further, Thompson made sure to emphasize the expansion of independent landowners on the island, and, echoing the early 1840s hopes for the Jamaica Mission, he linked together landownership with families and gendered order. "Thousands have become freeholders—settled in families, and begun to act like men and women, not slaves." The growth of piety, economic stability, and family life signaled emancipation's success, and Thompson also spoke favorably of the emergence of a political system "administered for the mass of the people as well as for the few," as the Colonial Assembly included "a goodly number of colored men." Thompson erased the distinctions of nation when he posed a question to the Reverend Woodhull: "Are the colored people of Newark better off by being free? So are the people of Jamaica."[34] Although more generally positive than his more private letters to the AMA, Thompson still remarked on the same markers of civilization and the end of slavery that had motivated him when he arrived in Jamaica in 1844. Landownership, Christian families, independence, and self-governance all entered into his account of Jamaican freed people.

A very different description of emancipation's positive qualities came from Sherman Wilson, a teacher who joined the mission in late 1859. A younger man than Thompson, who had come of age at a different moment in the abolitionist movement, Wilson failed to mention manly independence at all. Wilson identified his audience and what he assumed to be their fears: "I have seen many [Americans] who said they would be in favor of emancipation, but who deemed it very unsafe to liberate the slaves in our own land." White Americans did not worry about whether or not blacks would remain in dependency, Wilson believed; instead they concerned themselves about their own safety and about whether or not free black people would seek to be integrated into white society. Wilson saw it as his duty to counter these anti-emancipation arguments: "I do not know where a more quiet and influential people can be found, than the emancipated slaves of this island." Wilson went on to list the positive qualities of freed people in Jamaica, although his remarks bore little resemblance to the lofty plans once articulated by Amos Phelps and reiterated in Loren Thompson's letter. Wilson attested to the fact that freed people were "law-abiding and loyal, easily controlled and governed." The people were "ignorant and unenlightened (the result of the bondage to which they have been doomed)," but it was therefore that much more remarkable that "a people so ignorant are so easily controlled." White Americans who feared that "slaves would be too intrusive" or "would make themselves more intimate than would be desirable" should know that "no other people 'know their place' better than they, or are more cautious against intrusion."[35]

Wilson's praise for Jamaican freed people had little to do with manly independence and instead described them as passive people, eager for white oversight. The contrasting letters penned by Thompson and Wilson spoke to the way that the missionaries' views of the civilizing mission often depended on their age. A close friend to the Penfields, Sherman Wilson spoke for the younger generation of missionaries who had promulgated a new form of missionary domesticity structured around the idea that close supervision would help to "civilize" young Jamaicans where the older ministers' harsher methods of discipline would not. Just as Wilson and his like-minded colleagues wanted to raise compliant and obedient children in their homes, they also viewed adult Jamaicans in a similar light. These differences would be erased during the period of the Morant Bay Rebellion, although as soon as the danger had passed, the conflict reemerged around the governance of the Richmond School in 1866.

Months after the end of the Civil War, the American missionaries reported on the widespread drought that had affected the island. Missionary Joseph Fisher reported that the drought and a sickness had hurt his church members' incomes, and consequently things were at a low state at Brandon Hill.[36] At Chesterfield, Charles Venning dealt with a Native Baptist congregation that Julius Beardslee had reinvigorated. The Baptists had opened a school, and, according to Venning, they forbade their church members from sending their children to Venning's Chesterfield school.[37] For his part, Seth Wolcott had observed more specific signs of the impending hostilities that broke out at Morant Bay: "There seems to be a feeling of uneasiness general among the peasantry and in some places threatening signs of seditionary movements against the planters and government."[38] Since the late 1840s, enough black Jamaican men had joined with the island's colored and Jewish population in a loose alignment called the Town party, and the elected assemblymen often challenged the policies of the elite whites in the Planter party. The Town party gained in numbers in the 1850s, and many of the island's whites worried about a future when black men, a majority of the population, would rule. The Assembly passed a law in 1859 requiring each voter to pay a poll tax, effectively reducing the black electorate. From the late 1840s, the planter-dominated Assembly had shifted the tax burden away from themselves, and through import taxes and loopholes, the majority of the island's income came from freeholders and wage laborers. More recently, the costs of imported goods had skyrocketed during the American Civil War. As Thomas Holt notes, the "overall cost of living on the island rose sixty percent between 1859–61 and 1865."[39]

The Morant Bay Rebellion grew out of black Jamaicans' frustration with imperial policy and the legal hindrances they believed stood in the way of their full freedom. The island's attempts to reclaim and sell land abandoned by proprietors yet occupied by freed people lay at the heart of the uprising at Morant Bay. During a Saturday court session in Morant Bay in the parish of St. Thomas-in-the-East, the crowd protested when they felt a man had been unjustly punished for an assault charge. The protest gained momentum, and two days later, freeholders from the nearby village of Stony Gut showed up in court in defense of one of their neighbors, a farmer who had been arrested for trespassing after his land on an abandoned estate had been claimed and sold. On Tuesday, October 10, black police officers arrived in Stony Gut to arrest a local leader and a Native Baptist minister, Paul Bogle, and the villagers stopped the police, beating them. Bogle and his supporters petitioned the island's governor, Edward Eyre, for fair treatment under the law. The men and women at Stony Gut protested their dissatisfaction with the post-emancipation society they lived in and the failure of many of the island's white and colored lawmakers to live up to the former slaves' vision of a free country. Indeed, the subject had become the talk of the nation in the early part of 1865 as a letter penned by the secretary of the English Baptist Missionary Society, Edward Underhill, had been widely circulated in Jamaica. Underhill's letter complaining about the poor state of things in Jamaica had originally been written to the Colonial Office in London, and once it reached Jamaica's Governor Eyre, he distributed copies to whites throughout the island to gather their opinions. The renewed power of the Native Baptist churches during the Great Revival, a season of drought and sickness that had increased poverty and discontent, and the discussions of the "Underhill letter" around the island all came together in Stony Gut on Tuesday night, October 10.[40]

Bogle gave a letter to be sent to Spanish Town with an explanation of his feelings: "an outrageous assault was committed upon us by the policemen of this parish, by order of the Justices, which occasion an outbreaking, for which warrants have been issued against innocent parties of which we were compelled to resist," and the Stony Gut farmers asked for protection from the governor since they were "her Majesty's loyal subjects." The message to the governor "renders Bogle's intentions enigmatic," as Thomas Holt has argued.[41] Was he seeking recognition and justice, as his words indicated, or the more bloody vengeance of his actions that followed? On Wednesday afternoon, October 11, around five hundred men and women from Stony Gut entered into Morant Bay. The local official, the custos, guarded the Morant Bay courthouse, but his troops could not hold off Bogle and his supporters. The custos read the riot act to the angry crowd, who attacked him with a barrage of stones, but then the militia fired on the protesters. Bogle's supporters surged forward, ultimately killing the custos as well as a minister from the Anglican church, along with seven soldiers and over twenty civilians. Rumors circulated that the rebels had every intention of killing every white and brown person on the island, and the white missionaries were at the top of their list. This alleged revolution, however, never developed, because Governor Eyre responded with swift force on October 12. Eyre declared martial law for the parishes in the east, and he deployed ships carrying soldiers along with the island's Maroon soldiers; these men killed several hundred people, including Bogle and one of the governor's political enemies, the colored assemblyman, George William Gordon. Eyre called for Gordon's arrest in Kingston, and then Gordon was brought to Morant Bay where he was executed after a perfunctory military trial. News of the rebellion and of the expansive plot to kill all of the whites spread rapidly around Jamaica and back to England. Unlike the whites in Jamaica who supported Eyre and praised his fast response, whites in England looked at Eyre's actions as contrary to their own liberal and democratic principles of good governance. Eyre was recalled to England and investigated for his actions; ultimately he was pardoned for his actions and praised for preventing a major rebellion, even as they chastised him for imposing martial law for such an extended period of time.[42]

The American missionaries participated in the rumor mill, and Seth Wolcott sent an almost breathless letter to George Whipple in New York. Writing daily updates, Wolcott told of rioters yelling "no mercy here." Wolcott described the stories he had heard: "Some were pursued to their own homes and murdered in the presence of their wives and children—one minister and two of his sons thus perished. Another minister is said to have had his tongue cut out after he was dead, by the women." The rebellion had spread to Manchineal: "one Wesleyan minister said to be among the murdered victims."[43] Unsurprisingly, Wolcott focused on his fellow clerics, but he and his colleagues did not initially fear for themselves: "Almost to the present moment we have refused credit to the suspicion that the evil extended beyond the unfortunate locality." A week earlier, Wolcott wrote, he had been at Annotto Bay, "laughing at, as I then thought, the fears of alarmists." He continued, "Bad as I know many of our people to be I could not believe that I had near neighbors who could even approve of the least of what has been done—much less found to be plotting it." Yet things turned in a different direction when Wolcott had discovered that a man who had bought land at Richmond in the early 1860s had been apprehended, along with his daughter, who had been seen "wearing bloody garments with a large bundle of bloody clothing, gold chains, and sundry jewelry, etc. The property of the murdered people." According to Wolcott the police hanged this woman along with her mother at Annotto Bay on the evening of October 23; her father and her male companion had lesser punishments of fifty lashes.[44] Thornton Bigelow Penfield had a similar awakening when he learned from one of his church members at Brainerd, a constable, that he "had just apprehended a man who threatened the lives of Mr. Langbridge, my nearest white neighbor, and Mr. Rennie, Custos of St. Thos-Ye-Vale, living a little farther from me."[45]

The Americans were quick to lay the blame at the feet of the Native Baptists, just as Governor Eyre accused the English Baptist missionaries of being the root of the problem.[46] Wolcott insisted that "nothing short of an actual rising can convince me that the people under the influence of our mission can favorably contemplate sedition and murder." It was easy for him, however, to point the finger at "a few Native Baptists and the hatched and hatching Beardslee spawn who are ready for such work."[47] The connection linking Julius Beardslee to Morant Bay grew tighter when the American ministers heard of the execution of George William Gordon. "This Gordon," Wolcott reported, "has been operating about Hermitage and Chesterfield as a minister on Beardslee's account. He is or was a member of the House of Assembly, his chief aid at Morant Bay was a black preacher—one of those self-constitute independent fellows."[48] Penfield emphasized a similar point: "He was a large proprietor and professedly a great friend of the people and yet one who descended to the lowest and meanest trick to benefit his own pocket at their expense, and all under the cloak of a pretend religion."[49]

The Americans' antipathy toward Bogle, the Native Baptist preacher, was intense, but they reserved their most disparaging words for Gordon, a man who had been born into slavery, emancipated by his master-owner, and educated in England. For the American missionaries, he was their worst nightmare, proving the limits of missionary benevolence. Although he had been a member in good standing of the Presbyterian Church, he had left in the early 1860s, first going to James Phillippo's Baptist congregation, and then to the Native Baptists. Robert Stewart argues that Gordon embraced radical Baptist politics that informed his case for economic and political equality for the black peasantry and wage laborers.[50] He had received the gifts of civilization that had always been at the core of the Americans' civilizing mission: emancipation and freedom, an education, and property. He was "nearly white," in the words of Seth Wolcott, yet he, like Julius Beardslee, insisted on allying with "barbaric" Native Baptists. The poor peasantry might be forgiven, the missionaries thought, but a man such as Gordon had no excuse. "O poor deluded wickedly deceived people," lamented Wolcott, and, shifting his thoughts toward Gordon, "yet they are willingly deceived, choosing darkness rather than light."[51]

Several months after the excitement had passed, the ministers took the time to respond to the uproar in London over the violent retribution initiated by Governor Eyre. The Jamaica Assembly had already ended itself and the news from Britain was that the island was to become a Crown colony, ruled by a governor on appointment from the Queen and a council appointed by the governor. The Americans supported this move, on the whole, although Thornton Penfield wrote, "we all fear that the elective franchise will be abolished or so restricted as to amount to very nearly the same thing."[52] Seth Wolcott spoke more favorably about the change in government, even as he offered a very mild rebuke of Eyre's response to the riot. It is true, Wolcott wrote, "the man Gordon was, perhaps—I may say, I think, *probably* tried and condemned in form illegally. I *cannot* say *unjustly*." Wolcott also was willing to believe that "in the panic and excitement of putting down the riot many innocent persons suffered—many more or less guilty no doubt have been treated with unnecessary severity."[53] Newly returned to Jamaica, Charles Starbuck also commented on the new government, in "full operation" after he arrived in November 1866. Starbuck felt that even though the "massacres of a year ago" had been "dreadful," they had ushered in "a better system for the future." Jamaica was a "country so distracted by class factions" and now with all of the power concentrated in the governor's hands, "demagogues" like Gordon would be moot.[54]

The fact that England turned Jamaica into a Crown colony, effectively eliminating the franchise for blacks and whites, at the same moment that Radical Republicans in the U.S. Senate rallied their forces to extend suffrage to ex-slaves is striking. Thomas Holt has compellingly argued that the liberal supporters of emancipation had *always* preferred white rule in Jamaica to giving blacks political rights. Liberal declarations of the equality of men and political rights had limits: blacks, women, and those who did not share the same level of civilization as white Englishmen were not capable of or ready for these responsibilities.[55] During the political crisis of 1839, the colonial officials considered changing Jamaica into a Crown colony to gain authority over the recalcitrant white planters, while they gave no thought to expanding the black electorate as a means of making Jamaican society and politics more just. While the American missionaries shared some of these attitudes, their commitment to black manliness and their republican sensibilities had made them somewhat more skeptical of the control Britain exerted over Jamaica. Further, writing to the AMA at a moment of expanding black rights in the United States, the missionaries walked a delicate line in distinguishing between the need for British authority in Jamaica and black citizenship in the United States.

Historian Edward Rugemer has analyzed the varied coverage of Morant Bay from southern and northern newspapers, as well as its rhetorical uses in Congress. White southerners, and some Democrats in the North, drew a straight line connecting black political power to an ominous future of racial warfare in the South, while the economic and political inequities that led up to Morant Bay pushed Radical Republicans like Charles Sumner to agitate even more for equal rights in post-emancipation America.[56] It is therefore telling that the remaining American ministers in Jamaica at the end of 1866—Seth Wolcott, Sherman Wilson, and Charles Starbuck—and their British colleagues, Charles Venning and the newly hired John Thompson (no relation to Loren)—all spoke favorably of Eyre and the need for an authoritarian government on the island. The missionaries who had worked to "elevate" and "civilize" for thirty years still faced people who, as Seth Wolcott found, might listen to their sermons but did not necessarily believe what the ministers told them. Jamaica, with its predominantly black population, was fundamentally different from the U.S. South, where whites outnumbered blacks in most districts.

As these events unfolded, a different kind of crisis struck the Jamaica Mission concerning Seth Wolcott's leadership at the Richmond School. Wolcott's prickly personality and overbearing manner had not always endeared him to his colleagues. Sarah Penfield once incredulously told her friends back in Ohio about Wolcott's advice to her that she should limit her diet to green bananas and salt, as he had done when his family had gone through hard times during their many years in Jamaica. In the early 1860s, an Oberlin professor, George Allen, who taught at Richmond for a year, commented at length at his uneasy relationship with Wolcott. In the end, he reconciled himself to Wolcott's difficult manner, noting that his position of authority as a white minister among black freed people had transformed his character. Allen feared that Wolcott had "lived so long in the midst of a people who *cannot* be trusted, who must be *directed* and *commanded*" that he had become overly critical in all of his interpersonal relations. This meant, according to Allen, that "those that cannot fall in pretty nearly with his [Wolcott's] own views must of course be set down as wrong." He "severely criticized" nearly everyone and everything he encountered, from the mission's members to the island's government, to the English missionaries, and "especially the people of the country."[57]

An even more damning report came to the attention of the AMA in 1866, a date marking Wolcott's twentieth year on the island. Gardiner Greene Hubbard, a friend of the AMA's president, Edward Kirk, visited the Richmond Estate, and he painted a picture of Wolcott as a hard taskmaster, more interested in making money than in religious or civilizing work. He noted that Richmond's students "spend some four hours in the school and then as many hours more working in the field to pay for their board." This labor alone was apparently not enough to keep up Richmond's livestock and cane fields since Wolcott hired "some twenty or thirty laborers" and also had a store employing a clerk and a supervisor. After relaying Wolcott's business interests at Richmond, Hubbard noted that Seth Wolcott still received £29 from the AMA in addition to £50 from the Jamaican government for the school, and he questioned whether Wolcott should be on the AMA's payroll. The chief problem, he wrote, was that Wolcott's financial interests overpowered his commitment to missionary work. Hubbard wrote that Wolcott "occasionally takes the law into his own hand and inflicts summary punishment," a tactic that resulted "in the stealing of his crop and maiming of his cattle" in retribution.[58]

Hubbard also spent some time reflecting on Wolcott's personal deficiencies, writing, "I do not think a more unsuitable person for the Station could have been easily found." Wolcott was "not neat in his person," and more distressingly, "He has a very strong dislike to the negro, altho abolitionist of the ultra school by truth and education, he does not understand their character." More cryptically, Hubbard wrote that Wolcott "is disliked and almost hated by the negroes, altho known by all as perfectly honest and a truthful and reliable person in every respect."[59] This mixed assessment of Wolcott as hated yet respected is difficult to decipher. To shed some light on Hubbard's comments, consider a conversation Wolcott reported having with a fellow missionary. The other missionary complained about the persistent hypocrisy of the students at Richmond, and Wolcott countered, giving the example of "Thomas" who "is really trying to be good." The other missionary responded, "He takes good care to keep on the right side of you."[60] Although Wolcott dismissed his exceptionality, the other missionary's comments point to the fact that students at Richmond likely feared and respected Wolcott because of the power he had over their future. They might have viewed him as a fair broker who offered them an affordable education, reasonable prices on land, and access to his sugar works, even if they found him to be a moralizing and bossy character. Writing during the early years of Reconstruction in the United States, Gardiner Hubbard found Wolcott to be a demanding taskmaster with little sympathy toward black people, and he testified that he had "heard no one on the island speak so harshly of the blacks, or who sees so little hope in their future prosperity."[61]

Overall, the many pieces of evidence complaining of Wolcott's imperious and unpleasant character point to a man who was changed from an abolitionist in favor of black freedom to a racist who felt that black people in Jamaica would always require white supervision. This would be an easy conclusion to make, except for a few letters that suggest a more complicated explanation for Seth Wolcott's motivations. Charles Venning wrote several letters in the mid-1860s about Richmond and Wolcott's methods, and in his account, Wolcott had failed to institute the needed amount of discipline to control his workers and the school's students. In Venning's opinion, increased discipline and a greater willingness to expel troublemakers, along with a student body made up of wealthier and well-behaved students, would improve Richmond enormously. While Wolcott may have a "hearty benevolence and zeal for the best interest of the people of this Island," Venning observed, "his desire to do good to the worst and most degraded characters has induced him to take in young people without sufficient discrimination."[62] Venning had gone so far as to encourage Louis Kelly, one of the black Jamaican teachers in the mission, to attend the Moravian mission's school rather than Richmond.[63]

According to Venning, Seth Wolcott put too much faith in the "power of *moral* influence" instead of "the discipline of rules and penalties so essential to a proper training of our youth here."[64] A very similar estimation of Wolcott appeared in *Jamaica in 1866*, a book published by two English Quakers who visited Jamaica and the Richmond Estate. The writers, Thomas Harvey and William Brewin, endorsed the ideas behind the Richmond School, and its successes: "Of 168 pupils who have passed through the institution, 130 are known to have turned out well." Further, Wolcott, "a western American, with all the industrial energy and self-reliance of his class," not only taught in the school but also "put his hand to any description of useful labor." Yet Harvey and Brewin found that in practice, Richmond was "of a mixed character." Seth Wolcott was too trusting, and the school "suffered from the admission being made too easy and indiscriminate." Interestingly, and perhaps explaining the two men's biases, the very next paragraph remarked positively on Charles Venning's Chesterfield school.[65]

Confronted with conflicting accusations about his alleged racism on the one hand, and his overreliance on moral suasion instead of strict discipline on the other, Seth Wolcott defended his positions in a series of letters in 1866. Wolcott admitted to being surprised to hear of Venning's accusations that he had been "making concessions to the people, submitting to surrounding circumstances, etc." He answered, "I thought I was considered a 'hard case' in the opposite direction . . . stubbornly resisting and fighting against circumstances, especially of an immoral character."[66] Wolcott refused to change the school's structure or purpose. He asked Whipple to review the circulars that had been distributed in Richmond's first year, and he excerpted certain important quotations: "This institution is designed to furnish to children and youth of all classes the means of a practical English education adapted to the wants of common life," and "It aims to educate the masses." Because this was the school's primary goal, "We must of necessity accept of character as we find it," even if this meant accepting students who had a dubious moral character.[67] If the mission should abandon this principle and turn Richmond into a school like Kingston's Mico Institute or other more selective institutions, then it would be lost. Wolcott agreed that a special advanced department for training teachers could be created at Richmond, but this would require a greater investment from the AMA. He pointed this out, writing, "Let no one dream, however, that I expect to make Richmond equal in all desirable qualities to other institutions richly endowed and manned with from three to five teachers with large salaries."[68] He ended his letter on an interesting note, acknowledging that the "imagined" evils present at Richmond were certainly true—"that ignorance, idleness, strife, lying, theft, adultery, and many other bad things exist," but that as a missionary, Wolcott felt called to "deal with these things and counteract them" rather than to avoid confronting them at all.[69]

Seth Wolcott's demanding discipline appeared racist and vindictive to white visitors in Jamaica, while Charles Venning, an Englishman who had lived in Jamaica since the 1830s and who had married a colored woman, found Wolcott too interested in the plight of the poorest and least "civilized" black Jamaicans. This confluence of perspectives about the proper way to conduct a civilizing mission paints an interesting picture of racial ideology at this very meaningful moment in world history. In April 1865, the American Civil War had come to an end, and at the time of Gardiner Hubbard's visit to Jamaica, the Radical Republicans in Congress were laying out their plans for an interracial democracy in the United States. Meanwhile, in October 1865, the Morant Bay Rebellion had resulted in the declaration of martial law in Jamaica, and in 1866, Jamaica became a Crown colony. By the mid-1860s British citizens felt a duty to govern for black Jamaicans rather than to fight on behalf of their rights as Christian brothers and fellow citizens.[70] The British public had largely abandoned the idea that moral encouragement and missionary churches would "uplift" black Jamaicans, and they turned instead to industrial schools that taught girls how to sew and clean and that taught boys how to be menial laborers.⁷¹ This was not training for future landholders, or for the independent peasantry the Americans had once hoped to nurture in Jamaica. While Wolcott relied on sermons, lectures, and his moral example at Richmond, the Jamaican government began to send juvenile offenders and orphans to industrial schools in the 1870s, institutions that became one arm of the penal system, a far cry from the manual-labor experiment Richmond still aspired to be.

While Hubbard's take on Richmond and Wolcott likely reflected the fleeting egalitarian moment in the United States, Charles Venning's view represented the ascendant racial attitudes of the British Empire. Seth Wolcott satisfied neither. Wolcott's policy of reaching out to all students, even those of the lowest classes and who would potentially corrupt other students, derived from his own educational experience at Oberlin and his understanding of abolitionist missionary work that he learned in the 1830s and early 1840s. During Wolcott's formative years in Ohio, manual-labor education at the Oneida Institute and at Oberlin had been a means for poor boys to raise themselves up through their own labor. Abolitionist reformers had created black schools, white schools, and interracial schools on the principle of hard work and moral uplift, and Seth Wolcott had taken advantage of this new model of education himself. It took Wolcott almost ten years to finish his education at Oberlin because he paid for it entirely through his own labor.⁷² Men like Theodore Weld and Seth Wolcott had been forged into independent men while at these institutions, and this story became firmly implanted in Wolcott's worldview. Yet his years as a missionary had also shaped him into a commanding patriarch who was used to being obeyed, as George Allen observed. He made no room for separate standards for black students and white students, and, if Allen's testimony can be trusted, Wolcott was equally critical of all people, whether they were young white missionaries or licentious black students at Richmond. What had become most important to Wolcott was not the success of the civilizing mission, but his own soul's salvation through the hard work of being a farmer, a teacher, and a minister.

Epilogue

In the Jamaica Mission's final years, the remaining ministers hoped that the United States might consider annexing Jamaica, as the annexation of nearby Santo Domingo had become a much-touted subject in the halls of Congress.[1] If Jamaica were to remain in British control, wrote Charles Starbuck, "I should be faint-hearted enough. The English cannot get over that heathenish work of condescension. They hold the people off at arm's length and try to do them good by lecturing them." He offered his own opinion that "a respectable American infidel is a better Christian in social respects than an English minister."[2] Even after Morant Bay, the American ministers never felt entirely comfortable with British imperialism. The American missionaries believed that the United States, at this very moment entering into its short experiment with interracial democracy after the passage of the Reconstruction Act of 1867, would hold the best possible future for black Jamaicans. As citizens of the state of Jamaica, black Jamaicans would become full American citizens with voting rights instead of being subjected to a state of dependency as British subjects. It apparently did not occur to Starbuck that the majority of Jamaicans might want to be a nation in their own right, beholden to neither the United States nor Britain, or perhaps, subjects of Britain who had the same rights as white colonials in Canada. Starbuck's imagination encapsulates the driving dynamic behind the Jamaica Mission, and in a way, the impulse behind similar American attempts to force democracy, freedom, and "civilization" on other people. It is not that these governing principles were not respected and even desired, as freed Jamaicans clearly sought freedom and education. Instead, the problems arose when even the most benevolent Americans, in this case radical abolitionists, put themselves into a position of enforcing and commanding the rules of freedom.

When the mission began in the late 1830s, the American ministers thought in grand terms about what they might accomplish in an emancipated society. Unable to proselytize to southern slaves in the United States, they hoped that in Jamaica they could establish their interracial utopia. In the mid-1840s, Amos Phelps also dreamed of turning Jamaica into an island filled with industrious Yankee-minded farmers, and other missionaries, both men and women, transplanted their own aspirations onto the lives of black Jamaicans. The plans and execution of the Richmond Industrial School began a third phase of the mission, one that also failed to live up to the expectations of Seth Wolcott, Lewis Tappan, and, for that matter, the judgments of historians. When the two visions of freedom met in the Jamaica Mission, the American missionaries responded in the same way many English missionaries had done before them: they blamed the deficiencies they saw in black culture on the continued influence of the culture of slavery, and, less frequently, on the persistence of African traits tied to race. The abolitionist missionaries moved away from their adamant support for black independence and toward a discourse of the civilizing mission. They became more and more emphatic about church discipline and the hierarchy of the mission family as a way to keep tabs on the Jamaicans who participated in the mission community.

By the early 1880s, the Jamaica Mission had come to an end, but it still existed in the minds of old abolitionists, and they put a new spin on the mission to make it speak to the questions of the day. In 1883, Michael Strieby, an officer in the American Missionary Association and an Oberlin alumnus, gave a speech entitled "Oberlin and Missionary Work" at a celebration of the school's fiftieth year. The AMA's educational work in the South continued, even after the federal government had withdrawn troops and political support for freed people, and Strieby chose to reflect on the Jamaica Mission as a way to bolster support for domestic missionaries. Admittedly, he said, many people had come to consider the Jamaica Mission a failure, but it had important lessons for the United States. Strieby emphasized the need for ongoing northern support for black educational efforts in the South. As Jamaica had taught the United States, "Blacks need the presence and stimulus of the whites. When left in masses alone, they deteriorate into indolence, ignorance, and superstition."[3] For his audience filled with men and women who lived at a time of expanding foreign missions, reformers interested in civilizing Native Americans, and settlement houses intended to assimilate immigrants, he showed them how their abolitionism from the antebellum years should now be employed.

Michael Strieby saw the Jamaica Mission as an early example of how radical abolitionism and the civilizing mission could be fused together. In his reading of the mission, the experiences of the missionaries had proved that while all of God's people were equal, white Christians had a particular duty to "uplift" those who had not yet obtained Christian civilization. As the work in the South continued, Strieby hoped for an ever-expanding missionary agenda, one that resonated with the humanitarian justifications for the expansion of the British Empire in the 1880s, and that would become a commonly invoked reason for an American empire in the coming decade: "We must emancipate these people from color prejudice. Slavery was a cancer. It was not cured by emollients. The knife, or rather the sword, had to be used; but caste prejudice, its tap root is still left—a prejudice that, in the vast nations of heathen lands—in India, in China, in Japan—is the great hindrance of the gospel. We must conquer this in America for the world, as we conquered slavery."[4] The civilizing mission, and its inherent inequalities, would be required for the future endeavors of abolitionists.

The close links between radical abolitionism and the civilizing mission had not always been so happily united in the Jamaica Mission as Michael Strieby imagined, nor had the expectations of the American missionaries been fulfilled on the island. While the overarching narrative of the mission traced the ways in which the missionaries became increasingly committed to hierarchies and inserting themselves into the private lives of black

Jamaicans, the cultural encounter at the base of the mission made for shaky ground. As radicals from Oberlin College, the missionaries' abolitionist roots never disappeared entirely, and the unpredictability of the missionary encounter made it difficult to control. Far from being a simple precursor to American Reconstruction, or a model for future agents of cultural imperialism, the Jamaica Mission acted more like a crucible, testing the beliefs and practices of all of its participants.

NOTES

Introduction

1. Drescher, *Mighty Experiment*, 217–27; Rugemer, *Problem of Emancipation*, 260–86.
2. Woodward, *Origins of the New South*; Williamson, *Crucible of Race*; Silber, *Romance of Reunion*; Blight, *Race and Reunion*.
3. Davis, *Problem of Slavery*; Drescher, *Capitalism and Antislavery*; Christopher Brown, *Moral Capital*; James, *Black Jacobins*.
4. Rugemer, *Problem of Emancipation*, 114–32.
5. Egerton, "'Its Origin Is Not a Little Curious'"; Dorsey, *Reforming Men and Women*, 145–48.
6. McKivigan, *War against Proslavery Religion*. See also Strong, *Perfectionist Politics*, and Braude, *Radical Spirits*.
7. For an analysis of the debate about abolitionism's origins see Christopher Brown, *Moral Capital*, 3–24. On American abolitionism, see Kraditor, *Means and Ends*; Quarles, *Black Abolitionists*; Jeffrey, *Great Silent Army*; Newman, *Transformation of American Abolitionism*. For evangelical abolitionists, see James Stewart, *Holy Warriors*; Wyatt-Brown, *Lewis Tappan*; Abzug, *Passionate Liberator*.
8. DuBois, *Feminism and Suffrage*, 31; Midgeley, *Women against Slavery*, 158–67; Sklar, *Women's Rights Emerges within the Antislavery Movement*. More generally, see Sklar and Stewart, *Women's Rights and Transatlantic Slavery*; Yellin and Van Horne, *Abolitionist Sisterhood*; Hersh, *Slavery of Sex*.
9. Holt, "'Empire over the Mind'"; Cooper, Holt, and Scott, *Beyond Slavery*; Eudall, *Political Languages of Emancipation*; Scully and Paton, *Gender and Slave Emancipation*; Sklar and Stewart, *Women's Rights and Transatlantic Antislavery*; Scott, *Degrees of Freedom*.
10. Blackett, *Building an Antislavery Wall*; Rugemer, *Problem of Emancipation*; Guterl, *American Mediterranean*. See also McDaniel, "Our Country Is the World."
11. James Stewart, *Holy Warriors*, 56; McKivigan, "Christian Anti-Slavery Convention Movement"; Strong, *Perfectionist Politics*.
12. James Stewart, "Emergence of Racial Modernity." See also Rael, *Black Identity*, 203.
13. Andrew, *From Revivals to Removal*; McLoughlin, *Cherokees and Missionaries*.

14. See, for example, Rose, *Rehearsal for Reconstruction*; Richardson, *Christian Reconstruction*; Jones, *Soldiers of Light and Love*.

15. Fletcher, *History of Oberlin*, 290–96.

16. Jeffrey, *Great Silent Army*; Pierson, *Free Hearts and Free Homes*; Lasser, "Enacting Emancipation"; Baker, "Domestication of Politics." For an analysis connecting female antislavery to feminism, see Midgley, "Antislavery and the Roots of Imperial Feminism."

17. Catherine Hall, *Civilising Subjects*, 94–95, 189.

18. Fox-Genovese, *Within the Plantation Household*; Stoler, "Tense and Tender Ties."

19. Scully and Paton, *Gender and Slave Emancipation*, 14.

20. Kaplan, "Manifest Domesticity"; Stoler, "Tense and Tender Ties." See also Pascoe, *Relations of Rescue*; Louise Newman, *White Women's Rights*.

21. Frey and Wood, *Come Shouting*; Turner, *Slaves and Missionaries*; Robert Stewart, *Religion and Society*; Catherine Hall, *Civilising Subjects*; Warner-Lewis, *Archibald Monteath*.

22. Fuller, "'Christian' Morality in 'Heathen' Jamaica," and Gosselink, *Letters from Jamaica*.

23. Catherine Hall, *Civilising Subjects*, 137.

24. Holt, *Problem of Freedom*, 173.

25. Wolcott to Whipple, 1 May 1848, AMA Archives.

Part One Introduction

1. Ahlstrom, *Religious History*, 455; DeRogatis, *Moral Geography*, 4.

2. Hawley, *Journal*, 43.

3. Ibid., 48–49.

4. Ibid., 58–59.

5. Ibid., 73, 71.

6. John Shipherd to Z. R. Shipherd, 6 April 1831, Fletcher Papers, OCA.

7. Fletcher, *History of Oberlin*, 67–84, 87.

8. "An Appeal to the Philanthropists of Great Britain on Behalf of Oberlin College—by Theodore and Angelina Weld," *Weld-Grimké Letters*, 741–44.

9. Hutchison, *Errand to the World*, 45–51; Robert, *American Women in Mission*, 1–10.

10. Catherine Hall, *Civilising Subjects*, 88–89. For a similar case regarding British missionaries in South Africa, see Comaroff, "Images of Empire, Contests of Conscience," 166–67.

11. James Stewart, "New Haven Negro College," 326–27; Fletcher, *History of Oberlin*, 245–49.

12. Turner, *Slaves and Missionaries*, 7–23.

13. Byrd, *Captives and Voyagers*, 86–102; Besson, *Martha Brae*, 142–43; Turner, *Slaves and Missionaries*, 51–54; Austin-Broos, *Jamaica Genesis*, 50–59.

Chapter One. Revivals, Antislavery, and Christian Liberty

1. Cross, *Burned-Over District*; James Stewart, *Holy Warriors*; Mary Ryan, *Cradle of the Middle Class*.
2. Cott, *Bonds of Womanhood*, 156–58; Robert, *American Women in Mission*, 24–38.
3. Andrew, *From Revivals to Removal*, 264, 267. See also Goodman, "Manual Labor Movement," 365–67.
4. For Oberlin's racial conservatism, see James Stewart, "New Haven Negro College," 340–42.
5. A description of the types of frontier religious enthusiasm that frightened ministers like Beecher can be found in Boles, *Great Revival*; Hutchison, *Errand to the World*, 51–61.
6. Abzug, *Passionate Liberator*, 44.
7. Quoted in Cross, *Burned-Over District*, 174.
8. *Pastoral Letter of the Ministers of the Oneida Association, to the Churches Under Their Care, on the Subject of Revivals of Religion* (Utica, 1827), 14, quoted in Abzug, *Passionate Liberator*, 47.
9. Theodore Weld to the Grimkés, 26 August 1837, *Weld-Grimké Letters*, 433; Lyman Beecher, *Letters on "New Measures,"* 14–15.
10. Lyman Beecher, *Letters on the "New Measures,"* iv.
11. Ibid., 11. See also Mary Ryan, *Cradle of the Middle Class*, 67–71.
12. Gordon, *Mormon Question*, 22–23.
13. Cross, *Burned-Over District*, 18–19, 35–50.
14. Morris, *Fanny Wright*; Gordon, *Mormon Question*, 28–29.
15. Fenton, "Religious Liberties."
16. Wyatt-Brown, "Conscience and Career"; Dorsey, *Reforming Men and Women*, 130–31; Abzug, *Passionate Liberator*, 60–63.
17. Sklar, *Catharine Beecher*; Hardesty, *Women Called to Witness*; Welter, "Cult of True Womanhood"; Smith-Rosenberg, "Beauty, the Beast, and the Militant Woman."
18. Hewitt, *Women's Activism and Social Change*, 79–87.
19. Swerdlow, "Abolition's Conservative Sisters."
20. A series of similar narratives of like-minded abolitionists can be found in Goodman, *Of One Blood*, 81–121. See also Amos Dresser, Seth T. Wolcott, and Loren Thompson, Alumni Records, OCA.
21. Sernett, *Abolition's Axe*.
22. Goodman, *Of One Blood*, 83–84. See also Goodman, "Manual Labor."
23. *First Annual Report of the Society for Promoting Manual Labor in Literary Institutions*, 14, 37.
24. Abzug, *Passionate Liberator*, 52–53; Wyatt-Brown, *Lewis Tappan*, 98–99.
25. Lewis Tappan to Benjamin Tappan, 7 September 1831, Benjamin Tappan Papers, LOC, quoted in Thomas, *Theodore Weld*, 19. See Wyatt-Brown, *Lewis Tappan*, 297.
26. Abzug, *Passionate Liberator*, 62.

27. Weld to Gerrit Smith, 6 August 1839, *Weld-Grimké Letters*, 780–81.
28. C. S. Renshaw to Charles Finney, 15 July 1832, Finney Papers, OCA.
29. Abzug, *Passionate Liberator*, 82–89.
30. Thomas, *Theodore Weld*, 49.
31. Lyman Beecher, *Autobiography*, 2:321–22.
32. Lyman Beecher to William Beecher, 15 July 1835, in ibid., 2:345.
33. My account of the Lane Rebellion comes from Lesick, *Lane Rebels*.
34. Fletcher, *History of Oberlin*, 152; *Debate at Lane Seminary*, 3–4.
35. Lesick, *Lane Rebels*, 78–79.
36. *Debate at Lane Seminary*, 5.
37. Fletcher, *History of Oberlin*, 154.
38. "The Preamble and Constitution of the Anti-Slavery Society of Lane Seminary," *Cincinnati Journal*, 28 March 1834, quoted in Abzug, *Passionate Liberator*, 92–93.
39. *Report on the condition of the People of Color*, 2; James Stewart, "Emergence of Racial Modernity," 197–99; Wade, "Negro in Cincinnati," 50–51.
40. Lesick, *Lane Rebels*, 123; Dorsey, *Reforming Men and Women*, 150–54.
41. Lyman Beecher, *Autobiography*, 2:325.
42. Weld to Lewis Tappan, 9 March 1836, *Weld-Grimké Letters*, 273. See also Susan Ryan, *Grammar of Good Intentions*, 19.
43. Lesick, *Lane Rebels*, 92.
44. Fletcher, *History of Oberlin*, 160–61, citing Lane Seminary Trustees MS Minutes, 10 October 1834; *Cincinnati Journal*, 10 October 1834.
45. Lesick, *Lane Rebels*, 116–19.
46. Lyman Beecher to Nathaniel Wright, 7 September 1834, Western Reserve Historical Society, quoted in Lesick, *Lane Rebels*, 122.
47. Lane Seminary, Trustees Formal Minutes, meeting of 6 October 1834, quoted in Lesick, *Lane Rebels*, 127.
48. Weld, "Letter to James Hall, Editor," *Cincinnati Journal*, 30 May 1834.
49. Weld to Tappan, 9 March 1835, *Weld-Grimké Letters*, 272 (emphasis in original).
50. *Statement of the Reasons which Induced the Students of Lane Seminary to Dissolve Their Connection with That Institution*, quoted in Fletcher, *History of Oberlin*, 163.
51. *Statement of the Reasons*, 5, quoted in Lesick, *Lane Rebels*, 136.
52. Fletcher, *History of Oberlin*, 167–79.
53. Benjamin Woodbury to John J. Shipherd, 26 March 1835, Fletcher Papers, OCA.
54. John Morgan to Weld, 13 January 1835, in *Weld-Grimké Letters*, 198.
55. Phelps, *Slavery and Its Remedy*, 236. For more on Phelps, see Richard Newman, *Transformation of American Abolitionism*, 113–16, 135–44, 156.
56. Phelps, *Lectures on Slavery and Its Remedy*, 236–37.
57. Pierson, *Free Hearts and Free Homes*, 27–33.
58. Lerner, *Grimké Sisters*, 116–46; Sklar, "'Throne of My Heart,'" 228–33.
59. Kraditor, *Means and Ends*, 39–77; Hansen, *Strained Sisterhood*, 93–123; Pierson, *Free Hearts and Free Homes*, 32–33.

60. Fletcher, *History of Oberlin*, 681.
61. Goodman, "Manual Labor," 363–64.
62. Fletcher, *History of Oberlin*, 612.
63. Ibid., 641.
64. Ibid., 660–61.
65. Ibid., 746–51.
66. Mary Ann Adams, Ellen F. Griswold, and Elizabeth S. Peck to John Keep and William Dawes, 10 July 1839, Fletcher Papers, OCA.
67. *Laws and Regulations of the Female Department* 1852, 1859, 1865, quoted in Fletcher, *History of Oberlin*, 671–72.
68. Cowles to Mr. [Lewis] E[ly], 30 June 1841, Fletcher Papers, OCA.
69. Fletcher, *History of Oberlin*, 671; Lasser, "Enacting Emancipation," 328–29.
70. Lasser and Merrill, *Friends and Sisters*, 9–11.
71. Lucy Stone to her parents, 16 August 1846, quoted in Fletcher, *History of Oberlin*, 292.
72. Fletcher, *History of Oberlin*, 290–94; DuBois, *Feminism and Suffrage*, 24–31; Jeffrey, *Great Silent Army*, 199–204.
73. Oberlin Female Moral Reform Society MSS Minutes, 13 May 1836, in Fletcher Papers, OCA.

Chapter Two. Slavery and Freedom in Jamaica

1. Curtin, *Atlantic Slave Trade*, 268.
2. Byrd, *Captives and Voyagers*, 102. See also Eltis, *Rise of African Slavery*; Blackburn, *Making of New World Slavery*; Thornton, *Africa and Africans*.
3. Forret, "Conflict and the 'Slave Community.'"
4. Higman, *Slave Population and Economy*, 16.
5. For more on the rigorous debates over the meaning of "creole" in Caribbean history, see Braithwaite, *Development of Creole Society*, and Shepherd and Richards, *Questioning Creole*.
6. Rugemer, *Problem of Emancipation*, 164–70.
7. "Missionary Intelligence," *Oberlin Evangelist*, 7 October 1840.
8. Vincent Brown, "Spiritual Terror and Sacred Authority," 46.
9. Turner, *Slaves and Missionaries*, 55.
10. Bush, *Slave Women in Caribbean Society*, 73–77; Vincent Brown, "Spiritual Terror and Sacred Authority," 37.
11. Handler and Bilby, "On the Early Use and Origins of the Term 'Obeah.'" See also Frey and Wood, *Come Shouting*, 56–59; Richard Burton, *Afro-Creole*, 97–104; Holt, *Problem of Freedom*, 189–90.
12. Dianne Stewart, *Three Eyes*, 58–65.
13. Ibid., 47, 62, 58.
14. Schuler, *Alas, Alas, Kongo*, 33.
15. "Letters Showing the Rise and Progress of the Early Negro Churches," 69–92,

esp. 69–71. The letters have been culled from the *Baptist Annual Register*. Liele's autobiography has been republished in Carretta, *Unchained Voices*, 325–32, and discussed in Frey and Wood, *Come Shouting*, 115–17, 131–33.

16. Schuler, *Alas, Alas, Kongo*, 34.
17. "Letters Showing the Rise and Progress of the Early Negro Churches," 89.
18. Ibid., 85, 80–81, 76.
19. Dianne Stewart, *Three Eyes*, 89; Frey and Wood, *Come Shouting*, 131–32.
20. Turner, *Slaves and Missionaries*, 28–30.
21. Ibid., 92, 59.
22. Catherine Hall, *Civilising Subjects*, 150–61.
23. Renshaw, "Historical and Statistical View," 588.
24. A. M. Richardson to Whipple, 2 January 1852, AMA Archives.
25. This description of the Baptist War is from Turner, *Slaves and Missionaries*, 148–73. See also Craton, *Testing the Chains*, 291–321.
26. Turner, *Slaves and Missionaries*, 150.
27. Catherine Hall, *Civilising Subjects*, 105–6.
28. Drescher, *Mighty Experiment*, 144. For another analysis of apprenticeship, see Holt, *Problem of Freedom*, 94–112.
29. Holt, *Problem of Freedom*, 146–63; Besson, *Martha Brae*, 140–45.
30. Rugemer, *Problem of Emancipation*, 156–60. The two most notable abolitionist evaluations of the apprenticeship were Thome and Kimball, *Emancipation in the West Indies*, and Sturge and Harvey, *The West Indies*.
31. Thome and Kimball, *Emancipation in the West Indies*, 268.
32. Rugemer, *Problem of Emancipation*, 160–70. For more on Thome and Kimball, see Kenny, "Reconstructing a Different South."
33. Catherine Hall, *Civilising Subjects*, 319; Sheller, "Quasheba, Mother, Queen," 4–6.
34. Beckles, *Centering Women*, 141–44. For an analysis of the women in the Charleston market of the eighteenth century that explores why women in particular were allowed this degree of freedom, see Olwell, "'Loose, Idle and Disorderly.'"
35. Besson, *Martha Brae*, 87.
36. Taylor Memorandum, quoted in Holt, *Problem of Freedom*, 42–45.
37. Higman, *Plantation Jamaica*, 90–93; Accounts Produce for 1830, Libers 68–69, Jamaica Archives.
38. Samuel Diary, 199, 3 May 1835; 218, 18 July 1835, National Library of Jamaica.
39. Robert Stewart, *Religion and Society*, 70–72.
40. Samuel Diary, 218, 18 July 1835, National Library of Jamaica.
41. Cooper, "Reports," Montrose Cattle Pen, 18 April 1835, Jamaica Archives; Cooper, "Reports," Flint River Cattle Pen, 20 January 1835, Jamaica Archives.
42. Thome and Kimball, *Emancipation in the West Indies*, 268–69.
43. Cooper, "Reports," Flint River Cattle Pen, 20 January 1835, Jamaica Archives.
44. Catherine Hall, *Civilising Subjects*, 136–39.
45. Paton, "Flight from the Fields," 180; Drescher, *Mighty Experiment*, 158.

46. Quoted in Bolland, "Systems of Domination after Slavery," 599.
47. Wilmot, "'Females of Abandoned Character?'" 280.
48. For an overview of the debate about the flight from the estates, see Besson, *Martha Brae*, 140–45.
49. Drescher, *Mighty Experiment*; Holt, "Essence of the Contract;" Catherine Hall, *Civilising Subjects*, 347–63.
50. Robert Stewart, *Religion and Society*, 27–31; Catherine Hall, *Civilising Subjects*, 124–39.
51. Thome and Kimball, *Emancipation in the West Indies*, 31.
52. Ibid., 154.
53. Ibid., 287, 322, 339; see also Holt, *Problem of Freedom*, 64–65, and Paton, *No Bond But the Law*.
54. Thome and Kimball, *Emancipation in the West Indies*, 154.
55. Ibid., 324.
56. Ibid., 328.
57. Ibid., 83–84.
58. Diana Paton evaluates the literature on the question of why women left the fields in "Flight from the Fields," 184–85.
59. Brereton, "Family Strategies," 150; Sheller, "Quasheba, Mother, Queen," 98.
60. P.P. (XXXV), 1840, p. 44, T. McNell to Lionel Smith, 23 July 1839, Encl., quoted in Simmonds, "Civil Disturbances in Western Jamaica," 5.
61. Brereton, "Family Strategies," 152–54.
62. Paton, "Flight from the Fields," 186; Holt, *Problem of Freedom*, 170–76.
63. Besson, *Martha Brae*, 140.
64. Renshaw, "Historical and Statistical View," 572.
65. Paton, "Flight from the Fields," 191.
66. For an overview of gender in post-emancipation Jamaica, see Paton, "Flight from the Fields," 180–86. See also Holt, *Problem of Freedom*, 170–72; Brereton, "Family Strategies;" Higman, "Household Structure and Fertility," 534–36; Bush, "'The Family Tree is not Cut.'"
67. Brereton, "Family Strategies," 157.
68. Sheller, "Quasheba, Mother, Queen."
69. Terborg-Penn, "Through an African Feminist Theoretical Lens," 5.
70. Paton, "Flight from the Fields," 186–87.

Part Two Introduction

1. Ingraham to Phelps, 6 August 1839, Phelps Papers, Boston Public Library (emphasis in original).
2. Sarah Grimké and Angelina and Theodore Weld to Gerrit and Anne Smith, 18 June 1840, *Weld-Grimké Letters*, 841–43; Gerrit Smith to Theodore Weld, 11 July 1840, *Weld-Grimké Letters*, 849.
3. "Letters from Jamaica," *American Missionary*, June 1847.

4. Higman, *Slave Population*, 71–81; Holt, *Problem of Freedom*, 152–53; Paton, "Flight from the Fields."

5. Charles Stuart to Weld, 10 October 1839, *Weld-Grimké Letters*, 803.

6. Douglas Hall, "Flight from the Estates Reconsidered"; Besson, *Martha Brae*, 140–45; Holt, *Problem of Freedom*, 134–40; Paton, "Flight from the Fields; Bolland, "Systems of Domination after Slavery."

7. Barker, *Captain Charles Stuart*, 173–76.

8. Holt, "Essence of the Contract," 56.

9. Catherine Hall, *Civilising Subjects*, 137.

10. "Manual Labor with Study," *Oberlin Evangelist*, 13 May 1846.

11. "Phelps," *American Missionary*, September 1847; Hall to Whipple, 11 September 1851, and Beardslee to Tappan, 19 November 1851, AMA Archives.

12. James Stewart, "New Haven Negro College."

13. Olds to Renshaw, 15 March 1849, AMA Archives.

Chapter Three. Religion and the Civilizing Mission

1. *American Missionary*, June 1849, report reprinted from the Kingston *Jamaica Messenger*.

2. Charles Stuart to Weld, 10 October 1839, *Weld-Grimké Letters*, 803

3. Catherine Hall, *Civilising Subjects*, 165.

4. "West India Self-Supporting Missions," *Oberlin Evangelist*, 17 January 1844; "Interesting Movement at the Sandwich Islands," *Oberlin Evangelist*, 1 January 1845; "West India Missions," *Oberlin Evangelist*, 1 January 1845; "Self-Supporting Manual Labor School on Missionary Ground," *Oberlin Evangelist*, 15 January 1845; "The Self-Made Freedman of Canada West," *Oberlin Evangelist*, 5 November 1845.

5. "Letter from a planter in Port Morant," *Oberlin Evangelist*, 19 June 1839.

6. "Interesting Movement at the Sandwich Islands," *Oberlin Evangelist*, 1 January 1845.

7. "West India Missions," *Oberlin Evangelist*, 1 January 1845.

8. "West Indies," *Oberlin Evangelist*, 27 March 1839.

9. "Missionary Intelligence," *Oberlin Evangelist*, 7 October 1840.

10. Ibid.

11. Ingraham to Phelps, 6 August 1839, Phelps Papers, Boston Public Library.

12. Renshaw to Smith, *Weld-Grimké Letters*, 780.

13. Tyler to Henry Cowles, 20 March 1842, Ralph Tyler, Alumni Records, OCA.

14. Prince, *Narrative of Nancy Prince*, 50, 51.

15. Ibid., 53, 58.

16. Prince, *West Indies*, 8–9; 11.

17. "Rev. Charles B. Venning," *American Missionary*, March 1880.

18. Robert Stewart, *Religion and Society*, 89–94; Catherine Hall, *Civilising Subjects*, 192–99; Holt, *Problem of Freedom*, 189.

19. Catherine Hall, *Civilising Subjects*, 136.

20. "West India Mission Committee," *Oberlin Evangelist*, 28 August 1844.
21. "Instructive Christian Experience," *Oberlin Evangelist*, 5 August 1846.
22. Jeffrey, *Great Silent Army*, 138.
23. Hutchison, *Errand to the World*, 77–90; Robert, *American Women in Mission*, 69–70.
24. "The Doctrine of the American Board Respecting the Social and Moral Reforms of the Age," *Oberlin Evangelist*, 4 February 1846.
25. Wyatt-Brown, *Lewis Tappan*, 84–87. Arthur Tappan withdrew his generous financial support of the American Colonization Society in the early 1830s when he discovered that the American blacks relocated to Liberia conducted a brisk business in rum. Tappan's moral qualms with the society came less out of antiracist sentiments and more from his abhorrence of drink.
26. Maxfield, "Organic Sin," 9.
27. Beecher, "Dr. Beecher on Organic Sins," *Recorder* 30 (16 October 1845), 166, quoted in Maxfield, "Organic Sin," 10.
28. Beecher, "Dr. Beecher on Organic Sins," *Recorder* 30 (16 October 1845), 151, quoted in Maxfield, "Organic Sin," 9.
29. "The American Board and Slavery," *Recorder* (1 January 1846): 96, quoted in Maxfield, "Organic Sin," 22. Amos Phelps relied on a number of sources examining emancipation in the West Indies for his collection of abolitionist essays, *Lectures on Slavery and Its Remedy*.
30. Daly, *When Slavery Was Called Freedom*, 58–59.
31. Lewis Tappan, *History of the American Missionary Association*, 18–19.
32. Hutchison, *Errand to the World*, 62–90; Robert, *American Women in Mission*, 81–92.
33. "Instructions to Missionaries," *American Missionary*, March 1847.
34. "Jamaica Mission," *American Missionary*, February 1851.
35. "Jamaica Mission—Sailing of Missionaries," *American Missionary*, June 1851.
36. "Jamaica Mission," *American Missionary*, February 1855.
37. "Jamaica Mission," *American Missionary*, March 1852.
38. Olds to Whipple, 5 June 1851, AMA Archives.
39. "Statistics of Chesterfield Church," AMA Archives.
40. Paton, "Flight from the Fields," 186–87.
41. "Jamaica," *American Missionary*, July 1848.
42. Richardson to Whipple, 2 January 1852, AMA Archives (emphasis in original).
43. Olds to Whipple, 12 April 1853, AMA Archives.
44. Hall to Whipple, 10 August 1852, AMA Archives.
45. Hall to Whipple, 10 August 1852, AMA Archives.
46. Evarts to Whipple, June or July 1847, AMA Archives.
47. Evarts to Whipple, 12 October 1848, AMA Archives.
48. Ralph Tyler to Henry Cowles, 10 March 1842, Tyler, Alumni Records, OCA.
49. Wolcott to Whipple, 17 January 1848, AMA Archives.
50. Wolcott to Whipple, 1 May 1848, AMA Archives.

51. Renshaw, "Historical and Statistical View," 558.
52. Evarts to Whipple, 12 October 1848, AMA Archives.
53. Olds to Whipple, 19 July 1852, AMA Archives. See Gordon, *Mormon Question*, 47–48.
54. Evarts to Whipple, 12 October 1848, AMA Archives.
55. Hall to Whipple, 5 March 1856, AMA Archives.
56. Ibid.
57. Hall to Whipple, 29 May 1856, AMA Archives (emphasis in original).
58. Hall to Whipple, 29 May 1856, AMA Archives.
59. Olds to Whipple, 28 April 1852, AMA Archives.
60. Venning to Whipple, 21 April 1858, AMA Archives.
61. Ibid.; Olds to Whipple, 19 July 1852, AMA Archives.
62. Olds to Whipple, 2 July 1853, AMA Archives.

Chapter Four. From Spiritual Liberty to Sexual License

1. Thompson to Whipple, 24 July 1850; Thompson to Whipple, 8 August 1850, AMA Archives.
2. Thompson to Whipple, 18 May 1848, AMA Archives.
3. Hyde's perfectionism resembled that of John Humphrey Noyes, and his emphasis on individualism resembled that of Hicksite Quakers. For more on the radical religious context of central New York, see Cross, *Burned-Over District*; DeMaria, *Communal Love at Oneida*; Braude, *Radical Spirits*; Claw, *Without Sin*, 10–19.
4. Fuller, "'Christian' Morality in 'Heathen' Jamaica."
5. Dean to Whipple, 7 March 1849, AMA Archives.
6. Hyde to Whipple, 11 November 1849, AMA Archives.
7. Ibid.
8. Dean to Whipple, 14 August 1849, AMA Archives (emphasis in original).
9. Dean to Whipple, 18 October 1849; Wolcott to Whipple, 29 August 1849, AMA Archives.
10. Dean to Whipple, 12 March 1850, AMA Archives (emphasis in original).
11. Robert, *American Women in Mission*, 65–75.
12. Sklar, *Catharine Beecher*; Kaplan, "Manifest Domesticity," 589; Robert, *American Women in Mission*, 92–109.
13. Dean to Whipple, 18 October 1849; Dean to Whipple, 14 August 1849, AMA Archives (emphasis in original).
14. See chap. 6. Grimshaw, *Paths of Duty*, 171–75; Robert, *American Women in Mission*, 56–75.
15. Sophronia Brooks Hall (the younger sister of Abner Olds's wife, Ann Brooks Olds) was immortalized by her son, the chemist Charles Martin Hall, when he donated money to Oberlin College for a music auditorium named in her honor.
16. Hunt to Whipple, 7 January 1850; Beardslee to Whipple, 15 January 1850, AMA Archives.

17. Hunt to Whipple, 15 January 1850, AMA Archives.
18. Olds to Whipple, 18 March 1850; Evarts to Whipple, 15 June 1850; Dean to Whipple, 12 March 1850, AMA Archives.
19. Thompson to Whipple, 25 November 1850, AMA Archives.
20. Weld to Angelina Grimké Weld, 5 June 1846, Weld-Grimké Papers, William L. Clements Library (University of Michigan, Ann Arbor), quoted in Abzug, *Passionate Liberator*, 257.
21. Thompson to Whipple, 15 February 1848; Thompson to Whipple, 25 January 1850, AMA Archives; Thornton Bigelow Penfield to Henry Cowles and Minerva Penfield Cowles, 10 July 1860, *Letters from Jamaica*, 86.
22. Thompson to Whipple, 13 May 1850, AMA Archives.
23. Thompson to Whipple, 25 November 1850, AMA Archives.
24. Strong, *Perfectionist Politics*, 41–43.
25. Thompson to Whipple, 7 May 1850; Olds to Whipple, 8 May 1850, AMA Archives.
26. Beardslee to Whipple, 29 May 1850; Beardslee to Whipple, 21 June 1850, AMA Archives (emphasis in original).
27. Thompson to Whipple, 7 May 1850, AMA Archives.
28. Thompson to Whipple, 13 May 1850, AMA Archives.
29. Dean to Whipple, 28 May 1850; Venning to Whipple, Report on Brainerd School, July 1850, AMA Archives (emphasis in original).
30. Hall to George W. Hall, [July 1850], AMA Archives.
31. Wolcott to Whipple, 15 June 1850; also George Whipple's comments on the back of Abner Olds's letter, 8 May 1850, AMA Archives.
32. Wolcott to Whipple, 15 June 1850, AMA Archives.
33. Olds to Whipple, 8 May 1850, AMA Archives.
34. Hall to Whipple, 26 June 1850; Hall to Whipple, 1 July 1850, AMA Archives.
35. Evarts to Whipple, 16 July 1850; Hall to George W. Hall, [July 1850], AMA Archives. On spiritual hierarchy, see Braude, *Radical Spirits*, 23–24.
36. Evarts to Whipple, 16 July 1850, AMA Archives, ARC.
37. Thompson to Whipple, 17 December 1850, AMA Archives.
38. Wolcott to Whipple, 14 October 1850, AMA Archives (emphasis in original).
39. Thompson to Whipple, 21 August 1850, AMA Archives.
40. Thompson to Lewis Tappan, 8 August 1850, AMA Archives.
41. Wolcott to Whipple, 14 October 1850, AMA Archives.
42. Thompson to Lewis Tappan, 17 December 1850, AMA Archives.
43. Ibid.; Thompson to Whipple, 15 November 1850, AMA Archives.
44. Thompson to Whipple, 11 May 1851; Thompson to Whipple, 11 April 1851, AMA Archives.
45. Wolcott to Whipple, 10 March 1851, AMA Archives.
46. Richardson to Whipple, 6 June 1851 (emphasis in original); Hall to Whipple, 25 July 1851; Thompson to Whipple, 31 May 1852, AMA Archives.
47. Abzug, *Passionate Liberator*, 241.

48. William Henry Evarts, Alumni Records, OCA.
49. Richardson to Whipple, 21 January 1852, AMA Archives.
50. "Jamaica Mission," *American Missionary*, September 1851.
51. Dean to Whipple, 15 July 1852, AMA Archives.
52. Beardslee to Whipple, 31 May 1852, AMA Archives.
53. Mrs. Hyde to Whipple, 31 December 185[2], AMA Archives.
54. Mrs. Hyde to Whipple, 12 March 1853, AMA Archives.
55. Mrs. Hyde to Whipple, 2 May 1853, AMA Archives.
56. Wolcott to Tappan, 18 December 1855, AMA Archives.
57. H. B. Hall to Whipple, 2 October 1856, AMA Archives; Evarts, Alumni Records, and Allen Journal, Allen Papers, OCA.

Chapter Five. Cultivating Land, Cultivating Families

1. Cott, *Public Vows*, 57–68.
2. Dixon, *Perfecting the Family*, 92–98.
3. "Additional Hints in Regard to the West India Mission," *American Missionary*, September 1847.
4. Besson, *Martha Brae*, 87.
5. Paton, "Flight from the Fields," 180–86.
6. Catherine Hall, *Civilising Subjects*, 133–35.
7. "Additional Hints in Regard to the West India Mission," *American Missionary*, September 1847.
8. Phelps to Tappan, 12 January 1847, AMA Archives.
9. Phelps to Tappan, 12 January 1847, AMA Archives. Excerpts from this letter appeared in a letter to the *National Era* from "Clarkson" on 4 March 1847. While historians often refer to the independent farming and animal husbandry of Jamaican slaves as indicative of a 'protopeasantry,' Phelps uses the term in reference to a system that kept the former slaves tied to wage labor on the estates.
10. "First of August," *Oberlin Evangelist*, 14 August 1845.
11. Charles Stuart to Theodore Weld, 10 October 1839, *Weld-Grimké Letters*, 805.
12. Luckock, *Jamaica: Enslaved and Free*, 209.
13. "Jamaica Mission," *American Missionary*, August 1848. For more on the Americans' critique of wage labor and the creation of the Richmond Estate, see Kenny, "Reconstructing a Different South."
14. Wolcott to Whipple, 24 March 1854, AMA Archives.
15. "Letters from Jamaica," *American Missionary*, June 1847; Thompson to Whipple, 10 January 1848, AMA Archives.
16. Thompson to Whipple, 10 January 1848, FI-1385, AMA Archives; Account Produce for Charlottenburgh Estate in Metcalfe Parish, 1850–51, Liber 93, Jamaica Archives.
17. Thompson to Whipple, 14 January 1849, AMA Archives.

18. Cott, *Public Vows*; Gordon, *Mormon Question*, 82; Stanley, *From Bondage to Contract*, 35–59.
19. Grimshaw, *Paths of Duty*, 161–69.
20. Dixon, *Perfecting the Family*.
21. Renshaw, "Historical and Statistical View," 572. Thomas Holt notes that digging, for yams and sugar cane, was considered men's work, while women's work consisted of caring for other crops such as "oil nuts and beans" (*Problem of Freedom*, 171).
22. Wolcott to Whipple, 17 January 1848, AMA Archives.
23. "Jamaica Mission," *American Missionary*, February 1853.
24. Ibid.
25. Hall to Whipple, 20 December 1852, AMA Archives.
26. Stanley, *From Bondage to Contract*, 28–29; Cott, *Public Vows*, 81–103.
27. "Jamaica Mission," *American Missionary*, March 1852. Letter from A. D. Olds.
28. Venning to Whipple, 1858 Annual Report, AMA Archives.
29. Venning to Whipple, 14 November 1859, AMA Archives.
30. Ibid. (emphasis in original).
31. Wolcott to Whipple, 10 August 1854, AMA Archives.
32. Maria Hicks to Whipple, 17 March 1854, AMA Archives.
33. Wolcott to Tappan, 27 December 1854, AMA Archives.
34. Tappan to Richardson, 31 January 1855; Tappan to Olds, 24 December 1854, Lewis Tappan Papers, LOC; Wolcott to Whipple, 24 March 1854, and Wolcott to Whipple, 10 August 1854, AMA Archives.
35. Wyatt-Brown, *Lewis Tappan*, 296.
36. The major export for many was arrowroot.
37. Olds to Whipple, 2 December 1854, AMA Archives.
38. Thompson to Whipple, 6 October 1855, AMA Archives (emphasis in original).
39. Wyatt-Brown, *Lewis Tappan*, 297.
40. Wolcott to Tappan, 1 October 1858, AMA Archives.
41. Ibid.; circular (to shareholders in the United States) from Richmond, July 1859, AMA Archives.
42. Phelps to Tappan, 12 January 1847, AMA Archives.
43. Dean to Whipple, 14 October 1849, AMA Archives.
44. Dean to Whipple, 22 December 1855, AMA Archives.
45. "Jamaica Mission," *American Missionary*, April 1854; Carpenter to Whipple, 21 February 1854; Wolcott to Whipple, 24 March 1854, AMA Archives.
46. Wolcott to Whipple, 24 March 1854, AMA Archives.
47. Carpenter to Whipple, 24 February 1854, AMA Archives.
48. Tappan to Wolcott, 24 May 1855, Lewis Tappan Papers, LOC.
49. Wolcott to Whipple, 19 July 1855, AMA Archives.
50. Wolcott to Whipple, 10 August 1858, AMA Archives.
51. Wolcott to Tappan, 3 August 1855, AMA Archives.
52. Catherine Hall, *Civilising Subjects*, 248.

53. Ibid., 246–50; Holt, *Problem of Freedom*, 291; Robert Stewart, *Religion and Society*, 93–94.

54. Catherine Hall, *Civilising Subjects*, 250.

55. Wolcott to Tappan, 27 December 1854, AMA Archives (emphasis in original).

56. Richmond circular, December 1856; Wolcott to Tappan, 15 April 1857; Circular for Richmond, enclosed in the letter from Wolcott to Whipple, 8 April 1856; Wolcott to Whipple, 3 August 1857, AMA Archives.

57. Holt, *Problem of Freedom*, 194–95.

58. Wolcott to Whipple, 3 November 1856, AMA Archives (emphasis in original).

59. Catherine Hall, *Civilising Subjects*, 205. See also Heuman, *Between Black and White*.

60. Wolcott to Tappan, 27 December 1854, AMA Archives.

61. Wolcott to Whipple, 3 August 1857, AMA Archives.

62. Ibid.

63. Mary Adella Wolcott to Sir Arthur Richards, 9 January 1941, in "Richmond Estate, St. Mary, Offer for Sale to Government," Jamaica Archives.

64. Sehat, "Civilizing Mission of Booker T. Washington."

Part Three Introduction

1. Bigelow Penfield to Minerva Cowles, 19 July 1859, *Letters from Jamaica*, 52.

2. Fletcher, *History of Oberlin*, 301–2.

3. Ibid., 339.

4. Ibid., 683.

5. Butchart, "Mission Matters," 13–14.

6. Fletcher, *History of Oberlin*, 529–32.

7. Bigelow Penfield to Minerva Cowles, 19 July 1859, *Letters from Jamaica*, 52.

8. Antoinette Brown to Lucy Stone, June 1848, in *Friends and Sisters*, 42–43.

9. Lucy Stone to Antoinette Brown, August 1849, No. 2, in *Friends and Sisters*, 56.

10. Fletcher, *History of Oberlin*, 290–291.

11. Jeffrey, *Great Silent Army*, 96–126; Pierson, *Free Hearts*, 74; Dixon, *Perfecting the Family*, 3.

12. Kaplan, "Manifest Domesticity"; Pascoe, *Relations of Rescue*; Simonsen, *Making Home Work*.

13. Sarah Penfield to Minerva Cowles, 7 February 1859, *Letters from Jamaica*, 36.

14. Sarah Penfield to ? (Probably her parents-in-law), 3 January 1859, *Letters from Jamaica*, 26.

15. Sarah Penfield, "Missionary Correspondence," *Advocate and Family Guardian*, 15 September 1860, reprinted in *Letters from Jamaica*, 94.

Chapter Six. Civilizing Domesticity

1. Robert, *American Women in Mission*, 108.

2. Grimshaw, *Paths of Duty*; Brumberg, *Mission for Life*.
3. Hicks to Whipple, 10 July 1852, AMA Archives.
4. Fletcher, *History of Oberlin*, 246; Grimshaw, *Paths of Duty*, 115.
5. Kaplan, *Manifest Domesticity*.
6. Sarah Blakeley to Whipple, 30 July 1852, AMA Archives.
7. Sarah Moffat to Whipple, 28 January 1853, AMA Archives.
8. Thompson to Whipple, 3 January 1853, AMA Archives (emphasis in original).
9. Wolcott to Whipple, 10 September 1849, AMA Archives.
10. Richardson to Whipple, 2 January 1852, AMA Archives.
11. Sarah Blakeley to Whipple, 30 July 1852, AMA Archives.
12. Sarah Moffat to Whipple, 5 July 1853, AMA Archives.
13. Catharine Beecher, *Treatise on Domestic Economy*, 225–26.
14. Thompson to Whipple, 16 March 1853, AMA Archives.
15. Ibid.
16. Richardson to Whipple, 17 March 1853, AMA Archives.
17. Grimshaw, *Paths of Duty*, 100–127.
18. Dean to "George" [not Whipple], 15 September 1851, Amesville, Illinois, AMA Archives.
19. Elijah Griswold to Whipple, 8 November 1849, AMA Archives.
20. P. M. Way to Whipple, 1 January 1853; Hall to Whipple, 5 February 1856, AMA Archives.
21. Dean to Venning, 10 March 1857, AMA Archives.
22. "Jamaica Mission," *American Missionary*, August 1852.
23. Tappan to Dean, 1 April 1855; Tappan to Dean, 13 October 1856, Lewis Tappan Papers, LOC.
24. Tappan to Wolcott, 19 June 1855, Lewis Tappan Papers, LOC.
25. Tappan to Dean, 14 July 1855, Lewis Tappan Papers, LOC.
26. Dean to Whipple, 6 June 1852, AMA Archives.
27. Dean to Whipple, 2 December 1851, Shullsburgh, Wisconsin, AMA Archives.
28. Dean to Whipple, 6 June 1852, AMA Archives.
29. Dean to Whipple, 2 December 1851, Shullsburgh, Wisconsin, AMA Archives.
30. Dean to Tappan, 18 January 1854, AMA Archives.
31. Tappan to Dean, 28 November 1854, Lewis Tappan Papers, LOC.
32. Dean to Whipple, 27 June 1849; Dean to Whipple, 14 August 1849, AMA Archives.
33. Dean to Tappan, 2 May 1853, AMA Archives.
34. Dean to Whipple, 27 May 1853, AMA Archives.
35. Dean to Tappan, 2 May 1853, AMA Archives.
36. Dean to Whipple, 7 September 1855, AMA Archives.
37. Lucy Woodcock to Harry E. Woodcock, 4 January 1858, Woodcock Papers, OCA.
38. Ann Olds to Whipple, 15 August 1849, AMA Archives (emphasis in original).
39. Venning to Whipple, "Statistics of Church," June 1860, AMA Archives.

40. Elizabeth Mogg to Dean, 6 February 1858, AMA Archives.
41. Smith-Rosenberg, "Female World of Love and Ritual," 53–76; Mogg to Dean, 6 February 1858, AMA Archives.
42. Richardson to Whipple, 21 June 1852, AMA Archives.
43. Dean to Tappan, 2 May 1853, AMA Archives.
44. Wolcott to Tappan, 27 December 1854, AMA Archives.
45. Rose, *Rehearsal for Reconstruction*.
46. Dean to Venning, 10 March 1857 AMA Archives.
47. Ibid.
48. Ibid.
49. Hall to Whipple, 4 March 1857, AMA Archives.
50. Ibid.
51. Dean to Venning, 10 March 1857, AMA Archives (emphasis in original).
52. Ibid.
53. Dixon, *Perfecting the Family*, 28–34.
54. Sarah Penfield to Minerva Cowles, 8 November 1859, *Letters from Jamaica*, 61.
55. Ibid., 62.
56. Sarah Penfield to Minerva Cowles, 4 March 1859, *Letters from Jamaica*, 37.
57. "Missionary Correspondence," *Advocate and Family Guardian*, 16 April 1860, reprinted in *Letters from Jamaica*, 74.
58. Sarah Penfield to Minerva Cowles, 4 March 1859, *Letters from Jamaica*, 38–39.
59. Sarah Penfield to "Dear Friend," 31 January 1861, *Letters from Jamaica*, 104 (emphasis in original).
60. Sarah Penfield to Sarah Cowles, 14 March 1859, *Letters from Jamaica*, 41; Bigelow Penfield to Minerva Cowles, 21 June 1859, *Letters from Jamaica*, 47.
61. Sarah Penfield to Sarah Cowles, 14 March 1859, *Letters from Jamaica*, 41.
62. Sarah Penfield to Minerva Cowles, 4 April 1860, and 19 July 1859, *Letters from Jamaica*, 73, 53.
63. Sarah Penfield to Minerva Cowles, 4 April 1860, *Letters from Jamaica*, 73.
64. Sarah Penfield to Sarah Cowles, 14 March 1859, *Letters from Jamaica*, 41 (emphasis in original).
65. Sarah Penfield to Minerva Cowles, 4 April 1860, *Letters from Jamaica*, 73.
66. Ibid.; Bigelow Penfield to Minerva Cowles, 30 May 1860, *Letters from Jamaica*, 82.
67. Sarah Penfield to Sarah Cowles, 14 March 1859, *Letters from Jamaica*, 41.
68. Bigelow Penfield to Minerva Cowles, 19 July 1859, *Letters from Jamaica*, 50.
69. Sarah Penfield to Minerva Cowles, 30 June 1863, *Letters from Jamaica*, 159.
70. Bigelow Penfield to Charles Penfield, 11 April 1859, *Letters from Jamaica*, 43.
71. Sarah Penfield to Minerva Cowles, 4 March 1859 and 15 December 1859, *Letters from Jamaica*, 37 and 63 (emphasis in original).
72. Bigelow Penfield to Minerva Cowles, 19 July 1859, *Letters from Jamaica*, 51.
73. Penfield to Cowles, 7 October 1859, *Letters from Jamaica*, 58.
74. Ibid.

75. Hurtado, *Intimate Frontiers*; Stoler, "Tense and Tender Ties."
76. Sarah Penfield to Minerva Cowles, 3 March 1860, *Letters from Jamaica*, 68.
77. Ibid.
78. Sarah Penfield to Minerva Cowles, 6 July 1860, *Letters from Jamaica*, 84.
79. Wolcott to Whipple, November 1866, AMA Archives (emphasis in original).
80. Antoinette Burton, *Burdens of History*; Jayawardena, *White Woman's Other Burden*; Findlay, *Imposing Decency*; Tyrrell, *Women's World/Women's Empire*; Sneider, *Suffragists in an Imperial Age*.

Chapter Seven. Revival, Rebellions, and Colonial Subordination

1. Wolcott to Whipple, 23 October 1865, AMA Archives.
2. Ibid. (emphasis in original).
3. Wolcott to Whipple, 25 October 1866, AMA Archives. See also Heuman, *"Killing Time"*; Holt, *Problem of Freedom*, 289–302; Robert Stewart, *Religion and Society*, 153–70; Catherine Hall, *Civilising Subjects*, 57–65.
4. Robert Stewart, *Religion and Society*, 145–48.
5. Ibid., 145.
6. Sarah Penfield to Minerva Cowles, 18 January 1861, *Letters from Jamaica*, 102.
7. Thompson to Tappan, 24 January 1861, AMA Archives.
8. "Jamaica Mission," *American Missionary*, May 1861.
9. Ibid.
10. Thompson to Tappan, 24 January 1861, AMA Archives (emphasis in original).
11. "Jamaica Mission: The Revival," *American Missionary*, July 1861.
12. Thompson to Tappan, 24 January 1861, AMA Archives.
13. Thompson was not seen as a good preacher. Bigelow Penfield mentioned to his parents in confidence that the Eliot Church members said, "They have had so-so chat long enough, they want preaching, etc. etc. They would not probably give him a call again unless we pressed it exceedingly" (Bigelow Penfield to his parents, 2 October 1863, *Letters from Jamaica*, 169).
14. Bigelow Penfield to his parents, 28 February 1861, *Letters from Jamaica*, 105–6.
15. "Jamaica Mission: The Revival," *American Missionary*, July 1861.
16. Wolcott to Whipple, 13 June 1860, AMA Archives.
17. "Brownstone, Jamaica, May 28, 1861," *American Missionary*, September 1861.
18. Sarah Penfield to Henry Cowles, 16 April 1861, *Letters from Jamaica*, 109–10; "Missionary Correspondence," *American Missionary*, May 1861, reprinted in *Letters from Jamaica*, 112.
19. Allen Journal, 11 January 1864, Allen Papers, OCA.
20. Austin-Broos, *Jamaica Genesis*, 55; in regard to Beardslee: Bigelow Penfield to Minerva Cowles, 30 May 1860, *Letters from Jamaica*, 81.
21. Allen Journal, 11 January 1864, Allen Papers, OCA.
22. Bigelow Penfield to Minerva Cowles, 30 May 1860, *Letters from Jamaica*, 81.
23. Bigelow Penfield to Minerva Cowles, 2 July 1861, *Letters from Jamaica*, 115.

24. Ibid.
25. "Colored Refugees," *American Missionary*, February 1862.
26. Richardson, *Christian Reconstruction*, 3–7, 17–19.
27. Rose, *Rehearsal for Reconstruction*.
28. Bigelow Penfield to Whipple, 28 April 1865, AMA Archives.
29. Wolcott to Whipple, 23 September 1863, AMA Archives.
30. Thompson to Whipple, 24 November 1858, AMA Archives.
31. Ibid.
32. "The War—Its Cause and Remedy," *American Missionary*, June 1861.
33. Rugemer, *Problem of Emancipation*, 296–301.
34. "Happy Effects of Emancipation in the Island of Jamaica," *American Missionary*, October 1861.
35. "Jamaica Mission," *American Missionary*, February 1862.
36. Fisher to Whipple, 31 July 1865, AMA Archives.
37. Venning to Whipple, 31 July 1865, AMA Archives.
38. Wolcott to Whipple, 23 September 1865, AMA Archives.
39. Holt, *Problem of Freedom*, 265, 205–7, 250–58.
40. Ibid., 295, Catherine Hall, *Civilising Subjects*, 59–62; Robert Stewart, *Religion and Society*, 153–55.
41. Holt, *Problem of Freedom*, 297.
42. Ibid., 299, 304; Catherine Hall, *Civilising Subjects*, 59–63.
43. Wolcott to Whipple, 23 October 1865, AMA Archives.
44. Ibid.
45. Thornton Penfield to Henry and Minerva Cowles, 1 November 1865, *Letters from Jamaica*, 197. Gosselink's transcription reads "Mr. Rennals Castor of St. Thomas Ye Vale," and I interpret this to mean: Mr. Rennie, the custos of the parish.
46. Holt, *Problem of Freedom*, 254.
47. Wolcott to Whipple, 23 October 1865, AMA Archives.
48. Ibid.
49. Thornton Penfield to Henry and Minerva Cowles, 29 December 1865, *Letters from Jamaica*, 199.
50. Robert Stewart, *Religion and Society*, 161–63.
51. Wolcott to Whipple, 23 October 1865, AMA Archives.
52. Penfield to Whipple, 4 January 1866, AMA Archives.
53. Wolcott to Whipple, 5 January 1866, AMA Archives (emphasis in original).
54. Starbuck to Whipple, 26 November 1866, AMA Archives. See also Holt, *Problem of Freedom*, 307–9.
55. Holt, "Essence of Contract"; Mehta, "Liberal Strategies of Exclusion."
56. Rugemer, *Problem of Emancipation*, 294–99.
57. Sarah Penfield to Minerva Cowles, 15 December 1859, *Letters from Jamaica*, 63. Allen Journal, 9 January 1864, Allen Papers, OCA (emphasis in original).
58. Hubbard to Kirk, 2 April 1866, AMA Archives.
59. Ibid.

60. Wolcott to Whipple, November 1866, AMA Archives.
61. Hubbard to Kirk, 2 April 1866, AMA Archives.
62. Venning to Whipple, 1 October 1866, AMA Archives.
63. Venning to Whipple, 12 November 1866, AMA Archives.
64. Venning to Whipple, 1 October 1866, AMA Archives.
65. Harvey and Brewin, *Jamaica in 1866*, 63–64.
66. Wolcott to Whipple, 28 August 1866, AMA Archives.
67. Wolcott to Whipple, 30 October 1866, AMA Archives.
68. Wolcott to Whipple, November 1866, AMA Archives.
69. Wolcott to Whipple, 30 October 1866, AMA Archives.
70. Catherine Hall, *Civilising Subjects*, 424.
71. Bacchus, *Education As and For Legitimacy*, 128–31.
72. Wolcott, Alumni Records, OCA.

Epilogue

1. Sneider, *Suffragists in an Imperial Age*.
2. Starbuck to Whipple, 7 July 1868, AMA Archives.
3. Strieby, "Oberlin and Missionary Work," 121.
4. Ibid., 131.

BIBLIOGRAPHY

Primary Sources

MANUSCRIPT COLLECTIONS

Jamaica
Jamaica Archives, Spanish Town
    Accounts Produce, 1830–70, esp. 1830 and 1850–51.
    Cooper, John W. "Reports on the Properties of Simon Taylor, 1835." Call no. 7/177/1-8. Private gift.
    Richmond Estate, St. Mary, Offer of Sale to the Government. Call no. 18/5/77/9.
National Library of Jamaica, Kingston.
    Estate maps.
    Samuel, Peter. Diary and Letterbook (call no. MS 283).

United States
Allen, George N. Papers. Oberlin College Archives (OCA).
Alumni Records. Oberlin College Archives (OCA). Categorized by names of individual alumni.
American Missionary Association (AMA) Archives. Amistad Research Center (ARC), Tulane University.
Fletcher, Robert. Oberlin College Archives (OCA).
Phelps, Amos A. Papers. Antislavery Collection. Boston Public Library.
Shipherd, John Jay. Oberlin College Archives (OCA).
Tappan, Lewis. Papers, 1809–1903. Library of Congress (LOC), Washington, D.C.
Woodcock, Harry E. Oberlin College Archives (OCA).

PRINTED COLLECTIONS

"Letters Showing the Rise and Progress of the Early Negro Churches of Georgia and the West Indies, George Liele, Stephen Cooke, Abraham Marshall, Jonathan Clarke, Thomas Nichols Swigle." *Journal of Negro History* 1 (January 1916): 69–92.
Liele, George. In *Unchained Voices: An Anthology of Black Authors in the English Speaking World of the 18th Century*, edited by Vincent Carretta, 325–32. Lexington: University Press of Kentucky, 1996.

Penfield, Thornton Bigelow, and Sarah Ingraham Penfield. *Letters from Jamaica, 1858–1866.* Edited by Charles C. Gosselink. Silver Bay, N.Y.: Boat House Books, 2005.

Prince, Nancy. *Narrative and Travels of Mrs. Nancy Prince* (1850) and *The West Indies: Being a Description of the Islands, Progress of Christianity, Education, and Liberty among the Colored Population Generally* (1841) in *A Black Woman's Odyssey through Russia and Jamaica: The Narrative of Nancy Prince.* Edited by Ronald G. Walters. Princeton, N.J.: Markus Wiener, 1995.

Stone, Lucy, and Antoinette Brown Blackwell. *Friends and Sisters: Letters between Lucy Stone and Antoinette Brown Blackwell, 1846–93.* Edited by Carol Lasser and Marlene Deahl Merrill. Urbana: University of Illinois Press, 1987.

Weld, Theodore, et al. *Letters of Theodore Weld, Angelina Grimké Weld and Sarah Grimké, 1822–1844.* 2 vols. Edited by Gilbert H. Barnes and Dwight L. Dumond. New York: D. Appleton-Century Co., 1934.

PUBLISHED ARTICLES, PAMPHLETS, AND BOOKS

Beecher, Catharine. *Essays on Slavery and Abolitionism with Reference to the Duty of American Females.* Philadelphia, 1837.

———. *Treatise on Domestic Economy for the Use of Young Ladies at Home and at School.* Boston, 1843.

Beecher, Lyman. *The Autobiography of Lyman Beecher.* Edited by Charles Beecher. 2 vols. New York, 1865.

———, ed. *Letters of the Rev. Dr. Beecher and Rev. Mr. Nettleton, on the "New Measures" in conducting Revivals of Religion. With a Review of a Sermon, By Novanglus.* New York, 1828.

Child, Lydia Maria. *Appeal in Favor of that Class of Americans Called Africans.* Boston, 1833.

———. *The Freedman's Book.* Boston, 1865.

———. *The Right Way, the Safe Way.* Boston, 1860.

Debate at the Lane Seminary, Cincinnati; Speech of James A. Thome, of Kentucky, Delivered at the Annual Meeting of the American Anti-Slavery Society; Letter of the Rev. Dr. Samuel H. Cox, Against the American Colonization Society. Boston, 1834.

Duncan, Peter. *A Narrative of the Wesleyan Mission to Jamaica.* London, 1849.

First Annual Report of the Society for Promoting Manual Labor in Literary Institutions. New York, 1833.

Harvey, Thomas, and William Brewin. *Jamaica in 1866.* London, 1867.

Hawley, Zerah. *A Journal of a Tour through Connecticut, Massachusetts, New York, the North Part of Pennsylvania and Ohio.* New Haven, 1822.

Luckock, Benjamin. *Jamaica: Enslaved and Free.* New York, 1846.

Phelps, Amos A. *Lectures on Slavery and Its Remedy.* Boston, 1834.

Phillippo, James M. *Jamaica, Its Past and Present State.* London, 1843.

Renshaw, Charles Stewart. "Historical and Statistical View of the Working of Emancipation in Jamaica." *New Englander and Yale Review* (October 1848): 557–77.

———. "Religious State of Jamaica." *New Englander and Yale Review* (January 1846): 19–29.

Report on the Condition of the People of Color in the State of Ohio, Proceedings of the Ohio Anti-Slavery Convention. Putnam, Ohio, 1835.

Starbuck, C. C. "Emancipation in Jamaica." *Continental Monthly* (July 1863): 1–16.

———. "The Isle of Springs." *Continental Monthly* (September and October 1863): 284–92 and 433–44.

Strieby, Michael E. "Oberlin and Missionary Work." In *The Oberlin Jubilee, 1833–1883*, ed. W. G. Ballantine, 116–33. Oberlin, Ohio, 1883.

Sturge, Joseph, and Thomas Harvey. *The West Indies in 1837*. London, 1838.

Tappan, Lewis. *History of the American Missionary Association, Its Constitution and Principles*. New York, 1855.

Thome, James A. "Address to the Ladies of Ohio." In *Report of the First Anniversary of the Ohio Anti-Slavery Society*. Cincinnati, 1836.

———, and J. Horace Kimball. *Emancipation in the West Indies*. Boston, 1838.

PERIODICALS

Advocate and Family Guardian
American Missionary
Baptist Annual Register
Christian Recorder
Cincinnati Journal
Continental Monthly
Jamaica Gleaner
Liberator
National Era
New Englander and Yale Review
Oberlin Evangelist

Secondary Sources

Abzug, Robert H. *Cosmos Crumbling: American Reform and the Religious Imagination*. New York: Oxford University Press, 1994.

———. *Passionate Liberator: Theodore Dwight Weld and the Dilemma of Reform*. New York: Oxford University Press, 1980.

Ahlstrom, Sidney, *A Religious History of the American People*. 2nd ed. New Haven, Conn.: Yale University Press, 2004.

Andrew, John III. *From Revivals to Removal: Jeremiah Evarts, the Cherokee Nation, and the Search for the Soul of America*. Athens: University of Georgia Press, 1992.

Austin-Broos, Diane. *Jamaica Genesis: Religion and the Politics of Moral Orders.* Chicago: University of Chicago, 1997.

———. "Redefining the Moral Order: Interpretations of Christianity in Postemancipation Jamaica." In McGlynn and Drescher, *The Meaning of Freedom*, 221–44.

Bacchus. M. Kazim. *Education as and for Legitimacy: Developments in West Indian Education between 1846 and 1895.* Waterloo, Ontario: Wilfred Laurier University Press, 1994.

Baker, Paula. "The Domestication of Politics: Women and American Political Society." *American Historical Review* 89 (June 1984): 620–47.

Barker, Anthony J. *Captain Charles Stuart: Anglo-American Abolitionist.* Baton Rouge: Louisiana State University Press, 1986.

Barnes, Gilbert H. *The Antislavery Impulse, 1830–1844.* New York: D. Appleton-Century Company, 1933.

Barrow, Christine. *Family in the Caribbean: Themes and Perspectives.* Kingston, Jamaica: Ian Randle Publishers, 1996.

Bays, Daniel, and Grant Wacker, eds. *The Foreign Missionary Enterprise at Home: Explorations in North American Cultural History.* Tuscaloosa: University of Alabama Press, 2003.

Beckles, Hilary McD. *Centering Women: Gender Discourses in Caribbean Slave Society.* Kingston, Jamaica: Ian Randle, 1999.

Bender, Thomas, ed. *Rethinking American History in a Global Age.* Berkeley: University of California Press, 2002.

Berman, Carolyn. *Creole Crossings: Domestic Fiction and the Reform of Colonial Slavery.* Ithaca, N.Y.: Cornell University Press, 2006.

Besson, Jean. "Freedom and Community: The British West Indies." In McGlynn and Drescher, *The Meaning of Freedom*, 183–220.

———. *Martha Brae's Two Histories: European Expansion and Caribbean Culture-Building in Jamaica.* Chapel Hill: University of North Carolina Press, 2002.

———. "A Paradox in Caribbean Attitudes to Land." In *Land and Development in the Caribbean*, edited by Jean Besson and Janet Momsen, 13–45. London: Macmillan, 1987.

Blackburn, Robin. *The Making of New World Slavery: From the Baroque to the Modern, 1492–1800.* London: Verso, 1997.

Blackett, R. J. M. *Building an Antislavery Wall: Black Americans in the Atlantic Abolitionist Movement, 1830–1860.* Baton Rouge: Louisiana State University Press, 2001.

Blight, David. *Race and Reunion: The Civil War in American Memory.* Cambridge, Mass.: Harvard University Press, 2001.

Boles, John B. *The Great Revival, 1787–1805: The Origins of the Southern Evangelical Mind.* Lexington: University Press of Kentucky, 1972.

Bolland, O. Nigel. "The Politics of Freedom in the British Caribbean." In McGlynn and Drescher, *The Meaning of Freedom*, 113–46.

———. "Systems of Domination after Slavery: The Control of Land and Labor in the British West Indies after 1838." *Comparative Studies in Society and History* 23 (October 1981): 591–619.

Bolt, Christine. *The Anti-Slavery Movement and Reconstruction*. London: Oxford University Press, 1969.

Bosch, David. *Transforming Mission: Paradigm Shifts in Theology of Mission*. Maryknoll, N.Y.: Orbis Books, 1991.

Boylan, Anne. "Benevolence and Antislavery Activity among African-American Women in New York and Boston, 1820–1840." In Yellin and Van Horne, *The Abolitionist Sisterhood*, 119–37.

———. "Women in Groups: An Analysis of Women's Organizations in New York and Boston, 1797–1840." *Journal of American History* 71 (December 1984): 497–523.

Braithwaite, Edward K. *The Development of Creole Society in Jamaica, 1770–1820*. Oxford: Clarendon, 1971.

Braude, Ann. *Radical Spirits: Spiritualism and Women's Rights in Nineteenth-Century America*. Bloomington: Indiana University Press, 1989.

Brereton, Bridget. "Family Strategies, Gender, and the Shift to Wage Labor in the British Caribbean." In Scully and Paton, *Gender and Slave Emancipation in the Atlantic World*, 143–61.

Brown, Christopher. *Moral Capital: Foundations of British Abolitionism*. Chapel Hill: University of North Carolina Press, 2006.

Brown, Vincent. "Spiritual Terror and Sacred Authority in Jamaican Slave Society." *Slavery and Abolition* 24 (April 2003): 24–53.

Brumberg, Joan Jacobs. *Mission for Life: The Story of the Family of Adoniram Judson, the Dramatic Events of the First American Foreign Mission, and the ourse of Evangelical Religion in the Nineteenth Century*. New York: Free Press, 1980.

Bryan, Patrick E. "Aiding Imperialism: White Baptists in Nineteenth-Century Jamaica." *Small Axe* 7 (September 2003): 137–49.

Burton, Antoinette. *Burdens of History: British Feminists, Indian Women, and Imperial Culture*. Chapel Hill: University of North Carolina Press, 1994.

Burton, Richard D. E. *Afro-Creole: Power, Opposition, and Play in the Caribbean*. Ithaca, N.Y.: Cornell University Press, 1997.

Bush, Barbara. "'The Family Tree is not Cut': Women and Cultural Resistance in Slave Family Life in the British Caribbean." In *Resistance: Studies in African, Caribbean, and Afro-American History*, edited by Gary Y. Okihiro, 117–32. Amherst: University of Massachusetts Press, 1986.

———. *Slave Women in Caribbean Society, 1650–1838*. Bloomington: Indiana University Press, 1990.

Butchart, Ronald E. "Mission Matters: Mount Holyoke, Oberlin, and the Schooling of Southern Blacks, 1861–1917." *History of Education Quarterly* 42 (Spring 2002): 1–17.

———. *Northern Schools, Southern Blacks, and Reconstruction: Freedmen's Education, 1862–1875.* Westport, Conn.: Greenwood Press, 1980.
Byrd, Alexander. *Captives and Voyagers: Black Migrants across the Eighteenth-Century British Atlantic World.* Baton Rouge: Louisiana State University Press, 2008.
Campbell, Carl. "Early Post-Emancipation Jamaica: The Historiography of Plantation Culture, 1834–1865." In Montieth and Richards, *Jamaica in Slavery and Freedom*, 52–73.
Carretta, Vincent. *Unchained Voices: An Anthology of Black Authors in the English-Speaking World of the Eighteenth Century.* Lexington: University Press of Kentucky, 1996.
Chakrabarty, Dipesh. *Provincializing Europe.* Princeton, N.J.: Princeton University Press, 2000.
Chaudhuri, Nupur, and Margaret Strobel, eds. *Western Women and Imperialism: Complicity and Resistance.* Bloomington: University of Indiana Press, 1992.
Clarke, Edith. *My Mother Who Fathered Me.* London: George Allen and Unwin, 1957.
Claw, Spencer. *Without Sin: The Life and Death of the Oneida Community.* New York: Allen Lane, 1993.
Clayton, Nichola. "Managing the Transition to a Free Labor Society: American Interpretations of the British West Indies during the Civil War and Reconstruction." *American Nineteenth-Century History* 7 (March 2006): 89–108.
Comaroff, John L. "Images of Empire, Contests of Conscience: Models of Colonial Domination in South Africa." In Cooper and Stoler, *Tensions of Empire*, 163–97.
———, and Jean Comaroff. *Of Revelation and Revolution: Colonialism and Conscience in South Africa.* Chicago: University of Chicago Press, 1991.
Cooper, Frederick, Thomas Holt, and Rebecca Scott, eds. *Beyond Slavery: Explorations of Race, Labor, and Citizenship in Postemancipation Societies.* Chapel Hill: University of North Carolina Press, 2000.
Cooper, Frederick, and Ann Laura Stoler, eds. *Tensions of Empire: Colonial Cultures in a Bourgeois World.* Berkeley: University of California Press, 1997.
Cott, Nancy. *The Bonds of Womanhood: "Women's Sphere" in New England, 1780–1835.* 2nd ed. New Haven, Conn.: Yale University Press, 1997.
———. *Public Vows: A History of Marriage and the Nation.* Cambridge, Mass.: Harvard University Press, 2000.
Craton, Michael. *Testing the Chains: Resistance to Slavery in the British West Indies.* Ithaca, N.Y.: Cornell University Press, 1982.
Cross, Whitney. *The Burned-Over District: The Social and Intellectual History of Enthusiastic Religion in Western New York, 1800–1850.* Ithaca, N.Y.: Cornell University Press, 1950.
Curtin, Philip D. *The Atlantic Slave Trade: A Census.* Madison: University of Wisconsin Press, 1969.
———. *The Image of Africa: British Ideas and Action, 1780–1850.* 2 vols. Madison: University of Wisconsin Press, 1964.

———. *Two Jamaicas: The Role of Ideas in a Tropical Colony, 1830–1865*. Cambridge, Mass.: Harvard University Press, 1955.

Da Costa, Vittoria Emilia. *Crowns of Glory, Tears of Blood: The Demerara Slave Rebellion of 1823*. Oxford: Oxford University Press, 1994.

Dain, Bruce. *Hideous Monster of the Mind: American Race Theory in the Early Republic*. Cambridge, Mass.: Harvard University Press, 2002.

Daly, John. *When Slavery Was Called Freedom: Evangelicalism, Proslavery, and the Causes of the American Civil War*. Lexington: University Press of Kentucky, 2002.

Davis, David Brion. *Inhuman Bondage: The Rise and Fall of Slavery in the New World*. New York: Oxford University Press, 2006.

———. *The Problem of Slavery in the Age of Revolution, 1770–1823*. Ithaca, N.Y.: Cornell University Press, 1975.

DeMaria, Richard. *Communal Love at Oneida: A Perfectionist Vision of Authority, Property, and Sexual Order*. New York: E. Mellen Press, 1978.

DeRogatis, Amy. *Moral Geography: Maps, Missionaries, and the American Frontier*. New York: Columbia University Press, 2003.

Dixon, Chris. *Perfecting the Family: Antislavery Marriages in Nineteenth-Century America*. Amherst: University of Massachusetts Press, 1997.

Dorsey, Bruce. *Reforming Men and Women: Gender in the Antebellum City*. Chapel Hill: University of North Carolina Press, 2002.

Drescher, Seymour. *Capitalism and Antislavery: British Mobilization in Comparative Perspective*. New York: Oxford University Press, 1987.

———. *The Mighty Experiment: Free Labor Versus Slavery in British Emancipation*. New York: Oxford: 2002.

DuBois, Ellen Carol. *Feminism and Suffrage: The Emergence of an Independent Women's Movement in America, 1848–1869*. Ithaca, N.Y.: Cornell University Press, 1978.

Dubois, Laurent. *Avengers of the New World: The Story of the Haitian Revolution*. Cambridge, Mass.: Belknap Press of Harvard University, 2004.

Eisner, Gisela. *Jamaica, 1830–1930: A Study in Economic Growth*. Manchester: Manchester University Press, 1961.

Egerton, Douglass. "'Its Origin Is Not A Little Curious'": A New Look at the American Colonization Society." *Journal of the Early Republic* 5 (Winter 1985): 463–80.

Eltis, David. *The Rise of African Slavery in the Americas*. New York: Cambridge University Press, 2000.

———. "Abolitionist Perceptions of Society after Slavery." In *Slavery and British Society, 1776–1846*, edited by J. Walvin, 195–213 (London: Macmillan, 1982).

Eudall, Demetrius. *The Political Languages of Emancipation in the British Caribbean and the U.S. South*. Chapel Hill: University of North Carolina Press, 2002.

Evans, Julie. "Reassessing Missionary Conflict with Colonial Authorities: Sovereignty, Authority and the Civilising Mission in Jamaica." In *Evangelists of Empire? Missionaries in Colonial History*. Edited by Amanda Barry,

Joanna Cruickshank, Andrew Brown-May and Patricia Grimshaw. [Online] Melbourne: University of Melbourne eScholarship Research Centre, 2008. Available at http://msp.esrc.unimelb.edu.au/shs/missions.

Faust, Drew Gilpin, ed. *The Ideology of Slavery: Proslavery Thought in the Antebellum South, 1830–1860*. Baton Rouge: Louisiana State University Press, 1981.

Felt, Alice Tyler. *Freedom's Ferment: Phases of American Social History to 1860*. Minneapolis: University of Minnesota Press, 1944.

Fenton, Elizabeth. "Religious Liberties: Anti-Catholicism and Liberal Democracy in U.S. Literature and Culture, 1774–1889." PhD diss., Rice University, 2006.

Findlay, Eileen Suarez. *Imposing Decency: The Politics of Sexuality and Race in Puerto Rico, 1870–1920*. Durham, N.C.: Duke University Press, 1999.

Fladeland, Betty. *Men and Brothers: Anglo-American Antislavery Cooperation*. Urbana: University of Illinois Press, 1972.

Fletcher, Robert. *A History of Oberlin College from Its Foundation through the Civil War*. 2 vols. Oberlin, Ohio: Oberlin College, 1943.

Frederickson, George. *The Black Image in the White Mind: The Debate on Afro-American Character and Destiny, 1817–1914*. Hanover, N.H.: Wesleyan University Press, 1971.

Foner, Eric, *Free Soil, Free Labor, Free Men: The Ideology of the Republican Party before the Civil War*. New York: Oxford University Press, 1970.

———. *Nothing but Freedom: Emancipation and Its Legacy*. Baton Rouge: Louisiana State University Press, 1983.

Forret, Jeff. "Conflict and the 'Slave Community': Violence among Slaves in Upcountry South Carolina." *Journal of Southern History* 74 (August 2008): 551–88.

Fox-Genovese, Elizabeth. *Within the Plantation Household: Black and White Women of the Old South*. Chapel Hill: University of North Carolina Press, 1988.

Frey, Sylvia R., and Betty Wood. *Come Shouting to Zion: African American Protestantism in the American South and British Caribbean to 1830*. Chapel Hill: University of North Carolina Press, 1998.

Friedman, Lawrence. "Confidence and Pertinacity in Evangelical Abolitionism: Lewis Tappan's Circle." *American Quarterly* 31 (Spring 1979): 81–106.

Fuller, Barbara. "'Christian' Morality in 'Heathen' Jamaica: The American Missionary Association and the Case of Dr. Hyde, 1847–1858." *Journal of Caribbean History* 36, no. 1: 228–42.

Gaspar, David Barry, and Darlene Clark Hine, eds. *More Than Chattel: Black Women and Slavery in the Americas*. Bloomington: Indiana University Press, 1996.

Ginzberg, Lori D. *Women and the Work of Benevolence: Morality, Politics, and Class in the Nineteenth-Century United States*. New Haven, Conn.: Yale University Press, 1990.

Goodman, Paul. "The Manual Labor Movement and the Origins of Abolitionism." *Journal of the Early Republic* 13 (Fall 1993): 355–88.

———. *Of One Blood: Abolitionism and the Origins of Racial Equality.* Berkeley: University of California Press, 1996.

Gordon, Sarah Barringer. *The Mormon Question: Polygamy and Constitutional Conflict in Nineteenth-Century America.* Chapel Hill: University of North Carolina Press, 2002.

Gosselink, Charles C., ed. *Letters from Jamaica, 1858–1866.* Silver Bay, N.Y.: Boat House Books, 2005.

Greenberg, Amy S. *Manifest Manhood and the Antebellum American Empire.* New York: Cambridge University Press, 2005.

Grimshaw, Patricia. *Paths of Duty: American Missionary Wives in Nineteenth-Century Hawaii.* Honolulu: University of Hawaii Press, 1989.

Guterl, Matthew. *American Mediterranean: Southern Slaveholders in the Age of Emancipation.* Cambridge, Mass.: Harvard University Press, 2008.

Hall, Catherine. *Civilising Subjects: Metropole and Colony in the English Imagination, 1830–1867.* Chicago: University of Chicago Press, 2002.

———. "Gender Politics and Imperial Politics: Rethinking the Histories of Empire." In Shepherd, Brereton, and Bailey, *Engendering History: Caribbean Women in Historical Perspective*, 48–59.

Hall, Douglas. "The Flight from the Estates Reconsidered: The British West Indies, 1828–42." *Journal of Caribbean History* 10/11 (1978): 7–24.

Handler, J. S., and K. M. Bilby. "On the Early Use and Origins of the Term 'Obeah' in Barbados and the Anglophone Caribbean." *Slavery and Abolition* 22 (August 2001): 87–100.

Hansen, Debra Gold. *Strained Sisterhood: Gender and Class in the Boston Female Anti-Slavery Society.* Amherst: University of Massachusetts Press, 1993.

Hardesty, Nancy. *Women Called to Witness: Evangelical Feminism in the Nineteenth Century.* 1984; repr. Knoxville: University of Tennessee Press, 1999.

Hatch, Nathan. *The Democratization of American Christianity.* New Haven, Conn.: Yale University Press, 1989.

Hersh, Blanche Glassman. *The Slavery of Sex: Feminist Abolitionists in America.* Urbana: University of Illinois Press, 1978.

Heuman, Gad. *Between Black and White: Race, Politics, and the Free Coloreds in Jamaica, 1792–1865.* Westport, Conn.: Greenwood Press, 1981.

———. *"The Killing Time": The Morant Bay Rebellion in Jamaica.* London: Macmillan, 1994.

Hewitt, Nancy. "On Their Own Terms." In Yellin and Van Horne, *Abolitionist Sisterhood*, 23–30.

———. *Women's Activism and Social Change: Rochester, N.Y., 1822–1872.* Ithaca, N.Y.: Cornell University Press, 1984.

Higman, B. W. "Household Structure and Fertility on Jamaican Sugar Plantations: A Nineteenth-Century Example." *Population Studies* 27, no. 3 (November 1973): 527–50.

———. *Jamaica Surveyed: Plantation Maps and Plans of the Eighteenth and Nineteenth Centuries*. San Francisco: Institute of Jamaica Publications Ltd., 1998.

———. *Montpelier, Jamaica: A Plantation Community in Slavery and Freedom*. Kingston, Jamaica: University of the West Indies Press, 1998.

———. *Plantation Jamaica, 1750–1850: Capital and Control in a Colonial Economy*. Kingston, Jamaica: University of the West Indies Press, 2005.

———. *Slave Population and Economy in Jamaica, 1807–1834*. New York: Cambridge University Press, 1976.

Hoffert, Sylvia D. "Yankee Schoolmarms and the Domestication of the South." *Southern Studies* 24 (Summer 1985): 188–201.

Holt, Thomas C. "'An Empire over the Mind': Emancipation, Race and Ideology in the British West Indies and the American South." In *Region, Race, and Reconstruction: Essays in Honor of C. Vann Woodward*, edited by J. Morgan Kousser and James M. McPherson, 283–313. Oxford: Oxford University Press, 1982.

———. "The Essence of the Contract: The Articulation of Race, Gender, and Political Economy in British Emancipation Policy, 1838–1866." In Cooper, Holt, and Scott, *Beyond Slavery*, 33–61.

———. *The Problem of Freedom: Race, Labor and Politics in Jamaica and Britain, 1832–1938*. Baltimore: Johns Hopkins University Press, 1992.

Hurtado, Albert. *Intimate Frontiers: Sex, Gender, and Culture in Old California*. Albuquerque: University of New Mexico Press, 1993.

Hutchison, William R. *Errand to the World: American Protestant Thought and Foreign Missions*. Chicago: University of Chicago Press, 1987.

James, C. L. R. *The Black Jacobins*. 2nd ed. New York: Vintage, 1989.

Jayawardena, Kumari. *The White Woman's Other Burden: Western Women in South Asia during British Colonial Rule*. New York: Routledge Press, 1997.

Jeffrey, Julie Roy. *Abolitionists Remember: Antislavery Autobiographies and the Unfinished Work of Emancipation*. Chapel Hill: University of North Carolina Press, 2008.

———. *The Great Silent Army of Abolitionism: Ordinary Women in the Antislavery Movement*. Chapel Hill: University of North Carolina Press, 1998.

Johnson, Clifton H. "The American Missionary Association, 1846–1861: A Study of Christian Abolitionism." PhD diss., University of North Carolina, 1958.

Johnson, Curtis. *Islands of Holiness: Rural Religion in Upstate New York, 1790–1860*. Ithaca, N.Y.: Cornell University Press, 1989.

Johnson, Paul E. *The Shopkeeper's Millennium: Society and Revivals in Rochester, New York, 1815–1837*. New York: Hill and Wang, 1978.

Jones, Jacqueline. *Soldiers of Light and Love: Northern Teachers and Georgian Blacks, 1865–1877*. Chapel Hill: University of North Carolina Press, 1980.

Kachun, Mitch. "'Our Platform Is as Broad as Humanity': Transatlantic Freedom Movements and the Idea of Progress in Nineteenth-Century African American Thought and Activism." *Slavery and Abolition* 24 (December 2003): 1–23.

Kaplan, Amy. "Manifest Domesticity." *American Literature* 70 (September 1998): 581–606.

Kenny, Gale L. "Reconstructing a Different South: The American Missionary Association and Jamaica, 1834–65." *Slavery and Abolition* 30, no. 3 (September 2009): 445–66.

Kent, Eliza. *Converting Christians: Gender and Protestant Christianity in Colonial South India.* Oxford: Oxford University Press, 2004.

Kraditor, Aileen. *Means and Ends in American Abolitionism.* New York: Pantheon Books, 1969.

Lasser, Carol. "Enacting Emancipation: African American Women Abolitionists at Oberlin College and the Quest for Empowerment, Equality, and Respectability." In Sklar and Stewart, *Women's Rights and Transatlantic Antislavery,* 319–45.

———, and Marlene Deahl, eds. *Friends and Sisters: Letters Between Lucy Stone and Antoinette Brown Blackwell, 1846–93.* Urbana: University of Illinois Press, 1987.

Lerner, Gerda. *The Grimké Sisters of South Carolina: Pioneers for Women's Rights and Abolitionism.* 1967; Repr. and expanded ed., Chapel Hill: University of North Carolina Press, 2004.

Lesick, Lawrence. *The Lane Rebels: Evangelicalism and Antislavery in Antebellum America.* Metuchen, N.J.: Scarecrow Press, 1980.

Little, Thomas J. "George Liele and the Rise of Independent Black Baptist Churches in the Lower South and Jamaica." *Slavery and Abolition* 16 (August 1995): 188–204.

Loveland, Anne. "Abolitionism and 'Immediate Emancipation' in American Antislavery Thought." *Journal of Southern History* 32 (May 1966): 172–88.

Makdisi, Ussama. *Artillery of Heaven: American Missionaries, the Middle East, and the Question of Colonial Imperialism.* Ithaca, N.Y.: Cornell University Press, 2008.

Mathurin, Lucille. *The Rebel Woman in the British West Indies during Slavery.* Kingston: Institute of Jamaica Publications, 1975.

Matthews, Gelien. *Caribbean Slave Revolts and the British Abolitionist Movement.* Baton Rouge: Louisiana State University Press, 2006.

Maxfield, Charles. "The 1845 Organic Sin Debate: Slavery, Sin, and the American Board of Commissioners for Foreign Missions." In *North American Foreign Missions, 1810–1914: Theology, Theory, and Policy,* edited by Wilbert R. Shenk, 86–115. Grand Rapids: Eerdmans, 2004.

McDaniel, William Caleb. "The Fourth and the First: Abolitionist Holidays, Respectability, and Radical Interracial Reform." *American Quarterly* 57 (March 2005): 129–151.

———. "Our Country Is the World: Radical Abolitionists Abroad." PhD diss., Johns Hopkins University, 2006.

McGlynn, Frank, and Seymour Drescher, eds. *The Meaning of Freedom: Economics, Politics, and Culture after Slavery.* Pittsburgh: University of Pittsburgh Press, 1992.

McKivigan, John R. "The Christian Anti-Slavery Convention Movement of the Northwest." In *Abolitionism and American Reform*, vol. 1, *History of the American Abolitionist Movement: A Bibliography of Scholarly Articles*, edited by John R. McKivigan, 145–66. New York: Garland Publishing, 1999.

———. *The War against Proslavery Religion: Abolitionism and the Northern Churches, 1830–1865*. Ithaca, N.Y.: Cornell University Press, 1984.

McKivigan, John R., and Mitchell Snay, eds. *Religion and the Antebellum Debate over Slavery*. Athens: University of Georgia Press, 1998.

McLaughlin, William G. *Cherokees and Missionaries: 1789–1839*. New Haven, Conn.: Yale University Press.

———. *Revivals, Awakenings, and Reforms: An Essay on Religion and Social Change in America, 1607–1977*. Chicago: University of Chicago Press, 1980.

McPherson, James M. "The New Puritanism: Values and Goals of Freedmen's Education in America." In *The University in Society*, edited by Lawrence Stone, 611–42. Princeton, N.J.: Princeton University Press, 1974.

———. "Was West Indian Emancipation a Success? The Abolitionist Argument During the American Civil War." *Caribbean Studies* 4 (1964): 28–34.

Mehta, Uday. "Liberal Strategies of Exclusion." In Cooper and Stoler, *Tensions of Empire*, 59–86.

Melder, Keith. "Abby Kelley and the Process of Liberation." In Yellin and Van Horne, *Abolitionist Sisterhood*, 231–48.

Midgley, Claire. "Antislavery and the Roots of Imperial Feminism." In *Gender and Imperialism*, edited by Clare Midgley, 161–79. Manchester: Manchester University Press, 1998.

———. *Women against Slavery: The British Campaigns, 1780–1870*. London: Routledge, 1992.

Montieth, Kathleen E. A., and Glen Richards, eds. *Jamaica in Slavery and Freedom: History, Heritage, and Culture*. Kingston, Jamaica: University of West Indies Press, 2002.

Morris, Celia. *Fanny Wright: Rebel in America*. Cambridge, Mass.: Harvard University Press, 1984.

Newman, Louise Michele. *White Women's Rights: The Racial Origins of Feminism in the United States*. New York: Oxford University Press, 1999.

Newman, Richard S. *The Transformation of American Abolitionism: Fighting Slavery in the Early Republic*. Chapel Hill: University of North Carolina Press, 2002.

Olwell, Robert. "'Loose, Idle and Disorderly': Slave Women in the Eighteenth-Century Charleston Marketplace." In Gaspar and Hine, *More Than Chattel: Black Women and Slavery in the Americas*, 97–110.

Pascoe, Peggy. *Relations of Rescue: The Search for Female Moral Authority in the American West, 1874–1939*. New York: Oxford University Press, 1990.

Paton, Diana. "Flight from the Fields Reconsidered: Gender Ideologies and Women's Labor after Slavery in Jamaica." In *Reclaiming the Political in Latin American*

History, edited by Gilbert M. Joseph, 175–204. Durham, N.C.: Duke University Press, 2001.

———. *No Bond But the Law: Punishment, Race, and Gender in Jamaican State Formation, 1780–1870*. Durham, N.C.: Duke University Press, 2004.

Petley, Christer. "Slavery, Emancipation, and the World View of Jamaican Colonists, 1800–1834." *Slavery and Abolition* 26 (April 2005): 93–114.

Pierson, Michael. *Free Hearts and Free Homes: Gender and American Antislavery Politics*. Chapel Hill: University of North Carolina Press, 2003.

Porterfield, Amanda. *Mary Lyon and the Mount Holyoke Missionaries*. New York: Oxford University Press, 1997.

Quarles, Benjamin. *Black Abolitionists*. New York: Oxford University Press, 1969.

Raboteau, Albert. *Slave Religion: The "Invisible Institution" in the American South*. New York: Oxford University Press, 1978.

Rael, Patrick. *Black Identity and Black Protest in the Antebellum North*. Chapel Hill: University of North Carolina Press, 2002.

Rafael, Vincente. *White Love and Other Events in Filipino History*. Durham, N.C.: Duke University Press, 2000.

Richardson, Joe M. *Christian Reconstruction: The American Missionary Association and Southern Blacks, 1861–1890*. Athens: University of Georgia Press, 1986.

Robert, Dana. *American Women in Mission: A Social History of Their Thought and Practice*. Macon, Ga.: Mercer University Press, 1996.

Rose, Willie Lee. *Rehearsal for Reconstruction: The Port Royal Experiment*. Indianapolis, Ind.: Bobbs-Merrill Press, 1964.

Rugemer, Edward. *The Problem of Emancipation: The Caribbean Roots of the American Civil War*. Baton Rouge: Louisiana State University Press, 2008.

———. "Robert Monroe Harrison, British Abolition, Southern Anglophobia, and the Annexation of Texas." *Slavery and Abolition* 28 (August 2007): 169–91.

———. "The Southern Response to British Abolitionism: The Maturation of Proslavery Apologetics." *Journal of Southern History* 70 (May 2004): 221–48.

Ryan, Mary. *Cradle of the Middle Class: The Family in Oneida County, New York, 1790–1865*. Cambridge: Cambridge University Press, 1981.

Ryan, Susan. *The Grammar of Good Intentions: Race and the Antebellum Culture of Benevolence*. Ithaca, N.Y.: Cornell University Press, 2003.

Sanchez-Eppler, Karen. "Raising Empires Like Children: Race, Nation, and Religious Education." *American Literary History* 8 (1996): 399–425.

Schuler, Monica. *Alas, Alas Kongo: A Social History of Indentured African Immigration into Jamaica, 1841–1865*. Baltimore: Johns Hopkins University Press, 1980.

Scott, Rebecca J. *Degrees of Freedom: Louisiana and Cuba after Slavery*. Cambridge: Harvard University Press, 2005.

Scully, Pamela, and Diane Paton, eds. *Gender and Slave Emancipation in the Atlantic World*. Durham, N.C.: Duke University Press, 2005.

Sehat, David. "The Civilizing Mission of Booker T. Washington." *Journal of Southern History* 73 (May 2007): 323–62.

Sernett, Milton C. *Abolition's Axe: Beriah Green, Oneida Institute, and the Black Freedom Struggle.* Syracuse, N.Y.: Syracuse University Press, 1986.

Sheller, Mimi. *Democracy after Slavery: Black Publics and Peasant Radicalism in Haiti and Jamaica.* Gainesville: University of Florida Press, 2000.

———. "Quasheba, Mother, Queen: Black Women's Public Leadership and Political Protest in Post-Emancipation Jamaica." *Slavery and Abolition* 19, no. 3 (1998): 90–117.

———. "Subaltern Masculinities in Jamaica." In Scully and Paton, *Gender and Slave Emancipation in the Atlantic World,* 79–98.

Shepherd, Verene. "'Petticoat Rebellion'? The Black Woman's Body and Voice in the Struggles for Freedom in Colonial Jamaica." In *In the Shadow of the Plantation: Caribbean History and Legacy,* edited by Alvin O. Thompson and Woodville K. Marshall, 17–39. Kingston, Jamaica: Ian Randle Publishers, 2002.

———, and Glen Richards, eds. *Questioning Creole: Creolisation Discourses in Caribbean Culture.* Kingston, Jamaica: Ian Randle Press, 2002.

Shepherd, Verene, Bridget Brereton, and Barbara Bailey, eds. *Engendering History: Caribbean Women in Historical Perspective.* Kingston, Jamaica: Ian Randle Publishers, 1995.

Silber, Nina. *Romance of Reunion: Northerners and the South, 1865–1900.* Chapel Hill: University of North Carolina Press, 1997.

Simmonds, Lorna. "Civil Disturbances in Western Jamaica, 1838–1865." *Jamaica Historical Review* 14 (1984): 1–17.

Simonsen, Jane E. *Making Home Work: Domesticity and Native American Assimilation in the American West, 1860–1919.* Chapel Hill: University of North Carolina Press, 2006.

Sklar, Kathryn Kish. *Catharine Beecher: A Study in American Domesticity.* New Haven, Conn.: Yale University Press, 1974.

———. "'The Throne of My Heart': Religion, Oratory, and Transatlantic Community in Angelina Grimké's Launching of Women's Rights, 1828–1838." In Sklar and Stewart, *Women's Rights and Transatlantic Antislavery,* 211–41.

———. *Women's Rights Emerges within the Antislavery Movement, 1830–1870.* Boston: Bedford/St. Martin's, 2000.

———, and James Brewer Stewart, eds. *Women's Rights and Transatlantic Antislavery in the Era of Emancipation.* New Haven, Conn.: Yale University Press, 2007.

Smith, Raymond T. "The Matrifocal Family." In *The Character of Kinship,* edited by J. Goody, 121–44. Cambridge: Cambridge University Press, 1973.

Smith-Rosenberg, Carroll. "Beauty, the Beast, and the Militant Woman: A Case Study in Sex Roles and Social Stress in Jacksonian America." In Smith-Rosenberg, *Disorderly Conduct,* 109–28.

———. "The Cross and the Pedestal: Women, Anti-Ritualism and the Emergence of the American Bourgeoisie." In Smith-Rosenberg, *Disorderly Conduct,* 129–64.

———. *Disorderly Conduct: Visions of Gender in Victorian America.* Oxford: Oxford University Press, 1985.

———. "The Female World of Love and Ritual." In Smith-Rosenberg, *Disorderly Conduct: Visions of Gender in Victorian America*, 53–76.

Sneider, Allison. *Suffragists in an Imperial Age: U.S. Expansion and the Woman Question, 1870–1929.* New York: Oxford University Press, 2007.

Sorin, Gerald. *The New York Abolitionists: A Case Study in Political Radicalism.* Westport, Conn.: Greenwood Press, 1971.

Stanley, Amy Dru. *From Bondage to Contract: Wage Labor, Marriage and the Market in the Age of Slave Emancipation.* New York: Cambridge University Press, 1998.

Stauffer, John. *The Black Hearts of Men: Radical Abolitionists and the Transformation of Race.* Cambridge, Mass.: Harvard University Press, 2002.

Stewart, Dianne M. *Three Eyes for the Journey: African Dimensions of the Jamaican Religious Experience.* Oxford: Oxford University Press, 2005.

Stewart, James Brewer. "The Emergence of Racial Modernity and the Rise of the White North, 1790–1840." *Journal of the Early Republic* 18 (Summer 1998): 181–217.

———. *Holy Warriors: Abolitionists and American Slavery.* New York: Hill and Wang, 1976.

———. "Modernizing 'Difference': The Political Meanings of Color in the Free States, 1776–1840." *Journal of the Early Republic* 19 (Winter 1999): 691–712.

———. "The New Haven Negro College and the Meanings of Race in New England, 1776–1870." *New England Quarterly* 76 (September 2003): 323–55.

Stewart, Robert. *Religion and Society in Post-Emancipation Jamaica.* Knoxville: University of Tennessee Press, 1992.

Stoler, Ann Laura. *Carnal Knowledge and Imperial Power: Race and the Intimate in Colonial Rule.* Berkeley: University of California Press, 2002.

———. "Tense and Tender Ties." In *Haunted by Empire: Geographies of Intimacy in North American History*, edited by Ann Laura Stoler, 23–67. Durham, N.C.: Duke University Press, 2006.

Strong, Douglas. *Perfectionist Politics: Abolitionism and Religious Tensions of American Democracy.* Syracuse, N.Y.: Syracuse University Press, 1999.

Swerdlow, Amy. "Abolition's Conservative Sisters: The Ladies' New York City Anti-Slavery Societies, 1834–1840." In Yellin and Van Horne, *The Abolitionist Sisterhood*, 31–44.

Terborg-Penn, Rosalyn, "Through an African Feminist Theoretical Lens: Viewing Caribbean Women's History Cross-culturally." In Shepherd, Brereton, and Bailey, *Engendering History*, 3–19.

Thelan, David. "The Nation and Beyond: Transnational Perspectives on United States History." *Journal of American History* 86 (December 1999): 965–75.

Thomas, Benjamin. *Theodore Weld: Crusader for Freedom.* New Brunswick, N.J.: Rutgers University Press, 1950.

Thorne, Susan. *Congregational Missions and the Making of an Imperial Culture in 19th-Century England.* Stanford, Calif.: Stanford University Press, 1999.

Thornton, John. *Africa and Africans in the Making of the Atlantic World, 1440–1800.* 1992; repr. New York: Cambridge University Press, 1998.

Tompkins, Jane. *Sensational Designs: The Cultural Work of American Fiction, 1790–1860.* New York: Oxford University Press, 1985.

Turner, Mary. *Slaves and Missionaries: The Disintegration of Jamaican Slave Society, 1787–1834.* 1982; repr. Mona, Jamaica: University of West Indies Press, 1998.

Tyrrell, Ian. "American Exceptionalism in an Age of International History." *American Historical Review* 96 (October 1991): 1031–55.

———. *Woman's World/Woman's Empire: The Woman's Christian Temperance Union in International Perspective.* Chapel Hill: University of North Carolina Press, 1991.

Wade, Richard C. "The Negro in Cincinnati, 1800–1830." *Journal of Negro History* 39 (January 1954): 43–57.

Walters, Ronald G. *The Antislavery Appeal: American Abolitionism after 1830.* Baltimore: Johns Hopkins University Press, 1976.

Warner-Lewis, Maureen. *Archibald Monteath: Igbo, Jamaican, Moravian.* Kingston, Jamaica: University of the West Indies Press, 2007.

———. "The Character of African-Jamaican Culture." In Montieth and Richards, *Jamaica in Slavery and Freedom*, 89–114.

Welter, Barbara. "The Cult of True Womanhood." *American Quarterly* 18 (Summer 1966): 151–74.

Williamson, Joel. *Crucible of Race: Black-White Relations in the American South since Emancipation.* New York: Oxford University Press, 1984.

Wilmot, Swithin. "'Females of Abandoned Character?' Women and Protest in Jamaica, 1838–1865." In Shepherd, Brereton, and Bailey, *Engendering History*, 279–95.

———. "The Peacemakers: Baptist Missionaries and Ex-Slaves in West Jamaica 1838–40." *Jamaica Historical Review* 13 (1982): 42–48.

Woodward, C. Vann. *Origins of the New South, 1877–1913.* Baton Rouge: Louisiana State University Press, 1971.

Wyatt-Brown, Bertram. "Conscience and Career: Young Abolitionists and Missionaries." In *Anti-Slavery, Religion, and Reform: Essays in Memory of Roger Anstey*, edited by Christine Bolt and Seymour Drescher, 183–203. Hamden, Conn.: Archon Books, 1980.

———. *Lewis Tappan and the Evangelical War against Slavery.* Cleveland: Press of Case Western Reserve University, 1969.

Yellin, Jean Fagan. *Women and Sisters: The Antislavery Feminists in American Culture.* New Haven, Conn.: Yale University Press, 1989.

———, and John C. Van Horne, eds. *The Abolitionist Sisterhood: Women's Political Culture in Antebellum America.* Ithaca, N.Y.: Cornell University Press, 1994.

Zaeske, Susan. *Signatures of Citizenship: Petitioning, Antislavery, and Women's Political Identity.* Chapel Hill: University of North Carolina, 2003.

INDEX

AASS. *See* American Anti-Slavery Society
Abbott, Thomas, 81, 83, 97
Abolition Act. *See* Emancipation Act
abolitionism and abolitionists, 1, 8–9, 104; evangelical (*see* evangelical abolitionists); in Jamaica, 2, 4–5; radical abolitionism, 37, 38, 43, 44–45, 207, 208–9; in the United States, 3, 5–7; and women's rights, 6, 7, 38–39, 43, 137, 151–52, 165, 172
ACS. *See* American Colonization Society
Advocate and Family Guardian, 154, 173
African Americans, 6, 32–33
Allen, George, 188, 201, 205
AMA. *See* American Missionary Association
American and Foreign Anti-Slavery Society, 151
American Anti-Slavery Society (AASS): formation of, 6; and Lane Seminary, 31, 32; schisms in, 6; and the West Indies, 48, 57, 70; and the woman question, 38, 42
American Board of Commissioners for Foreign Missions, 5, 8, 26; establishment of, 18; focus on spiritual rather than social transformation, 85, 87; and marriage, 136; single women employed by, 156; on slavery, 85–86, 87
American Colonization Society (ACS), 5, 30, 32, 33, 85

American Congregationalists, 11
American Missionary, 126, 131, 137; and church discipline, 88–89; on Dean, 163; and the Great Revival, 184, 187, 188; as immediate emancipation advocate, 193; term for American ex-slaves discussed in, 190
American Missionary Association (AMA): and abolition, 44, 77, 85–86; and the Baptist War, 55; and church discipline, 87–88; and Dean's criticism of Hyde, 107–8, 109; establishment of, 77, 86–87; Evarts dismissed by, 122–23, 124; fields of mission labor, 87; and funding, 134, 140; and Hunt, 100; and Hyde, 103, 104, 107–8, 109, 115, 122–23, 124, 126; and missionaries' antiauthoritarianism, 107–8, 115; missionaries' letters to, 11; origins of, 84–86; and Richmond, 140, 141; in the U.S. South, 8, 183, 190–91, 208; withdrawal of support for Jamaica Mission, 155, 190, 191–92; and the woman question, 39; and women missionaries, 156; mentioned, 78, 82, 207
Anderson, Rufus, 85, 87
Andrew, John, 22
Anglican Church, 4, 18, 53
antiabolitionism, 6, 33–34
anti-Catholicism, 25, 86

{ 247 }

Antigua, 1, 57
antislavery movement. *See* abolitionism and abolitionists
apprenticeship program, 1, 56–58, 60, 62–63

baptism, 53, 76, 94–95, 188
Baptist Church, 23; and adult baptism, 94–95; African American, 19, 51–53, 138; English (*see* English Baptists); European cultural values of, 52–53; and marriage, 138; Native (*see* Native Baptist churches); ticket system in, 52, 54–55
Baptist War of 1831–32, 5, 19, 55–56
Barbados, 1, 46, 57
Bateman, Josephine Penfield, 150
Beardslee, Julius: and the AMA, 122; and Hyde, 114; and the Morant Bay Rebellion, 198; and the Native Baptists, 188–89, 195, 199; and self-supporting churches, 77
Beecher, Catherine, 30, 32, 39, 106, 161
Beecher, Edward, 85, 86
Beecher, Henry Ward, 150
Beecher, Lyman: on emancipation, 30, 31; and family order, 35–36; Finney criticized by, 25; and interracial socializing, 33; and Lane Seminary, 30, 33, 34; revivalists' techniques adopted by, 24–25; mentioned, 85
Bernard, Letitia, 90
Besson, Jean, 58, 64–65
Blackett, Richard, 7
black Jamaicans: American missionaries viewed by, 2–3, 11–12, 18, 67, 71, 81–83, 111; Christian morality viewed by, 181–82; church membership sought by, 12, 75–77, 88–91, 138–39; English missionaries viewed by, 70–71, 81–83; family structure, 65–66; and freedom, 3, 20, 44–45, 48, 56, 67, 76; and the ideology of domesticity, 10, 63, 67–68, 71; sexual behavior of, 70, 71, 93, 113, 132, 137–38; viewed by American missionaries, 2, 3, 8, 18, 67, 69–71, 74, 76–77, 93, 95, 97–98, 116, 123–24, 160, 194–95, 202, 207; viewed by Wolcott, 202; viewed in Britain, 204–5; and wage labor, 55–62, 66, 67–68, 71–72, 79–80, 133–34; women (*see* women, black Jamaican)
Blakeley, Sarah. *See* Moffat, Sarah Blakeley
Bogle, Paul, 196–97, 199
Bradley, James, 31
Brereton, Bridget, 64
Brewin, William, *Jamaica in 1866*, 203
Britain: black Jamaicans viewed in, 204–5; experiment of emancipation, 1, 2, 4, 5, 73, 131–32
Brown, Antoinette, 42, 43, 151
Brown, Vincent, 49
Brumberg, Joan Jacobs, 156
Byrd, Alexander, 47

Calvinism, 23, 24, 26
Campbell, John, 128
Campbell, Urania, 90
Campbellism, 188, 189
Carlyle, Thomas, 2, 61
Carpenter, Ruth E., 142, 143
Catholicism, 25
Cherokee, 8, 85
cholera, 88, 144
Church Missionary Society, 19
Cincinnati, Ohio, 32–33, 33–35
Civil War: end of, 204; and immediate emancipation, 193; and the Jamaica Mission, 155, 183, 190; mentioned, 7, 8, 47
Clark, John, 187
Colonial Assembly, 194, 195
colonization, 5, 31, 32
Congregationalists, 19, 23, 186, 188
Connecticut Missionary Society, 15–17

Cooper, John, 59–60
Cott, Nancy, 136
coverture, 64–65
Cowles, Alice Welch, 40, 150
Cowles, Betsey, 43
Cowles, Henry, 150, 172
Cowles, Mary Welch, 39
Cowles, Minerva Penfield, 150, 172
creoles, 47, 48, 49; religion (*see* Myal religion)
Cromwell, Oliver, 46
Cushman, Richard, 151

Dean, Mary: and church discipline, 113; and family prayer, 106–7; Hyde criticized by, 102, 104–5, 105–6, 108, 115–16, 121, 126; and the ideology of domesticity, 162, 163, 164, 166, 179; influence in homes of black families, 141–42; living with the Wolcotts, 169; matriarchal relationship with Jamaican children, 166, 167, 168–70, 173, 177; other missionaries criticized by, 115, 149, 163, 164, 165, 166, 169, 170–71; relocated to remote Chesterfield, 157, 162–63, 164; relocated to Rock River, 166–67; returns to the U.S., 125, 162, 171; and Richmond, 142, 144, 163, 169; and sexual inequalities in the mission, 164–66, 171; and Urania Hunt, 108–9, 109–10, 112–13; viewed by other missionaries, 104, 107–8, 110, 112–13, 120, 152, 162, 163; mentioned, 119, 128
Disciples of Christ, 188
domesticity, 20; and abolitionism, 26, 27, 39, 136–37, 171–72; and black Jamaicans, 3, 63, 64, 67–68, 71; categories of civilized and uncivilized created by, 10, 179; and the civilizing mission, 152, 158, 172; clash in generational views of, 153, 172, 195; and female moral authority, 9–10, 105–6, 152, 153, 158, 164, 167, 168, 172, 179; and the Jamaica Mission, 3, 9–10, 20, 107, 172; at Oberlin, 20, 37–38; and race, 10, 158; and ties of affection, 179–80; transformation of ideology of, 137
Dowson, Thomas, 83
Drescher, Seymour, 57
Dresser, Amos, 49, 77

Edmondson, Mary and Emily, 150
Elgin, Lord, 83
emancipation: and black independence, 193, 194, 195; and black wage labor, 56–62, 67; Britain's experiment in, 1, 131–32, 200; and extramarital sex, 63; and freed women working in the fields, 63–64; immediate, 57, 193; in Jamaica, 63, 193; obstacles to, 45; and suffrage, 200; viewed by America missionaries, 2, 76, 193–95; viewed by black Jamaicans, 58, 196; viewed by radical abolitionists, 44–45
Emancipation Act: of 1833, 1, 6, 19, 56; of 1838, 56
Emancipation in the West Indies (Thorne and Kimball), 57, 63, 70
English Baptist Missionary Society, 53, 54, 56, 143, 196
English Baptists, 77; and the Baptist War, 55–56; classes in, 81; free villages of, 60–61, 83; and Jamaican emancipation, 73; missionaries of (*see* missionaries, English); and the Morant Bay Rebellion, 198; and the ticket system, 54–55; in the West Indies, 53
evangelical abolitionists, 5; anti-Catholicism of, 86; and Christian perfectionism, 7–8, 12, 98; exclusionism of, 51; and gender ideology, 26, 27, 39, 136–37, 151, 164, 171–72; and self-reliance, 44; slavery viewed as sin by, 7, 84–85; southern patriarchy

INDEX { 249 }

evangelical abolitionists (*continued*)
criticized by, 172; women viewed by, 171–72
Evangelical Alliance, 184
evangelical revivalism, and the antislavery movement, 5–6
Evarts, Henry, 70; and the AMA, 119, 122–23; antiauthoritarianism, 119; at Brainerd Station, 117, 118; children of, 123, 124, 125, 128; death of, 127; and family authority, 123; freedom viewed by, 119; and Hunt, 108, 117, 118, 120; and Hyde, 104–5, 114, 117; Native Baptist church leaders viewed by, 92, 93–94; and spiritual hierarchy, 118–19; viewed by other missionaries, 121–22, 123
Evarts, Jeremiah, 22, 23
Evarts, Lucy: children of, 123, 124, 125, 127–28; and family authority, 123; and Hunt, 108, 117, 127; marriage rejected by, 123; reform activities at Oberlin, 157; relationship with Hyde, 117, 120–21, 123, 125, 126, 127, 127–28, 158; and sexual experimentation at Brainerd Station, 118, 120–21
Eyre, Edward John, 182, 196, 197, 199, 200

Fairchild, James, 150
Finney, Charles Grandison: converts of, 28, 29; criticism of, 24, 25, 34, 77; new moral order called for, 21–22, 24, 44, 104; and Oberlin, 36, 150; and women speaking in public, 24, 151; mentioned, 23, 26, 30, 84, 105
Fisher, Joseph, 195
Fletcher, Robert, 151
Foster, Abby Kelley, 38, 39, 42–43
Foster, Stephen, 42–43
freedom: conflicting ideas about, 12, 76; and landownership and family practices, 3; radical interpretation of, 125; relationship to religion, gender, and race, 19; viewed by American missionaries, 2–3, 56, 67, 74, 76, 101, 102, 113–14, 207; viewed by black Jamaicans, 3, 20, 44–45, 48, 56, 67, 76
freed people. *See* black Jamaicans
Frémont, Jesse Benton, 151–52
Frémont, John, 152
Fugitive Slave Act, 126, 151
funerals, 54

Garrison, William Lloyd, 6, 30, 42, 44, 86; and women's rights, 38, 151
gender ideology: and the civilizing mission, 10, 150–51; and evangelical abolitionists, 38, 151, 152, 153, 164; and independence, 161–62; Jamaican, 10, 62, 63, 64, 65–68; and Weld, 27–28
Goodman, Paul, 28
Gordon, George William, 182, 197, 198, 199, 200
Gordon, Sarah, 136
Great Awakening, 19, 51
Great Revival, 183–88, 190, 196
Grimké, Angelina. *See* Weld, Angelina Grimké
Grimké, Sarah, 38, 39, 165, 172
Grimshaw, Patricia, 156
Griswold, Elijah, 162
Guterl, Matthew, 7

Haitian revolution, 5
Hall, Catherine, 9, 11, 73, 77, 83, 144
Hall, Heman: and church discipline, 113; and Dean, 170; Evarts children adopted by, 125; and family prayer, 117; and Hyde, 113, 115–16, 118, 124; and Jamaican morality, 91, 92, 137, 138; on Native Baptist churches, 91, 92, 94–96, 98; return to the U.S., 187; treatment of black Jamaicans, 170, 173, 176–77; mentioned, 108, 119, 128, 176

Hall, Sophronia Brooks, 108, 176–77
Hartson, Elizabeth, 69
Harvey, Thomas, 57; *Jamaica in 1866*, 203
Hawley, Zerah, 16, 18
Henderson, George, 143
Hicks, Maria, 157
Higman, Barry, 48
Hill, Richard, 145
Holley, Sallie, 43
Holt, Thomas, 11, 73, 196, 197, 200
Hovey, George, 77
Howe, Mary, 161, 162, 166, 179
Hubbard, Gardiner Greene, 201–2, 204, 205
Hunt, Urania: antiauthoritarianism of, 111, 117; at Brainerd Station, 117, 118, 120, 127; and corporal punishment, 115–16; and Dean, 108–9, 112; death of, 127; and the feminine civilizing mission, 111, 162; and Hyde, 108, 109–10, 116, 127; and the ideology of domesticity, 179; other missionaries' complaints about, 100, 110, 112–13, 114; return to Jamaica, 127; as single woman, 108; and the Thompsons, 110, 111–12, 115; mentioned, 128, 159
Hurtado, Albert, 177
Hyde, John: and the AMA, 103, 104, 107–8, 109, 115, 122–23, 124, 126; antiauthoritarianism of, 104, 111, 117, 119; beliefs of, 101–2, 116, 117, 127; at Brainerd Station, 118, 120–21; children of, 124, 127; and the civilizing mission, 112, 128; Dean's criticism of, 102, 106–7, 108, 121, 126; and family prayer, 102, 106–7; on fellow missionaries, 103, 104; and Hunt, 108, 109–10, 120, 127; language of religious liberty and individual freedom used by, 103–4; lessons learned by missionaries from, 129, 189; marriage rejected by, 117–18, 123; mission hierarchies dismantled by, 119, 123, 152; Olds attacked by, 117; relationship with his wife, 123, 126–27; relationship with Lucy Evarts, 120–21, 123, 125, 126, 127–28, 137, 158; and Thompson's church, 110–12; viewed by other missionaries, 107–8, 110, 112–13, 114, 117, 121, 123, 164, 168

industrial schools, 204–5
Ingraham, David, 67, 77, 80, 150, 191; and antislavery, 69–70; and the wage-labor disputes, 79–80, 133

Jamaica: agricultural production in, 46–48; antislavery movement in, 4–5; British capture of, 46; compared with U.S. South, 200, 201; creole religion in (*see* Myal religion); as a Crown colony, 199–200, 204, 206; harsh conditions in, 19, 47; history of missionary efforts in, 18–19, 51–56; post-emancipation, 2, 71–72; U.S. annexation of, 206–7
Jamaica Congregational Association, 83
Jamaica in 1866 (Harvey and Brewin), 203
Jamaica Mission: and abolitionism, 44, 129–30, 132; and the American Civil War, 155, 183, 190; and church discipline, 3, 7–8, 71, 75, 77, 81–82, 84, 87, 92, 94, 95, 98–99, 113, 132, 137–38, 160–61, 207; clash between generations of missionaries at, 11, 150, 152, 155; decline of, 155, 183; end of, 207; and evangelical abolitionism, 74, 149; and freedom, 101, 125, 129, 131–32; funding for, 80, 83–84, 126; and gender ideology, 10, 11, 27–28, 107, 152–53, 164, 170, 172; goals of, 207; hierarchies of, 3–4, 43, 152–53, 208; mission family in 1850, 108; recruiting converts from Native

Jamaica Mission (*continued*)
    Baptists, 71; schools of, 116, 117; and self-supporting churches, 77–78, 83, 84; sex scandal at, 117–18, 119–21, 123, 124, 125, 128, 129; single women employed by, 156–57; withdrawal of AMA support for, 155, 190, 191–92
Jamaicans, black. *See* black Jamaicans
Judson, Adoniram, 156

Kaplan, Amy, 10, 158
Kelley, Abby. *See* Foster, Abby Kelley
Kelly, Louis, 203
Kimball, J. Horace, 48, 57, 62–63, 76; *Emancipation in the West Indies*, 57, 63, 70
Kirk, Edward, 201
Knibb, William, 11

Lamb, Mary Ann, 192–93
landownership: and independence for black men, 62, 70, 71, 130, 134, 136; and reform of Jamaican family life, 129–30, 132–33, 136, 146; viewed by black Jamaicans, 58, 60, 62, 64–65, 130
Lane Anti-Slavery Society, 32–33
Lane Rebels, 23, 31–36, 42, 104, 107; mentioned, 57, 62, 85, 151
Lane Seminary, 23, 30, 74, 107; rebellion at (*see* Lane Rebels)
Lasser, Carol, 42
Latter-Day Saints, 25
Lee, Ann, 25
Liberator, 30
Liberty Party, 39
Liele, George, 51–52, 53
Lindop, William, 59
Livingston, Thomas, 101, 117, 125; and Hunt, 100, 110, 111, 115
Loyalists, 4, 10, 51
Luckock, Benjamin, 133
Lyon, Mary, 106

Mahan, Asa, 105, 150
manual-labor schools, 20, 22, 26, 27, 28, 44; at Richmond Estate (*see* Richmond Industrial and Normal School)
Maroons, 47
marriage, 25, 37, 68, 117–18, 136, 137; Jamaican, 64–65, 66, 130, 136, 137, 138
May, Samuel, 105
Methodists, 19, 23
missionaries, African American, 10, 51–53
missionaries, American: and accounts of post-emancipation Jamaica, 11; and black independence, 36, 62, 70, 71, 130, 134, 189, 207; black Jamaicans viewed by, 2, 3, 8, 18, 67, 69–71, 74, 76–77, 93, 95, 97–98, 116, 123–24, 160, 194–95, 202, 207; and black sexual behavior, 11, 113, 137–38; Britain viewed by, 74, 206; British treatment of emancipation viewed by, 131–32; and church discipline, 3, 7–8, 71, 75, 77, 81–82, 84, 87, 92, 94, 95, 98–99, 113, 132, 137–38, 160–61, 207; and church membership, 75–77, 88–89, 91, 181; and English missionaries, 11, 18, 73–74, 81, 131, 206; and family prayer, 117; freeholds viewed by, 133–34; and gender hierarchies, 102, 107, 113–14, 122, 129, 172; generational differences, 11, 172; goals of, 2, 7, 11, 74; and the Great Revival, 183–88; hierarchies of, 3, 107, 176, 207, 208; Hunt viewed by, 113; and a less dogmatic Christianity, 97–98; relationship with black church leaders, 48–49, 78, 81, 83, 93–94, 101, 128, 189; self-supported mission desired by, 77–78, 134–35; sexual experimentation among, 102, 117–18, 119–21, 123, 124, 125, 128; and U.S. annexation of Jamaica, 206–7; viewed by black Jamaicans, 2–3, 11–12, 18, 67, 71, 81–83, 111; and wage-labor disputes, 79–80

missionaries, American women, 106; absence of organization for, in Jamaica, 157–58; civilizing through sentimental attachments, 153–54, 160; expectations of, 157–58, 161–62, 163; and moral authority, 9–10, 38, 106, 152, 153, 158, 172; unmarried, 156–57, 158
missionaries, black Baptist, 10, 51–53
missionaries, English, 10, 19, 53–54; and free peoples' needs, 131; and the Native Baptist churches, 54–56, 70, 82–83; planters' policies viewed by, 133; relationship with black Jamaicans, 70–71, 82–83; viewed by America missionaries, 81, 131, 206
missionary movement, 8, 16
Mission Institute, 102, 162
Moffat, Addison, 159
Moffat, Sarah Blakeley, 159–61, 162, 179
Mogg, Elizabeth, 168
Mogg, John, 168
Mogg, Letitia, 168
moral reform societies, 22, 26
Morant Bay Rebellion, 146, 155, 197, 198, 204; and the American missionaries, 182–83; causes of, 195–96
Moravians, 18–19, 53
Morgan, John, 37, 151
Mormonism, 77, 188
Mount Holyoke Female Seminary, 106
Myal religion, 48, 49–51, 53, 67, 96; and the Great Revival, 183, 186; revival of, 50, 70, 83

National Era, 131
Native Americans, 18, 208
Native Baptist churches, 49, 77, 199; and African American Baptists, 51–53; and the American missionaries, 71, 91–94, 96, 98, 99, 123, 124, 134, 182; and the Baptist War, 55; and the English missionaries, 52, 54–56, 70, 82–83; and the Great Revival, 184, 196; and marriage as requisite to church membership, 138, 139; missionary churches left for, 89; and the Morant Bay Rebellion, 182, 198; and Myalism, 50; pluralism of, 67; as the religion of slavery, 94; and sexual behavior, 93; and the ticket system, 54
Nelson, David, 105
New York City Female Moral Reform Society, 26
New York Female Moral Reform Society, 43, 173

Obeah men, 50, 54, 187
Oberlin, Ohio, 17, 62, 153
"Oberlin and Missionary Work" (Strieby), 207–8
Oberlin College: African Americans at, 2, 17, 18, 23, 36–37, 74; black women at, 42; criticism of, 36–37, 42; domesticity at, 37–38, 39–40, 43, 44; gendered manual-labor requirements at, 40–41; ideology of, 2, 9, 20, 23, 26, 37–38, 39, 83; and the Lane Rebels, 36; manual-labor education at, 26, 40–41, 144, 205; radicalism of, 2, 9; slavery viewed as sin by founders of, 2, 84; social interactions between sexes at, 41–42; women at, 17, 23, 36–37, 42, 107, 157; and women's rights, 39–40, 42–44, 62, 151, 157; mentioned, 28, 67, 102, 105, 132, 147, 209
Oberlin Evangelist, 49, 70, 78, 79, 85, 132, 150
Oberlin Female Moral Reform Society, 43, 150
Oberlin Institute. *See* Oberlin College
"Occasional Discourses on the Negro (Nigger) Question" (Carlyle), 2, 61
Ohio Anti-Slavery Convention, 32
Ojibwe Indians, 87
Olds, Abner, 119; black Jamaicans viewed

Olds, Abner (*continued*)
by, 93, 96–97; and church discipline, 113; confrontation with other missionaries, 116; and Dean, 102–3, 104, 108; Evarts children adopted by, 125, 128; expansive interpretation of Christianity, 97–98; and family prayer, 117; and Hunt, 109, 112–13; and Hyde, 104, 116; on marriage and church membership, 138; and Richmond, 140; treatment of adopted Jamaican children, 173; views challenged by congregation of, 89–90
Olds, Ann Brooks, 102–3, 167–68, 173
Oneida Commune, 71
Oneida Institute, 22, 23, 28, 31, 41; independence and self-reliance at, 83; manual-labor education at, 29–30, 144, 205; and missionary work, 29–30; northern blacks at, 74; perfectionism of, 124; students of, at Lane Seminary, 31
Oughton, Samuel, 143–44
Oughton, Thomas, 143, 157

Paton, Diana, 10, 65, 66
Penfield, Bigelow. *See* Penfield, Thornton Bigelow
Penfield, Josephine, 151
Penfield, Mary Cowles, 177
Penfield, Sarah Ingraham: accounts written about meeting her former nurse, 154–55; age of, 172; and Beardslee, 189; criticized by older missionaries, 158, 176, 177–78; criticizes other missionaries, 149, 172; death of, 191; discipline through emotion, 174; and domestic ideology, 179; and the Great Revival, 183, 186–88; on her domestic life, 174–75; and issues concerning single women, 172–73; and the Jamaica Mission, 149, 150, 154, 172; Jamaican children adopted in family of, 173, 174–76, 177–78; on Jamaican women living with men before marriage, 173–74; on Wolcott, 201
Penfield, Thornton Bigelow: age of, 172; and Beardslee, 188–89; criticized by older missionaries, 158, 177–78; criticizes other missionaries, 149, 150, 154, 172, 177–78; and decreased AMA funding, 191; and the Great Revival, 186–87, 188; intervention in Jamaican domestic dispute, 174; on Jamaica as a Crown colony, 199; Jamaica Mission viewed by, 149, 150, 155; and the Morant Bay Rebellion, 198–99; name change, 191; and Oberlin, 150; return to the U.S., 191
Pennock, Thomas, 82, 83
Phelps, Amos, 80, 83, 194; AMA established by, 86–87; and American treatment of emancipation, 131–32; and black independence from white landowners, 136; black landownership viewed by, 130, 131, 141, 146; British compensation of slaveholders viewed by, 132; on British missionaries, 131; freeholds viewed by, 133–34; goals for the Jamaica Mission, 207; and interracial marriage, 37
Phillippo, James, 83, 199
Pierson, Michael, 39
Plan of Union, 23
Plea for the West, A (Beecher), 25
Presbyterians, 23, 199
Prince, Nancy, 81–82, 97
prostitution, 26–27
provision grounds, 60, 68; and estate labor, 58–59; freed peoples' attachment to, 133; and Jamaica's marketing culture, 63, 71; and rent, 61, 133–34

Quakers, 4, 25

racial ideology, 204

racism, 10, 45, 77
radical abolitionism: and the civilizing mission, 208–9; emancipated society imagined by, 44–45; and enforcing freedom, 207; gender roles challenged in, 38; and interracial socializing, 37; and the woman question, 43
Radical Republicans, 200, 204
Reconstruction Act of 1867, 206
Rehearsal for Reconstruction (Rose), 190–91
Renshaw, Charles Stewart, 49, 77, 80, 89; and the daughters of Thomas Livingston, 111; on Jamaican landownership, 65; on Jamaican men, 137; Native Baptist church leaders criticized by, 93; at Oneida, 29; on the ticket system, 54
Renshaw, Stewart. *See* Renshaw, Charles Stewart
Richards, Sir Arthur, 147
Richardson, Albert, 98, 124, 125; on church membership, 91; on inquiry meetings, 89; on mission teachers, 162, 163; and Richmond, 140
Richmond Estate, 131, 135, 139, 140–41, 143, 187; discipline at, 203; manual labor at, 201, 205 (*see also* Richmond Industrial and Normal School)
Richmond Industrial and Normal School: discipline at, 145–46, 147, 203; enrollment at, 144, 145; funding for, 145; goals of, 146; governance of, 195, 201–4; manual labor at, 205; and missionary influence on Jamaican society, 139–40, 141–43, 207; mixed results of, 203; patterned after the New England family, 142, 144, 145, 146, 152, 169; mentioned, 178
Richmond Normal School. *See* Richmond Industrial and Normal School
Rose, Willie Lee, 190–91
Rugemer, Edward, 7, 200

Salem Female Anti-Slavery Society, 84
Samuel, Peter, 58–59
Sandwich Islands, 16, 18
Schuler, Monica, 51
Scully, Pamela, 10
Second Great Awakening, 6, 8, 21, 26, 49, 186–87
Shakers, 25
Sharpe, Sam, 55
Shipherd, John Jay, 18, 19; and Oberlin, 17, 36, 39, 153
Sierra Leone, 5, 87
Simms, Lydia, 90
slave drivers, 48, 54
slave rebellion, 4, 19
slavery: American Board debate on, 85–86, 87; in Jamaica (*see* slaves, Jamaican); in the United States, 47; viewed as sin, 84–85, 86
slaves, Jamaican, 46, 47–48, 62–63; land owned by (*see* provision grounds)
Smith, Gerrit, 70, 80
Smith, Joseph, 25
Smith, Sir Lionel, 73
Society for the Promotion of Manual Labor, 28–29
Society for the Propagation of the Gospel, 18
spiritualist movement, 119, 120
Stanley, Amy Dru, 136
Stanton, Elizabeth Cady, 7, 34
Stanton, Henry B., 34
Starbuck, Charles, 173, 176, 184, 199–200, 206, 207
Statement of the Reasons Which Induced the Students of Lane Seminary, to Dissolve Their Connection with that Institution, 35
Stewart, Diana, 50
Stewart, James Brewer, 8, 32
Stewart, Robert, 183, 199
Stoler, Ann Laura, 10
Stone, Lucy, 42–43, 151

Stowe, Calvin, 85, 86
Stowe, Harriet Beecher, 85, 126, 150, 152
Strieby, Michael, 207–8
Strobie, Catherine, 102, 108, 159, 162
Stuart, Charles, 71, 73, 133
Sturge, Joseph, 57, 141
suffrage, 27, 151, 179, 200
sugar, 1–2, 46, 61, 72
Sumner, Charles, 200

Tappan, Arthur, 29, 30–31, 36, 85
Tappan, Benjamin, 29
Tappan, Lewis: AMA established by, 86–87; and the American Anti-Slavery Society, 6, 38; British compensation of slaveholders viewed by, 132; and Dean, 163–64, 165–66, 171; frustration with Jamaica Mission, 149; on Hyde, 164; and Lane Seminary, 30; and manual-labor education, 28; and moral reform, 29; and Oberlin, 36; and radical abolitionism, 30–31, 84; and Richmond, 140, 142–43, 207; and women's rights, 151; mentioned, 124, 131, 141, 186
Taylor, Henry, 58
Taylor, Simon, 58, 59, 60
temperance, 12, 15–16
Temperance Society, 80
Thompson, John, 200
Thompson, Loren, 149; and the AMA, 122; and Beardslee, 189; and black independence from white landowners, 136; on the Blakeleys' marriage, 159; conversions at church of, 88; and the daughters of Thomas Livingston, 111–12; and domestic ideology, 179; Eliot trustees supported by, 100–101; on emancipation in Jamaica, 193–94, 195; and family prayer, 122; and the Great Revival, 184, 185–86, 187; on Howe, 161; and Hunt, 108, 109–11; 114–15, 119–20; and Hyde, 104–5, 114, 116, 121, 122–23; and Lambe, 192; and landownership, 135–36, 194; and Richmond, 141; and treatment of adopted Jamaican children, 173, 177–78; viewed by Bigelow Penfield, 150
Thompson, Nancy, 108, 109–10, 159
Thorne, James A., 31, 42, 48, 57, 62–63, 76; *Emancipation in the West Indies*, 57, 63, 70; and the Lane Seminary rebellion, 34, 35
Treat, Sarah, 186–87
"Truth's Hindrances" (Weld), 124
Tuskegee, 147, 148
Tyler, Ralph, 49, 77, 80, 81, 92

Uncle Tom's Cabin (Stowe), 126, 152
Underhill, Edward, 196
Union Missionary Society, 87
Unitarians, 23
United States, 2, 5–6, 207
Universalists, 77
Upson, Sarah, 145

Venning, Charles: and the AMA, 122; and Beardslee, 189; and British racial attitudes, 82, 205; and Dean, 163, 170, 171; Eyre viewed by, 200; on the Great Revival, 185; and Hyde's ideas about education, 115–16; and Jamaica as a Crown colony, 200; on marriage and church membership, 138–39; Wolcott viewed by, 178, 202–3, 204; mentioned, 90, 108, 195

wage disputes: for black Jamaicans, 55–62, 66, 67–68, 71–72, 79–80, 133–34; in Jamaica Mission, 79–80
Washington, Booker T., 28, 148
Wattles, Augustus, 32, 34
Weld, Angelina Grimké, 17, 27, 38, 39, 165, 172

Weld, Theodore Dwight: and the daughters of Thomas Livingston, 111; ideology of evangelical manhood developed by, 27–28, 124; and interracial socializing, 33; and the Lane Seminary rebellion, 23, 31, 34, 35; and manual-labor education, 28–29, 30, 40; and Oberlin, 17; and radical abolitionism, 30–31; and women's rights, 24, 27; mentioned, 37, 57, 70, 71, 205

Wesleyan Missionary Society, 88

Wesleyans, 52, 53, 54, 56

Western Evangelical Mission Society, 87

Western Monthly Magazine, 34

Western Reserve, 15–17

West India Mission Committee, 83–84, 86, 87, 131

West Indies, 1, 4, 53, 70, 79

Westmorland, Henry, 135

Whipple, George, 142, 157; Ann Olds's letters to, 167, 168; and complaints about Urania Hunt, 100; and Dean, 105, 162, 165, 166, 167; and the Eliot Station's school, 100, 101; and Hyde, 107, 127; and the Lane Seminary rebellion, 35; Moffat's letters to, 160; and the upheavals at Jamaica Mission, 116–17; Wolcott's letters to, 134, 197, 203–4

Wilson, Sherman, 177, 194–95, 200

Wolcott, Henry B., 147

Wolcott, Mary, 108

Wolcott, Mary Adella, 147

Wolcott, Seth, 98, 108, 142; and the AMA, 122, 191–92; and Beardslee, 189; and church membership and school attendance, 92–93, 181; and Dean, 105, 126, 163, 164, 169, 170; disapproval of charity to black Jamaicans, 170; and discipline, 145, 205; domestic influence viewed by, 178; and Evarts, 121–22, 123; Evarts children adopted by, 125, 128; Eyre viewed by, 200; on Gordon, 199; and the Great Revival, 187; and Hunt, 120; and Hyde, 104–5, 114, 117, 121, 123, 126; and Jamaica as a Crown colony, 199, 200; on Jamaican marriage, 137; on ministerial authority, 160; and the Morant Bay Rebellion, 182, 195, 197–98, 199; at Oberlin, 205; patriarchal hierarchy used by, 152, 169, 205; and Richmond Estate, 131, 139–40, 141, 143, 145, 147; and Richmond School, 142, 144, 145, 178, 201–4, 205, 207; and a self-supporting mission, 134–35; and treatment of adopted Jamaican children, 173; viewed by other missionaries, 150, 178, 201–5

woman question. *See* women's rights

women, American missionary. *See* missionaries, American women

women, black Jamaican: and the Anglo-American family model, 138; and church membership, 89; working in the fields, 62–64

women, evangelical: and abolitionism, 27, 38; and moral reform, 22, 26–27; in the North, 171–72

women's rights, 9–10; and abolitionists, 6, 7, 38–39, 43, 137, 151–52, 165, 172; and the AMA, 39; and freed women working in the fields, 62–64; and Oberlin, 39–40, 42–44, 62, 151, 157

Woodcock, Lucy, 167

World's Anti-Slavery Convention, 7, 81

Wright, Frances, 25

Wyatt-Brown, Bertram, 141

Zion Revivalism, 186

RACE IN THE ATLANTIC WORLD, 1700–1900

The Hanging of Angélique: The Untold Story of Canadian Slavery and the Burning of Old Montréal
by Afua Cooper

Christian Ritual and the Creation of British Slave Societies, 1650–1780
by Nicholas M. Beasley

African American Life in the Georgia Lowcountry: The Atlantic World and the Gullah Geechee
edited by Philip Morgan

The Horrible Gift of Freedom: Atlantic Slavery and the Representation of Emancipation
by Marcus Wood

The Life and Letters of Philip Quaque, the First African Anglican Missionary
edited by Vincent Carretta and Ty M. Reese

In Search of Brightest Africa: Reimagining the Dark Continent in American Culture, 1884–1936
by Jeannette Eileen Jones

Contentious Liberties: American Abolitionists in Post-emancipation Jamaica, 1834–1866
by Gale L. Kenny

We Are the Revolutionists: German-Speaking Immigrants and American Abolitionists after 1848
by Mischa Honeck

The American Dreams of John B. Prentis, Slave Trader
by Kari J. Winter

Missing Links: The African and American Worlds of R. L. Garner, Primate Collector
by Jeremy Rich

www.ingramcontent.com/pod-product-compliance
Lightning Source LLC
Chambersburg PA
CBHW011744220426
43666CB00018B/2895